SHAKESPEARE
SET FREE

Also from the Teaching Shakespeare Institute

Shakespeare Set Free: Teaching *Hamlet* and *Henry IV, Part 1*
Shakespeare Set Free: Teaching *Romeo and Juliet, Macbeth,* and
  A Midsummer Night's Dream

Published by WASHINGTON SQUARE PRESS

For orders other than by individual consumers, Washington Square Press grants a discount on the purchase of **10 or more** copies of single titles for special markets or premium use. For further details, please write to the Vice-President of Special Markets, Pocket Books, 1230 Avenue of the Americas, New York, NY 10020.

For information on how individual consumers can place orders, please write to Mail Order Department, Paramount Publishing, 200 Old Tappan Road, Old Tappan, NJ 07675.

SHAKESPEARE

&

SET FREE

&

TEACHING

TWELFTH NIGHT

•

OTHELLO

PEGGY O'BRIEN, GENERAL EDITOR
JEANNE ADDISON ROBERTS, SCHOLARSHIP EDITOR
MICHAEL TOLAYDO, PERFORMANCE EDITOR
NANCY GOODWIN, CURRICULUM EDITOR

•

Teaching Shakespeare Institute
Folger Shakespeare Library
Washington, D.C.

WASHINGTON SQUARE PRESS
PUBLISHED BY POCKET BOOKS
New York   London   Toronto   Sydney   Tokyo   Singapore

A WASHINGTON SQUARE PRESS *Original* Publication

A Washington Square Press Publication of
POCKET BOOKS, a division of Simon & Schuster Inc.
1230 Avenue of the Americas, New York, NY 10020

Library of Congress Catalog Card Number: 95-68952

ISBN: 0-671-76047-5

First Washington Square Press printing September 1995

10 9 8 7 6 5 4 3 2 1

WASHINGTON SQUARE PRESS and colophon are registered trademarks of Simon & Schuster Inc.

Cover illustrations by Kinuko Y. Craft

Printed in the U.S.A.

CONTENTS

ACKNOWLEDGMENTS   vii

INTRODUCTION   xi
"Didn't She Tell Us This Already?"
PEGGY O'BRIEN

ठ | Part One
    THINKING ABOUT THE PLAYS
    JEANNE ADDISON ROBERTS, EDITOR

Sex, Lies, and Shakespearean Drama   3
RUSS MCDONALD

Women and the Tyranny of Dramatic Genres   11
JEANNE ADDISON ROBERTS

***Twelfth Night* and *Othello,* Those Extraordinary Twins**   22
STEPHEN BOOTH

No Cloven Hooves   33
DORIS ADLER

ठ | Part Two
    **TEACHING SHAKESPEARE THROUGH
    PERFORMANCE**
    MICHAEL TOLAYDO, EDITOR

**Up on Your Feet with Shakespeare: The Wrong Way
and the Right**   41
MICHAEL TOLAYDO

"A Touch, a Touch, I Do Confess": Sword Fighting in the Classroom   50
MICHAEL TOLAYDO

  Part Three
IN THE CLASSROOM
NANCY GOODWIN, EDITOR

Twelfth Night   61
MARTHA HARRIS, EDITOR

Othello   133
LOUISA FOULKE NEWLIN AND MARY WINSLOW POOLE, EDITORS

Unfinished Business: An African-American Teacher Talks Race and *Othello*   215
DONNA DENIZÉ

Whole-Brained Shakespeare   223
NANCY GOODWIN

ACKNOWLEDGMENTS

The three volumes of *Shakespeare Set Free* have been a project of the Folger Library's Teaching Shakespeare Institute. The institute—a whirligig of scholars, actors, and secondary-school teachers in varying and endless combination—goes about its business today with backbone it derived twelve years ago from the wisdom and high standards of Carolynn Reid-Wallace. Every minute since then, I—along with thousands of teachers and students—have been grateful to her, and to the National Endowment for the Humanities for its continued confidence and support.

The idea of a set of sourcebooks for the teaching of Shakespeare began rattling around my head as early as 1986. Janet Alexander Griffin, director of the Folger's Museum and Public Programs and godmother to every Library education program, responded with enthusiasm. The National Endowment for the Humanities agreed to fund a special 1988–89 summer institute and follow-up conference focused on teaching Shakespeare's language. To some of the forty participating teachers, scholars, actors, and directors, it was a grand experiment; to others, a great leap of faith. Some of these smart and splendid people weren't sure that they could hunker down for the summer and really come up with the practical tools by which students could make Shakespeare's language—and by extension his plays—their own. I knew they could. And they did. Even the ones who thought I was crazy.

Nevertheless, these folks know what uncertainty, pressure, humidity, exhilaration, frustration, exhaustion, and satisfaction are all about. In their labors, they were supported by the great good work of Lauri Lewis, Heather Lester, and the ever famous Mr. Freddie Lindsay. In large and small ways, most everybody collaborated toward creation. Their important work makes up the curriculum section of this book:

Andrea Alsup, *Woodstock, Vt.*
Tom Berger, *Canton, N.Y.*
Susan Biondo-Hench, *Carlisle, Pa.*
Stephen Booth, *Berkeley, Calif.*
Kathleen Breen, *Louisville, Ky.*
Susan Cahill, *Sparta, N.J.*
Carlos Castillo, *Denver, Colo.*
Martha Christian, *Kingston, Mass.*
Barbara Crabb, *Helena, Ark.*
Donna Denizé, *Arlington, Va.*
Ellen Diem, *Inola, Okla.*
Judy Dill, *Columbia, S.C.*
Susan Donnell, *St. Louis, Mo.*
Judith Elstein, *Somers Point, N.J.*

Lynn Frick, *Madison, Wis.*
Nancy Goodwin, *Clinton, Okla.*
Martha Harris, *Golden Valley, Minn.*
Diane Herr, *Lansdale, Pa.*
Tony Hill, *Stratford-upon-Avon, U.K.*
Judith Klau, *Groton, Mass.*
Michael LoMonico, *Stony Brook, N.Y.*
Jerry Maguire, *Columbus, Ind.*
Mary Beth Maitoza, *North Providence, R.I.*
Russ McDonald, *Greensboro, N.C.*
Diane Mertens, *Madison, Wis.*
Barbara Mowat, *Washington, D.C.*
John Murphy, *Claremont, Calif.*

Louisa Newlin, *Washington, D.C.*

Skip Nicholson, *Los Angeles, Calif.*

Suzanne Peters, *Tucson, Ariz.*

Mary Winslow Poole, *Washington, D.C.*

Christopher Renino, *New York, N.Y.*

Randal Robinson, *East Lansing, Mich.*

John Scott, *Hampton, Va.*

Susan Snyder, *Swarthmore, Pa.*

Annie Stafford, *New York, N.Y.*

Everett Stern, *Toledo, Ohio*

Robin Tatu, *Washington, D.C.*

Pat Thisted, *Colorado Springs, Colo.*

Michael Tolaydo, *Washington, D.C.*

George Wright, *Minneapolis, Minn.*

Subsequently, this project benefited enormously from the support of Barbara Mowat and Paul Werstine, editors of the New Folger editions of Shakespeare—fresh texts edited with beautiful clarity; from the blessing of Werner Gundersheimer, director of the Folger Shakespeare Library; from the support and insight of Jane Rosenman, our editor at Washington Square Press; and from the participation of hundreds of students across the country.

These books would not exist without the talent and dedication of the Folger Library's education staff. They are my home. Molly Haws, Louisa Newlin, Becky Jones, and Anne Turner know that my gratitude far exceeds my ability with language. Members of the Reading Room staff—in particular Betsy Walsh, LuEllen DeHaven, Rosalind Larry, David Ressa, and Georgianna Zeigler—have aided not only in the preparation of *Shakespeare Set Free* but in all of the institute's work. My thanks to them, to the wise Missy Pearson, to the docents of the Folger Library, and to Mary Tonkinson, *Shakespeare Set Free*'s official dial-a-grammarian. She's brutal, she's funny, and she's *always* right.

All Library education efforts would suffer without the consistently honest, creative, and joyful attention of the Department of Public Programs. Janice Delaney, Chris Shreeve, Jane Bissonette, Stephanie DeMouche, Katy O'Grady, Anna Flye, Saskia Hamilton, Bill Fecke, Susanne Oldham, Heather Thomas, and Kate Mazetti: thank you for *everything*.

This book, this series, my life have been enriched and enlarged by the Institute's Founding Feminist, scholarship editor Jeanne Addison Roberts, and by the creative and ruthless genius of curriculum editor Nancy Goodwin. They are candidates for canonization, as is editor—and worrier—Michael LoMonico.

I am packing this—the last volume in the *Shakespeare Set Free* series—off to publication at about the same time that I am packing myself off to a new job as Director of Education Programs at the Corporation for Public Broadcasting. What ever could lure me away from working on behalf of teachers at the Folger? Only two things: The possibility of working on behalf of teachers in a larger and amazingly powerful ballpark. And the certainty that the Folger Shakespeare Library and its Teaching Shakespeare Institute will always support, educate, and celebrate people doing the world's most important work. The beat goes on no matter what—at CPB, and at the Folger where the NET will continue to grow and prosper.

At this moment, then, I am overwhelmed with the reality that the Teaching Shakespeare Institute has been for me, as it has been for so many others, a life-changing experience. My work, my brains, my heart and my soul have been completely overhauled—in particular by the ubiquitous Mike LoMonico, Nancy Goodwin, Jeanne

Roberts, Michael Tolaydo, and Louisa Newlin, and equally by the likes of Stephen Booth (who loves me but hates gush like this), Russ McDonald, Skip Nicholson, Martha Harris, Andrea Alsup, John Scott, Martha Christian Mutrie, Chris Renino, Donna Denizé, and Paul Sullivan. They have over and over given to the Folger, to this nation's teachers, and to me, gifts beyond measure.

And oh: A prized member of the institute faculty, actor, director, and born teacher Michael Tolaydo also is, along with John O'Brien and Beth O'Brien, my own life's treasure. No writer could find words big and deep enough to describe my gratitude for his energy and generosity, love and steadfastness. Not even Shakespeare.

P.O'B.

INTRODUCTION

"Didn't She Tell Us This Already?"

❧

A LETTER FROM PEGGY O'BRIEN

The notion of a set of intellectually stimulating and perfectly practical sourcebooks on the teaching of Shakespeare sprang—like so many other things in my life—from my unwavering belief in the supreme value of teachers. And from my belief in the value of a teacher's voice. In all of the present, past, and certainly future cacophony about education, the most important voice is heard the least.

Why couldn't curriculum be written, not in the sterile robotlike prose of education books, but by real classroom teachers in their real voices? Why couldn't this *Shakespeare Set Free* series fill the needs of real teachers and therefore include scholarship *and* curriculum? (Content and methodology? In a book about teaching? *Together?* Gasp.) And so it went.

I like that these books resonate with teachers' voices because perhaps the greatest strength of the Teaching Shakespeare Institute is the fullness of its disparate voices—teachers, scholars, and actors, each one different, from different schools, or different schools of thought. The mix of these voices is vigorous, compelling, and exciting beyond belief. When these voices take hold of each other and of the Folger Shakespeare Library—the world's largest and perhaps most significant collection of materials pertaining to the English and Continental Renaissance—the result is education at its best.

In this kind of fine education, I have had the good fortune to serve as both instigator and beneficiary, and in work with tens of thousands of teachers and students, I've had a chance to develop and perpetually refine my own beliefs about teaching, and about teaching Shakespeare. I began writing about these beliefs in *Shakespeare Set Free: Teaching* Romeo and Juliet, Macbeth, *and* A Midsummer Night's Dream, retooled and expanded them right into *Shakespeare Set Free: Teaching* Hamlet *and* Henry IV, Part 1, and I'm still chewing on them right now.

If you are new to this series, you might want to cast your eyes over the introductions to the first two books. I generally have a healthy disrespect for introductions in books, but in this case, they provide the philosophical underpinnings for all that follows. This is important because, while *Shakespeare Set Free* is a collection of 600 surefire things for your sixth-period class, that's not *all* it is. *Shakespeare Set Free* is support for the art, the craft, the significant magic of teaching. It is food for your brain *and* a lively piece of work for your students. It points the way toward students and teachers actively engaging with text in ways that are intellectually sophisticated and stimulating *and* a hell of a good time besides. This is the best kind of teaching and learning.

Here then, from the home office slightly east of Sioux City, Iowa:

Peggy O'Brien's List of Top Eight Essentials About Teaching Shakespeare

8. **The people who know the most and best about teaching are the people who do it every day with real kids in real classrooms.** Yes!

7. **Shakespeare is for all students, of all ability levels and reading levels, of every ethnic origin, in every kind of school.** This book has been written by secondary-school and college teachers, but for every kind of teacher and all of their students. You're a good teacher, so you'll know what to reshape, extend, add, or trim so that your fifth graders can have a wonderful experience in Illyria, or your graduate students will find the study of *Othello* suitably challenging.

Scholars Jeanne Roberts, Doris Adler, Stephen Booth, and Russ McDonald give us new ways to look at old plays; Michael Tolaydo lays out "The Tolaydo Method" for a piece of *Othello;* and high-school teachers Mary Poole, Louisa Newlin, and Martha Harris offer us practical plans for teaching *Twelfth Night* and *Othello,* fashioned and refashioned between reading their own students' essays and journals. *Shakespeare Set Free* is only a beginning. Start with us and stir in yourself and your own students.

6. **The most important and powerful part of teaching Shakespeare has to do with teaching Shakespeare's** *language.* Shakespeare's words are where the power lies. Your students' active connection with these words is the greatest gift you can give them. In dozens of different ways, *Shakespeare Set Free* works toward putting his words in students' mouths. You just set up the connections and step back. Direct engagement

O'BRIEN'S UNFINISHED TAXONOMY

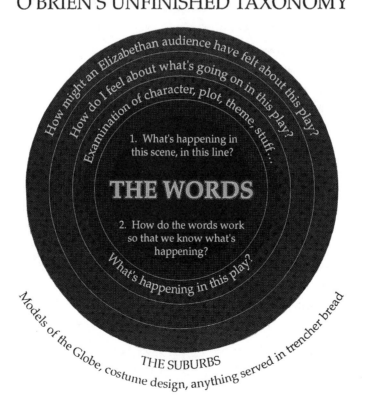

with Shakespeare's language is central, whatever the route you take to get there. The facing diagram is another way of showing that models of the Globe (even though no scholar is sure what it looked like) can be fun, and discussion of things *about* Shakespeare's plays are OK. But the moment of truth is when, in speaking his language, your students discover their natural affinity for this guy and his plays. Fasten your seatbelt and enjoy the ride. It's a fabulous trip.

5. **The teaching of literature has not changed much in a hundred years.** And you know it needs to. Check out p. xii of *Shakespeare Set Free: Teaching* Hamlet *and* Henry IV, Part 1 for a brief demo on the *how* of literature teaching that will shock and amaze you. If your English classes tend to feature a lot of you and your insights while your students are remembering facts, you will be doubly amazed. And may this jolt propel you into a new life.

Things aren't so great in the content department either. The secondary-school curriculum has been stuck for about a hundred years. *JC* was once the play of choice because it perfectly complemented a turn-of-the-century classical education heavy with emphasis on Latin and rhetoric. Now it seems we might be saddled forever with *Caesar* as well as *Mac*, *Ham*, and *Romeo* because we have let tradition and the publishers of textbook anthologies dictate which plays we teach. Are *Julius Caesar, Macbeth, Hamlet,* and *Romeo and Juliet* good plays? Absolutely. Are they the four best plays Shakespeare wrote? Or the four best choices for students? Don't you believe it.

4. **Many of Shakespeare's *other* thirty-four plays are terrific for students.** You already know this because you are on to *Othello* or *Twelfth Night* or both. Your students will have a superb literary experience, and something else besides. In this world torn apart by intolerance of "the other," the study of an *Othello* or a *Merchant* will give your students the opportunity to learn about Shakespeare *and* themselves too. The Teaching Shakespeare Institute's late, great class of 1994 took on both of these plays and in that process shared anonymously the patterns of their own prejudice. The session was honest and uncomfortable, the kind of discomfort that leads to recognition and real learning. It was an impressive afternoon.

3. **Shakespeare study can and should be active, intellectual, energizing, and a pleasure for teacher and student.**

2. **There are no standards like high standards.** The world is cold for teachers. We are undermined, underpaid, overlooked, dissed with regularity. Many of us take our orders from administrators who know less than we do—about students, about schools, about almost everything. On the other hand, our students need everything. And then there are their parents.

Still, or maybe because, we have to keep on keeping on—holding ourselves, our colleagues, our administrators, and our students to the highest standards. If we don't, who will?

1. **The most significant work *in the world* goes on in your classroom. Period.**
You know all this. Now just do it. Godspeed.

Peggy O'Brien

PEGGY O'BRIEN
Folger Shakespeare Library
October 1994

PART ONE

Thinking About the Plays

·

JEANNE ADDISON ROBERTS

EDITOR

Sex, Lies, and Shakespearean Drama

Russ McDonald
UNIVERSITY OF NORTH CAROLINA AT GREENSBORO

"Look how imagination blows him."—Twelfth Night

Around the turn of the seventeenth century, just in mid-career, Shakespeare shifts from comedy to tragedy. Why? Explanations range from the biographical (a psychological crisis darkened Shakespeare's view of human experience) to the commercial (audience taste and thus company policy motivated the change to tragedy) to the artistic (Shakespeare grew tired of one mode and wanted to experiment) to the cultural (in Shakespeare's work, as in England generally, the post-Armada optimism of the 1590s yielded to Jacobean skepticism). The truth is that we do not know. But what is sometimes obscured in discussion of this shift is that comedy and tragedy can be different ways of exploring the same topic.

A productive way of thinking about Shakespeare's change of mind is to regard it not as a turn from affirmation to pessimism but rather as an adjustment of perspective. If we think of comedy and tragedy not as binary opposites but as two ends of a continuum, we can identify structural parallels between the two forms and recognize in both modes some of the same thematic concerns. The terms "comedy" and "tragedy" are after all codes, shorthand terms for a set of dramatic conventions—e.g., marriage in one form, death in the other—that help artists to organize their perceptions about human experience and guide the spectators' responses to those perceptions. Virtually all human action is liable to opposing interpretations, depending mainly upon distance: to take the familiar case of the banana peel, the fall is painful to the slipper, hilarious to the spectator across the street. The two contrasting dramatic modes encourage complementary responses to the dualities of all human endeavor, and some awareness of the claims of both—birth and death, joy and despair, heroism and folly—is implicit in every great example of either mode. Sometimes the balance of those claims can be so delicate that it is difficult to distinguish one form from the other. Thomas Mann remarked of comedy and tragedy that "a shift of lighting suffices to convert one into the other," and it will be useful to think about the middle of Shakespeare's career in just these terms.

Twelfth Night (1601–2) and *Othello* (1604), a comedy and a tragedy, lead us to very different conclusions about the possibility for human happiness, yet they are built out of some of the same narrative materials: schemes, disguises, duels, lies about love.

Moreover, they engage their audiences with many of the same human problems: the unreliability of language, our propensity for self-delusion, the potency of the human will, and the uses and abuses of the imagination. *Twelfth Night* marks the end of a phase in which the effects of the imagination are mostly benevolent; *Othello*, written three or so years later, reveals the hideous consequences of the poisonous imagination. Both plays depend upon the manipulation of images, and for Shakespeare, words are the most powerful images of reality.

I

The third act of *Twelfth Night* begins with an informal dialogue about words:

Enter Viola and Feste, the Fool, playing a tabor.

VIOLA   Save thee, friend, and thy music. Dost thou live by thy tabor?
FOOL   No, sir, I live by the church.
VIOLA   Art thou a churchman?
FOOL   No such matter, sir. I do live by the church, for I do live at my house, and my house doth stand by the church.
VIOLA   So thou mayst say the king lies by a beggar if a beggar dwell near him, or the church stands by thy tabor if thy tabor stand by the church.
FOOL   You have said, sir. To see this age! A sentence is but a chev'ril glove to a good wit. How quickly the wrong side may be turned outward!
VIOLA   Nay, that's certain. They that dally nicely with words may quickly make them wanton.
FOOL   I would therefore my sister had had no name, sir.
VIOLA   Why, man?
FOOL   Why, sir, her name's a word, and to dally with that word might make my sister wanton. But, indeed, words are very rascals since bonds disgraced them.
VIOLA   Thy reason, man?
FOOL   Troth, sir, I can yield you none without words, and words are grown so false I am loath to prove reason with them.

(3.1.1–26)[1]

The two speakers toy with each other, playing a witty game of one-upmanship that is described later in the scene as a species of verbal sword fight. Preceded by the broad hilarity of Malvolio's letter scene, written in prose without any big lyrical speeches, and doing nothing to advance the plot, this is one of those episodes that directors often cut and readers tend to skim. But its apparent irrelevance actually indicates its importance. The medium is the message: Viola and the Fool deplore, even as they playfully illustrate, the dangerous flexibility of language.

Throughout *Twelfth Night* Shakespeare makes his audience aware that words are unreliable images of reality. In the quoted lines, the Fool squeezes a single phrase to produce three different meanings:

live by = support oneself
live by = follow the doctrines of
live by = reside near

---

[1] Except where otherwise noted, all references to Shakespeare's works are taken from the New Folger edition (New York: Simon & Schuster, 1992).

This capacity of one set of sounds to yield multiple senses was known to Renaissance literary critics as "amphibologie" or "ambiguitas"; it is described by George Puttenham, in *The Art of English Poesie* (1589), as "when we speake or write doubtfully and that the sense may be taken two wayes." The key to this rhetorical turn is likeness in difference, or one term with multiple senses, and it seems particularly relevant to a plot that turns on the confusion of twins. Sebastian and Viola share a single appearance or image susceptible to two very different meanings and functions, male and female. Shakespeare thus engages his audience directly, by sight and sound, in the problem of identity, whether a thing actually *is* what it looks like or what it sounds like. As Viola catches onto the Clown's method, she milks the phrases "lies by" and "stands by," whereupon the two jokesters begin to explore the ethical implications of their practice, noting that "a good wit" can turn any utterance inside out (3.1.11–13) and that such clever manipulation can cause words to lose their reputation: "they that dally nicely with words may quickly make them wanton." Words are "rascals"; they have "grown so false" as to be worthless.

It is illuminating to notice that in the center of *Othello* Shakespeare creates a parallel scene. The Clown in the tragedy is a negligible figure whose two brief appearances are calculated to illustrate that words are untrustworthy, that they quickly slither from one sense to another:

> CASSIO   Dost thou hear, mine honest friend?
> CLOWN   No, I hear not your honest friend. I hear you.
> CASSIO   Prithee, keep up thy quillets.
> (3.1.22–24)

"Quillets" are quibbles, puns, deliberate misreadings of verbal signs. In this case, the Clown ignores a verbal stop sign, a punctuation mark indicating a pause, to convert the sentence from one meaning to another. Even from such nonsensical turns meaning emerges: Cassio's "honest friend" would be Iago, or as he is repeatedly known, "honest Iago." And yet, as we also know, Othello (as well as Cassio) "thinks men honest that but seem to be so" (1.3.443). Misunderstanding, whether verbal or visual, is the human weakness on which the action of *Othello* depends; the plot itself is a quillet, a misreading of signs. In that same third-act exchange in *Twelfth Night*, Feste insists that he is not the Lady Olivia's fool, but her "corrupter of words." In *Othello*, the role of the Clown has been usurped by Iago, who is probably Shakespeare's supreme corrupter of words.

II

Feste complains that since his sister's "name's a word," playing around with that word will damage her reputation. The issue beneath the joke is the relation of image to reality: will the playing with his sister's name make his "sister" wanton, or make his sister wanton? What is the relation of "sister" to sister, of reputation to reality, of signifier to signified? Verbal signs may become promiscuous, may lose their capacity for being faithful, and so it is with all images. *Othello* is a play in which a man dallies with a woman's name and thereby makes her wanton to the vulnerable imagination of her husband; Iago's success is a result of his gift for creating and exploiting images of sensuality and betrayal. The equivocal properties of language that in the comedy produce amusing puns and hilarious misunderstandings become in the tragedy obscene insinuations and deadly lies.

Throughout *Twelfth Night* the audience is delighted with the deformation of images and the power of language to alter images of reality. Viola herself demonstrates the power of a false image in her disguise as Cesario, and several characters are manipulators who depend upon this interplay between perception and truth. Sir Toby Belch encourages the feckless Sir Andrew Aguecheek to imagine himself a successful suitor to Olivia and persuades him to read Olivia's overtures to Cesario as deliberate incitements to his own masculinity: "She did show favor to the youth in your sight only to exasperate you, to awake your dormouse valor, to put fire in your heart and brimstone in your liver" (3.2.17–20). Likewise, the sword fight that Toby arranges between two unlikely duelists, Sir Andrew and Viola, a half-witted coward and a young woman, depends upon the creation of parallel personas of furious courage. Fabian to Viola about Andrew: "He is indeed, sir, the most skillful, bloody, and fatal opposite that you could possibly have found in any part of Illyria" (3.4.276–78). Toby to Andrew about Viola: "Why, man, he's a very devil. I have not seen such a firago. . . . They say he has been fencer to the Sophy" (3.4.284–85, 289–90). After the duel is interrupted by Antonio, who mistakes the image of Viola for that of Sebastian and rescues her, Toby extends the sport by refashioning the image of Viola from "a very devil" to "a very dishonest, paltry boy, and more a coward than a hare." To Sir Toby this game of gulling is a witty exercise calculated to amuse himself and his friends and to line his pockets.

As Toby is to Andrew, so, in *Othello,* Iago is to Roderigo. In fact, Iago is quick to assure the audience that he isn't actually a friend of such an idiot: "For I mine own gained knowledge should profane / If I would time expend with such a snipe / But for my sport and profit" (1.3.427–29). In tragedy, the game of images and reputations is deadly. At Iago's prompting, Roderigo resolves to sell all his land, disguise himself, and follow Othello's party to Cyprus, a scheme like something out of *Twelfth Night:* Iago takes money from Roderigo in return for promises that Desdemona will ultimately be his, much as Sir Toby promises Sir Andrew that cash and persistence will ultimately win him Olivia. The sword fight that Toby arranges finally yields nothing more dangerous than "a bloody coxcomb" for himself and Sir Andrew: comedy protects its fools from serious harm. But in Act 5 of the tragedy, Roderigo, incited by Iago to attack his rival in a corresponding fray, is injured by that rival (Cassio) and then murdered by Iago, his deceiver and instigator of the scheme.

In both comedy and tragedy Shakespeare is fascinated with the mechanics of deception or delusion (from *ludere,* "to play"), particularly self-delusion. Self-delusion involves playing games with reality, construing images and words in ways that correspond to one's wishes, and in both dramatic modes Shakespeare identifies the tendency to self-deception with the force of desire, the overpowering human "will."

In comedy this will is often amorous, with would-be lovers regularly attempting to refashion the facts:

> OLIVIA
> Stay. I prithee, tell me what thou think'st of me.
> VIOLA
> That you do think you are not what you are.
> OLIVIA
> If I think so, I think the same of you.
> VIOLA
> Then think you right. I am not what I am.
> OLIVIA
> I would you were as I would have you be.
> (3.1.145–49)

The irony underlying this exchange, of course, is that Viola, dressed as a boy, already presents a false image to the world, but the crucial statement is Olivia's last line. In comedy such force of will usually leads to hilarity, as it does here, but sometimes it can lead to scornful laughter and even humiliation, as in the case of Malvolio, whose illegitimate desires are implicit in his name, which translates as "ill will."

In Shakespeare's day a synonym for the noun "will" was "carnal appetite," or the sexual urge. When this sense is applied to *Twelfth Night*, the scrambled relations of Orsino, Olivia, Viola, and Sebastian become all the more heated and amusing, and the connection to *Othello* becomes especially clear. Iago, thwarted in his wish for promotion and driven by the desire for revenge on the general, manipulates Othello by magnifying Desdemona's sexual appetites, particularly her refusal of the Venetian bachelors she might have married: "Foh! One may smell in such a will most rank, / Foul disproportion, thoughts unnatural" (3.3.272–73). Iago presses the sexual connotations of the noun when he tells Roderigo that love "is merely a lust of the blood and a permission of the will," and when he goads Othello with the suggestion that Cassio "did . . . Lie . . . With her—on her—what you will." (4.1.38–42) And in *Twelfth Night* the theme of sexual desire, its urge for fulfillment, and its demand for transformation are indicated in the punning subtitle, *What You Will*.

III

Twelfth Night and *Othello* examine not only the strength of the human will but also the strength of human wit, particularly the powers of the imagination or invention. The etymological connection of "image" with "imagination" indicates that both the misreading of images by the victims and the deliberate transformation of images (for good or ill) originate in the imaginative faculty. Shakespeare's attention to the unreliability of visual and verbal signs is an outgrowth of his concern for the positive and negative possibilities of the human wit, the imaginative faculty, and of his worries about the role of fiction in general. Comedy and tragedy delight and horrify us with the consequences of misinterpretation and invention.

The most spectacular instance in *Twelfth Night* of fictional delusion is Maria's scheme to bamboozle Malvolio with the fake letter. Forgery offers a textbook case of confused images—"I can write very like my lady your niece; on a forgotten matter, we can hardly make distinction of our hands" (2.3.158–60)—and the steward's misreading of the letter involves his own erroneous manipulation of verbal signs: he vainly assumes that he is "the unknown beloved" mentioned in it, that its cryptic words actually make sense, and that they pertain to him. Even before finding the letter he creates mental pictures that transform him into the lover of the Countess and master of the house: as one of the onlookers puts it, "Look how imagination blows him." Malvolio's own imagination has puffed him up, made him vulnerable to abuse by the creative imagination of another, and so he is tricked into misinterpretation, seduced by words into thinking himself the object of desire. Self-deception is usually a precondition for deception.

Maria has made the letter look as if it comes from Olivia ("By my life, this is my lady's hand!"; "And the impressure of her Lucrece, with which she uses to seal"); it sounds as if it does ("her very phrases!"); and Malvolio adjusts the image of the addressee to suit his conception of himself ("If this should be thee, Malvolio!"). The verbs in the following passage illustrate Malvolio's attempts to make reality conform to his willful conception of it: "'M.O.A.I. doth sway my life,' Nay, but first let me see, let me see, let me see. . . . If I could make that resemble something in me! Softly! 'M.O.A.I.'—. . . . This simulation is not as the former, and yet to crush this a little, it would bow to me, for every one of these letters are in my name" (2.5.113–45). The truth, however, is confusing, as the anagrammatical relation of letters in the characters' names indicates: O-l-i-v-i-a loves not M-a-l-v-o-l-i-o but V-i-o-l-a. (Those anagrams, moreover, indicate that these characters' desires are not so different from one another's.) In its second phase, Maria's ingenious scheme further disturbs Malvolio's imagination: as Sir Toby puts it immediately after the letter scene, "Why, thou hast put him in such a dream that when the image of it leaves him he must run mad."

Othello is like a dream—a nightmare—in which the hero effectively runs mad as Iago infects his brain with images of bestiality and betrayal. The grotesque corruption of Othello's imagination at the hands of Iago represents a tragic version of the humiliating deception that Maria perpetrates on Malvolio: whereas she deceives a would-be lover into thinking himself desired, Iago deceives a husband into thinking himself displaced. Both schemers create verbal pictures of sex-starved women, Maria of a frustrated Olivia pining silently for her steward, Iago of a ruttish young wife finding satisfaction outside marriage. The deceivers even express their aims similarly. Maria will make Malvolio "a common recreation," an "ass"; the scheme "cannot but turn him into a notable contempt" (2.5.207–8); Olivia describes his parading before her in cross-garters as "midsummer madness." Iago's plot against Othello involves "making him egregiously an ass / And practicing upon his peace and quiet / Even to madness" (2.1.331–33).

The correspondences of comedy and tragedy begin to emerge even more clearly when we observe that there are also connections between the imaginative designs of Viola and Iago. Both present false images to the world and declare their misrepresentation in precisely the same language, Iago to Roderigo and Viola to Olivia: "I am not what I am" (*Twelfth Night*, 3.1.148; *Othello*, 1.1.71). When arranging with the Sea Captain for her male disguise, Viola asks him, "Only shape thou thy silence to my wit" (1.2.64). In comedy that "wit" is creative intelligence, a capacity for play benevolently employed, and Viola's mask is only physical and temporary. In tragedy the term takes on more sinister applications. When Iago tells Roderigo, "Thou know'st we work by wit and not by witchcraft," the denial ironically imparts a demonic quality to his ingenuity, and the effects of his hypocrisy, what amounts to a psychological disguise, are fatal. In fact, in considering the word "wit" as a synonym for imagination in *Othello*, we may see Iago not only as the manipulator of fictions but as victim of them too. As Othello becomes more and more cruel to his wife, Emilia complains to Iago that villains must have slandered Desdemona: "O, fie upon them! Some such squire he was / That turned your wit the seamy side without / And made you to suspect me with the Moor" (4.2.171–73). Iago's imaginative aggression may be a result of imaginative injury.

The plot to poison Othello's imagination is a tour de force of ingenuity. Its most obvious component is Iago's wearing of a mask, his playing the role of "honest Iago," trusted friend. Highlights include the staging of scenes, such as Roderigo's planted insult to Cassio that leads to the brawl, or Cassio's "guilty-like" parting from Desdemona. The most theatrically effective scene involves a stage prop, Desdemona's handkerchief, especially when Bianca returns it to Cassio with Othello as audience. Narrative fictions are employed strategically, particularly Iago's recital of Cassio's nocturnal dream in the barracks, ending with "'Cursèd fate that gave thee to the Moor!'" (3.3.467–82). (This episode raises the fascinating question of whether Cassio might have had such a dream and whether in fact he might feel an attraction to Desdemona; in that case Iago's talent would consist of using what he finds as well as making up his evidence.) Othello's imagination is most immediately affected by the salacious images Iago conjures for it: "Would you, the supervisor, grossly gape on, / Behold her topped?" (3.3.451–52). Iago evades the demand for "ocular proof" by offering filthy pictures to the mind's eye: "It is impossible you should see this, / Were they as prime as goats, as hot as monkeys, / As salt as wolves in pride . . ." (3.3.459–61). And the simple substitution of a preposition—"lie on" for "lie with"—creates a verbal image so potent that it brings on Othello's epilepsy. Originally, as Othello reports in the speech to the Senate, he won Desdemona's affection with his imaginative narration of his past, and once Iago succeeds in stimulating that fertile imagination with pornographic fictions, Othello is finished.

IV

As Shakespeare's own imagination began to darken, his perception of the contradictions and discontinuities in our nature began to intensify, and comedy began to metamorphose into tragedy. The mature plays attest to Shakespeare's recognition of the mutuality of comedy and tragedy, his awareness that the two modes inevitably shade into each other, that the potentially tragic strain can heighten the joys of comedy, just as the comic affiliations of tragedy can seem to relieve and therefore intensify its darkness. *Twelfth Night* and *Othello* especially reveal this mutuality because Shakespeare seems to be concerned with similar topics—the slipperiness of words, the unreliability of all representational systems, and the immense range of the human imagination. The well-meaning deceptions of a Viola and the psychotic plots of an Iago have their different modes, but those modes may be more alike than we have been taught to think. *Twelfth Night* concludes with the Clown's melancholy song about the misery of marriage, the inevitability of failure, and the constancy of the wind and the rain; at the Globe performances, on the other hand, performances of a tragedy like *Othello* would have been followed by dances, festive songs, and acts of clowning. Konstantin Stanislavsky, the great Russian director who first staged Chekhov's plays, considered *The Cherry Orchard* a tragedy; the author disagreed, insisting that he had written a comedy. Audiences since then have not been able to make up their minds, and it is appropriate that they should not. For Chekhov, for Shakespeare, for all great artists, and for audiences and readers as well, artistic forms are very good servants but very bad masters.

Women and the Tyranny of Dramatic Genres

èð

JEANNE ADDISON ROBERTS
THE AMERICAN UNIVERSITY

Thinking about *Twelfth Night* and *Othello* together raises some questions about dramatic genres. We know, or think we know, that plays take two basic forms—comedy and tragedy; and we often see individual works in terms of these genres. We know that the editors of the Shakespeare First Folio, two actors from Shakespeare's acting company, classified *Twelfth Night* as a comedy and *Othello* as a tragedy. And yet there are questions. *Twelfth Night* has been described as "dark comedy" and *Othello* starts out like a comedy and departs from tragic tradition in its domestic setting. Russ McDonald shows how the two forms may overlap and helpfully suggests that we imagine the two genres not as separate types but as poles of a dramatic continuum that permits and encourages variations, blendings, and alternative perspectives.

I suggest that we consider modifying even this binary paradigm and think rather of dramatic materials as comparable to a sculptor's lump of clay that may be shaped into permutations almost infinite. It may take the form of a bust, human figure, an animal, a flower, an unidentifiable monster, or a totally abstract design. Success is limited only by the imagination of the artist and the appreciative capabilities of the audience. It is true that human beings seem to think in terms of categories, and categories change slowly; but they do change. Drama does not have to be either comedy or tragedy as we have traditionally defined them, and it is refreshing to free ourselves from the tyranny of genre. You will observe that few modern playwrights give generic tags to their works and that television directories favor the catchall term "drama."

Having said this, however, I must add that the categories of comedy and tragedy are perhaps essential to a study of Shakespeare since he and his age demonstrably thought in terms of such categories. (That the categories were showing signs of disintegration may be indicated by Polonius's meticulous catalog of such subcategories as history, pastoral, pastoral-comical, historical-pastoral, tragical-historical, and tragical-comical-historical-pastoral [*Hamlet* 2.2.421–23].) I should like to consider briefly how Shakespeare's comedy and tragedy conform to inherited traditions, how they radically depart from traditions, and how they are limited by those traditions.

11

Shakespeare was writing under the influence of classical drama. There is no evidence that he knew Greek comedy or tragedy in the original language but he certainly knew the Latin works of Plautus and Terence who continued the traditions of Menander, inventor of New Comedy, so-called to distinguish it from the Old Comedy of Aristophanes. The scripts of Seneca's Latin tragedy, which drew on Greek tragedy, were also well known to English Renaissance writers. The dramatic traditions that Shakespeare inherited were constructed by men and for men in patriarchal cultures.

Drama is closely related to the society that produces it. It typically focuses on the tensions and conflicts of the culture surrounding it. As cultures change, drama changes, and indeed drama may be an instrument of change. As Freud suggests, humor grows out of tensions and conflicts in society. Laughter is a nervous response that affords temporary relief from an underlying anxiety. Traditional happy endings suppress doubts and fulfill social hopes for harmonious resolutions. Unhappy endings focus also on tensions and conflicts, exposing them overtly and playing out the catastrophic consequences inherent in the conflicts.

But the relation of drama to society is not necessarily that of a mirror up to nature. It is a striking anomaly that in Greek tragedy, produced by a culture where women were clearly subordinated and relatively powerless, female characters loom very large and often very threateningly. Clytemnestra, Electra, Jocasta, Antigone, Phaedra, Medea, and the Bacchae are murderous, incestuous, and rebellious, and they are developed in some detail. Even though they suffer death or exile, they are forces to be feared and reckoned with by the masculine society. Indeed, they seem to be magnified expressions of male nightmares.

By contrast, most of Shakespeare's tragedies are, as their titles suggest, affairs between men. Such women as Lady Macbeth, the witches, Gertrude, and Lear's daughters may also be male nightmares and causes of disaster, but they are subordinate characters. Others, like Ophelia, Lady Macduff, Cordelia, and Desdemona, fulfill, on the other hand, the roles of innocent victims. Lady Macbeth and Desdemona, initially strong-minded women, dwindle to near ciphers by the middle of their plays. Lady Macbeth is mad, and the confident Desdemona who has stood up resolutely to her father accepts a role as a passively dutiful wife. The women may die, but they are not "tragic heroes" and act only incidentally as major forces of the plot. In *Romeo and Juliet* and *Antony and Cleopatra* Shakespeare does become a daring innovator, directing attention more to Juliet than to Romeo and devoting a whole final act to the death of Cleopatra. In these two plays tragedy actually shows signs of evolution to a newer and more radical form, which includes women in roles more complex than those of villains and victims. Shakespeare's late romances also modify tragic norms by offsetting them with patterns of comedy. In accepting traditional forms of tragedy, Shakespeare is limited by his restricted interest in women, but he also explores the possibility of redrawing boundaries.

My chief interest here, however, is in the evolution of comedy, and it is to that topic that I will address my attention in the rest of this article.

If classical tragedy expressed male nightmares, classical comedy seems more like male wish fulfillment. In Aristophanes women are occasionally necessary pawns; but, except in *Lysistrata*, they are all but invisible. The pairing off of marriageable children does not seem to generate enough anxiety to be a dramatic subject for the early Greek playwright.

Only with the arrival of Menander, father of both the Greek and Roman drama called New Comedy, does marriage and the establishment of a new generation become the subject of comedy. I suspect that this development reflects a cultural change that began to make the subject problematic. With this change a few "women," played on stage by male actors, began to appear, but the form was still constructed by men and for men in a patriarchal society where marriages were arranged for the security and convenience of men. Female characters appear in predictable stereotypes—mother, nurse, wife, servant, prostitute, old lady, and the virgin who is the subject of the negotiations but is usually a mere cipher. The arrangement of marriage is clearly a male prerogative and is carried on between men.

The two Roman models that Shakespeare must have known well were Plautus and Terence. Both regard marriage as the focal point of the comic plot, but the interested parties are men. In Plautus's *Casina* there are two wives and a maid, but the marital object of the two men never appears on the stage. The struggle is between father and son. Courtesans and low-class women abound in Plautus's plays, and marriages and promises of marriage constitute a regular resolution, but the virgins are minor players and are rarely individualized.

In Terence again and again there are paired male suitors, but one or both of the objects of their suits remain invisible. Courtesans may be attractive, and extramarital sex is not uncommon; but the virgins on whom the future depends are merely the counters of male negotiation. The plays are funny because of their satiric portrayals of socially disruptive stock characters like the lecherous old man, the rich miser, and the manipulative servant, but the happy endings depend on disposing of the virgins. In this rigidly patriarchal society there seems to be no interest whatever in the personality, desire, or individuality of virtuous young women of the upper classes. The comedy recapitulates almost ritualistically a parade of faceless daughters married off in ways that support custom. But drama is not ritual, and dramatic forms change. Shakespeare's comedies are within the tradition but with notable innovations.

When I ask my college students how they recognize drama as comic, they invariably say "It's funny and it ends happily." At this point I used to give my lecture on C. L. Barber's analysis of Shakespeare's comedy as festive, providing the release of the holiday after the monotony of the everyday. I followed this lecture by one on Northrop Frye's analysis of Shakespeare's comedy as a celebration of the triumph of the younger generation over the old and the founding of a new, potentially fertile family—the ritual passing of winter into spring. After dazzling them with these lectures, I would ask again for a definition of comedy, and my students would blithely repeat that they recognize the form because it is funny and ends happily. So much for pedagogy.

I have gradually come to conclude that my students are more useful than Barber and Frye in putting Shakespeare's comedy in perspective. Instead of neatly explaining, their definition presents us with basic questions—What makes drama funny and what constitutes a happy ending? And are these qualities constant and "universal"?

At the time that Shakespeare was writing his comedies, especially in the last decade of the sixteenth century, major changes were taking place in English society. Whether men liked it or not, great political power was in the hands of Queen Elizabeth, an unmarried woman. Education, limited though it was, was becoming increasingly available to women. And, at least in theory, parent-arranged marriages were beginning to give way to companionate marriages arranged by the couples themselves. Arranged marriages were in fact still overwhelmingly the norm, but social changes seem to have brought young women increasingly into the focus of Shakespeare's comedy. Whereas the Greeks and Romans had expressed in tragedy their anxiety about the murderous power of women, the ancients were apparently confident enough about their marriage machinery to suppress the female participant and represent the tensions as clearly between men.

Shakespeare's variations on this New Comedy theme are truly astonishing. Perhaps because by 1596 he was the father only of daughters, or perhaps because he was unusually sensitive to male tensions and dilemmas, and to social upheavals, his comedies give very unusual scope to women. He explores male/female tensions between the young as well as the old, and reveals the ambiguities of their resolution.

Shakespeare's greatest comic innovation is his portrayal of women as major players in marital negotiations. His comic heroines—Rosalind, Beatrice, Portia, and the Helena of *All's Well That Ends Well* are powerful, resourceful, and articulate. They are also vividly individualized. The Viola of *Twelfth Night* is a transitional figure from these strong-minded women to the more passive heroines of the romances. (She finds the knots of her situation too difficult to untie and leaves the resolution to time— 2.3.40–41.) But she too is a memorable character. However, all the heroines of Shakespeare's romantic comedies have in common one thing that ties them to earlier patterns. All are virgins and all end their stories either married or with the prospect of marriage. Indeed, in Shakespeare's first eleven comedies there are thirty-two marriages either accomplished or expected; and the overwhelming majority of brides are virgins. (Shakespeare never applies the word to men—the sexual status of the males is apparently of no interest.) Many theorists have pointed out that, as in New Comedy, the business of Shakespearean comedy is marriage.

In a few plays there are strong resemblances to the model of Plautus and Terence, but even in these there are interesting modifications. *The Comedy of Errors*, written very early in Shakespeare's career, is closely based on Plautus's *The Twin Menaechmi;* but Shakespeare has seemingly feminized it, cleaned it up, and broadened its focus. Whereas Plautus is concerned with the tensions in an established marriage and the mechanics of restoring to it at least superficial order, Shakespeare has added an older generation, a long-separated father and mother, and Luciana, a marriageable sister, as a prospective wife. Thus young lovers become part of the standard New Comedy plot, modifying Plautus's untypical interest in the already-married. Shakespeare has also toned down the prostitute and left the relationship between her and the married Antipholus ambiguous enough so that at least one distinguished critic has described it as a platonic friendship.

Shakespeare has added women; but looking closely, we find that they are the standard stereotypes—wife, whore, and mother. The real interest of the comedy is still in the males. Splitting the hero into twins provides a perfect device for representing the recurrent male dilemma of trying to reconcile the images of chaste virgin and promiscuous whore so as to imagine an acceptable wife. Chastity prevails. The prostitute is domesticated. The virgin sister is a suitable bride. The mother has been desexualized by thirty years in a convent, and at the play's end only the fat, lecherous Luce remains a threat to Dromio. The abbess becomes a mouthpiece for the patriarchal voice as she blames the abused wife for her husband's presumed madness:

> The venom clamors of a jealous woman
> Poisons more deadly than a mad dog's tooth.
> It seems his sleeps were hind'red by thy railing,
> And thereof comes it that his head is light.
> Thou say'st his meat was sauc'd with thy upbraidings . . .
> The consequence is then, thy jealous fits
> Hath scar'd thy husband from the use of wits.
>
> (5.1.69–86)[2]

As in Plautus and Terence, in *The Comedy of Errors*, the marriageable virgin Luciana has very few lines and very little personality. Like Sebastian who magically appears to provide a spouse for Olivia at the end of *Twelfth Night*, Luciana is a device to assure a conventional New Comedy ending. These marriages are not arranged, but the prospects for long-term success of such "love" marriages may seem a bit dubious.

The Merry Wives of Windsor is also in some ways like Roman comedy. The double plot and multiple lovers reflect Terence, and the negotiation over the marriageable virgin is Plautine. We feel we know Anne Page as a lively and engaging young woman, and hers is the plan behind her marriage to the man of her choice. But Shakespeare has given her only thirty-three lines. His true innovation is the focus on the wives, and his satire of both jealous husbands and would-be seducers. The blame for both lechery and jealousy is now shifted firmly onto the men. And marriage in defiance of parental approval is both celebrated and presumed successful. Whether or not Shakespeare wrote this play for Queen Elizabeth, as has been suggested, it seems within its limits to qualify as a genuinely feminist play.

Love marriages are not, of course, always so happy. In both *Romeo and Juliet* and *Othello* they end disastrously. Juliet's father advances the traditional view of parental prerogative most vociferously, concluding when Juliet tries to resist:

> An you be mine, I'll give you to my friend.
> An you be not, hang, beg, starve, die in the streets,
> For, by my soul, I'll ne'er acknowledge thee
> Nor what is mine shall never do thee good.
>
> (3.5.203–6)

Desdemona's father, Brabantio, actually dies as a result of his daughter's defection.

---

[2] *The Riverside Shakespeare*, edited by G. Blakemore Evans (Boston: Houghton Mifflin, 1974).

Other plays are more ambiguous about love marriages vs. arranged marriages, but the topic was clearly timely. In *The Taming of the Shrew* the improbable parentally arranged marriage between Kate and Petruchio seems to turn out well—it promises to be a companionate marriage between equals (notwithstanding Kate's final praise of obedient wives) because the two have gradually learned to play the marriage game together. The marriages of Hortensio to his widow and Bianca to Lucentio, arranged by the principals themselves, look less promising—at least from a male point of view; neither Bianca nor the widow seems likely to be a duly docile wife.

Paternal forces are weakened but not forgotten in Shakespeare's comedies. Dead fathers are usually assets for his comic heroines. In the early comedy *Love's Labour's Lost*, Shakespeare presents us with four eligible men and four eligible women whom convention ineluctably persuades us to see as potential wives. But in the end, at precisely the juncture where the Princess of France receives the news of her father's death, she and her ladies in waiting reject the marriage offers of their suitors, forcing them to wait a year for a final decision. Rational appraisal of the men suggests that the women are right in not taking them too seriously. As the Princess says, the courtship has seemed like pleasant jest and bombastic passing of the time. It has been perceived by the women as mere merriment (5.2.777–84, *The Riverside Shakespeare*). And yet rational appraisal is not necessarily the stuff of comedy, and even a modern audience may share the mood of Berowne's wry conclusion:

> Our wooing doth not end like an old play:
> Jack hath not Gill. These ladies' courtesy
> Might well have made our sport a comedy.
> (5.2.874–76, *The Riverside Shakespeare*)

And a twelve-month wait, as he says, is "too long for a play." The only immediate hope for fertility in this play is a child of doubtful paternity conceived out of wedlock by a country wench. It is an imagined emblem of collapsing patriarchy. Conventional comedy has been severely challenged.

Other comic heroines who seem to benefit by absent fathers are Beatrice of *Much Ado*, Viola of *Twelfth Night*, Rosalind of *As You Like It*, Portia of *The Merchant of Venice*, Isabella of *Measure for Measure*, and Helena of *All's Well that Ends Well*. But the case is never quite clear. Beatrice benefits from the benevolence of her uncle Leonato, who colludes in "arranging" to make her fall in love with Benedict. Viola is forced into fending quite imaginatively for herself when deprived of father and brother, but she has sought refuge with Orsino, a duke known to her father; and she ends up marrying him.

Rosalind actually arranges her own marriage and presides over her play but chooses the son of her father's friend and manages to marry in her father's presence. Portia, perhaps the most powerful of the heroines, refuses to marry except by the device of the caskets arranged by her now-dead father and, before her marriage, she recites a conventional declaration of submission to her husband-to-be as "her lord, her governor, her king" (3.2.161–75). But even at the play's end she is displaying her dominance over Bassanio in the matter of the rings. Ironically, even modern audiences who may admire strong, intelligent, resourceful women often find Portia a bit overwhelming. Without a father, Isabella finds refuge in a convent and successfully resists seduction, but in order to do so she accepts the guidance of a new "father" figure in the form of the Duke disguised as a priest and may or may not succumb to his proposal of marriage. Helena uses her medical skill inherited from a dead father to cure a king and to win a husband but is only very belatedly successful in winning her reluctant spouse's cooperation in the match.

The transition from arranged to love marriage is not a clean break. Shakespeare seems acutely aware of the complex interaction of fathers and daughters. Daughters who actually defy their fathers rarely achieve unambiguously happy endings, and for Juliet and Desdemona the consequences are, of course, tragic. Daughters, no matter how powerful, are still not free agents. The prevailing male/female hierarchy of all the plays manifests itself in the use of disguise.

The disguise of men as women, which occurs only very rarely in Shakespeare, is degrading. But the experience of Rosalind, and Portia, and Viola as men is freeing and empowering. Even the rather docile Viola discovers in disguise her own attractions and succeeds in getting her man. A man disguised as a woman is descending on the Chain of Being. A woman experiencing life as a man is moving upward.

Shakespeare's comedies are funny—the mistaken identities of *The Comedy of Errors*, the male/female confrontation of *The Taming of the Shrew*, the clever tricks of *The Merry Wives*, the merry war between Beatrice and Benedict, and the riotous drunkards vs. the Puritan Malvolio in *Twelfth Night*. Perhaps most delicious is the humor that arises from sexual tensions; and the delay of consummation may be more pleasurable than the final resolution. Because all the women are more or less eager to be married, the conventional New Comedy nuptials do constitute happy endings—even if shadowed by doubts. Shakespeare's radical innovation is the sustained representation on stage of the women whose futures are at stake.

The forces of change at work in Elizabethan England and perhaps Shakespeare's own predilections and sensitivities profoundly changed the shape of comic drama in his time. The potential power of women and even their threat of dominance was publicly represented. It is possible that the fact that the audience knew that the "women" were actually men may have undermined the sense of these characters' threat as women. And one might argue that male anxiety was alleviated by the promise that these women are or will be safely confined within the bounds of matrimony. Shakespeare's later works in the comedy/romance mode change the emphasis from young lovers to the problems of the older generation. Happy endings are achieved only by miracles or supernatural intervention.

It may have occurred to you before now to note that all the playwrights and critics mentioned so far are men, writing primarily for male audiences. And it may even occur to you to ask what a happy ending might be for a female writing for a female audience. Given the scarcity of early female playwrights, there is not much material on which to base a theory. But there are two fascinating and suggestive examples that are worth mentioning.

In the Europe of the Middle Ages, the growth of convents made possible the development of female communities whose values differed somewhat from those of the surrounding culture. At the German convent of Gandersheim, a tenth-century nun named Hrosvitha wrote plays—six of which have survived. She says quite specifically that her plays are in emulation of Terence, and she calls her plays comedies. But she adds that she wishes to show the chastity of Christian virgins rather than the "shameless acts of licentious women" and to avoid the "pernicious voluptuousness of pagan writers" (*Hrosvitha of Gandersheim: Her Life, Times, and Works, and a Comprehensive Bibliography*, ed. Haight [1965], 20). (She must have had in mind the courtesans since there is little sign of voluptuousness among the salable virgins.)

Hrosvitha's most famous play, *Dulcitius*, deals with two very tense topics for women—forced obedience and rape. It is funny precisely because of its ridicule of men and the exhilarating prospect of their ultimate defeat. A would-be rapist becomes so deluded that he ends up kissing pots and pans in the kitchen where he is so begrimed in the process that he goes away "befouled and . . . defiled" with soot (*Dulcitius, A Mediaval Comedy*, trans. McCann [1933], 9). Curiously the play is named for this villain; but the central characters, three holy virgins, Agape, Chionia, and Irene, have a common goal, and it is not earthly marriage. They are determined to preserve their virginity against the assaults of lust and their religion against the threats of paganism. For Hrosvitha the happy ending for these virgins is Christian martyrdom. Agape and Chionia die in fire, and Irene is shot with arrows. Rejoicing Irene says, "The more cruelly I am tortured, the more will I glory and rejoice" (13). And she prepares to "enter the heavenly bridal chamber of the Eternal King." The ending is marriage, but with a notable difference. This ending may simply substitute one kind of patriarchal ideal for another, but it shatters the mold of traditional New Comedy in focusing on women and in frustrating the social goal of earthly matrimony. It is funny and it has a happy ending, but it rejects the focus on males and the pressure toward fertility that would establish a new human generation. This is indeed new comedy, but of a strikingly untraditional sort.

My second example of comedy by a woman is the seventeenth-century work of Margaret Cavendish, duchess of Newcastle, a play called *The Convent of Pleasure*, based roughly on Shakespeare's *Love's Labour's Lost*. Published in 1668 after the Restoration, when females had begun to act on the stage, the play seems never to have been performed. Cavendish had seen female actors on the Continent, however; and when she reports that she played scenes in her head, she was very likely imagining genuine women as players. Her heroine is Lady Happy, young, beautiful, very rich, and free of patriarchal restraints because of the recent death of her father. She resolves to retire with her female friends to an abbey where they may, as she says, "enjoy pleasure, and not bury [themselves] from it" (from *Plays Never Before Printed* [London, 1668], 6). Only poor women, she adds, need men "who make the Female sex their slaves." Accordingly her cloister is to be a "place for freedom, not to vex the Senses but to please them" (7). Men are duly excluded.

Cavendish's play focuses almost exclusively on women. Like *Love's Labour's Lost*, *The Convent of Pleasure* has a play within a play and a masque. But unlike Shakespeare's abortive play of the nine worthies "celebrating" farcically the great men of history, Cavendish provides nine scenes from the lives of average women. Her internal plays are a grim and extended catalog of the woes of women. They feature in rapid succession: (1) women who pull their drunken husbands out of the ale house, expecting to be beaten when they get home; (2) a sick pregnant woman; (3) male gamblers who waste their estates and entertain whores; (4) a mother of a dead child; (5) women drinking to cure their melancholy over their unfaithful husbands; (6) a woman painfully giving birth; (7) ancient ladies discussing the trials of motherhood; (8) a dead child born to a dead mother; (9) a married man pursuing a virgin (3.2–3.10, pp. 24–30). The Epilogue to this internal play declares quite understandably after what we have seen that

> Marriage is a Curse we find,
> Especially to women kind. (30)

Cavendish clearly thought of her play as a comedy. These scenes are certainly not funny, but the grim realism is safely offset by the utopian female world of the convent. Humor is directed at male would-be suitors who consider such drastic measures as knocking down the walls, setting the convent on fire, and even disguising themselves as women. In male drama, as we have seen, such disguise would be a movement down the Chain of Being—Falstaff disguised as Mother Prat in *The Merry Wives* sinks to ignominious disgrace. The male plan in Cavendish seems ludicrous in part because it is conceived by the males as such a desperate measure and finally rejected. But there is another side to the story. In Cavendish's play a foreign Princess appears and wins the love of Lady Happy. The play flirts quite openly with scenes of lesbian possibility. The scenes are funny partly because they are so flagrantly transgressive of social norms.

Cavendish herself seems to have been happily married to an admiring husband, and it is perhaps not surprising that the happy ending of her play reveals that the visiting Princess is actually a man so that he and Lady Happy can be safely wedded. But the sustained disguise of the man in female dress is a revolutionary and rarely imitated innovation. Cavendish concludes with a rather muted praise of marriage

> . . . though some few be unhappy in Marriage, yet there are many more that are so happy that they would not change their condition.
>
> (3.10, p. 31)

She has, in the end, accepted the convention of marriage as the end of New Comedy, but her vivid exposure of the pains of marriage for women leaves a stronger impression than her conclusion. And her opening up of the possibility of an unconventional lesbian union, like Hrosvitha's alternative happy ending, casts doubt over the inevitability of the pattern of New Comedy. Marriage may not always be a happy ending for women.

Elizabeth Cary in her play *The Tragedy of Mariam, The Fair Queen of Jewry*, probably written about the same time as *Othello,* gives these lines to Salome, who has been speaking of divorce:

> Why should such privilege to man be given?
> Or given to them, why barr'd from women then?
> Are men than we in greater grace with Heaven?
> Or cannot women hate as well as men?
> I'll be the custom-breaker: and begin
> To show my sex the way to freedom's door. . . .
> (1.4.305–10, eds. Barry Weller and
> Margaret W. Ferguson, Berkeley:
> University of California, 1994)

Admittedly Salome, already on her second husband and soon to take a third, is a villain; but her voicing of these rebellious lines is still electrifying in a world where women are taught to be chaste, silent, and obedient.

Shakespeare's comedies preserve the form of New Comedy with its focus on marriage, but with their acceptance of strong-minded women they reflect a new spirit in his age and open up the possibility of modifying the genre. Change was in the air. Female actors and female playwrights were on the horizon. Women actors sparked the revival of Shakespeare's comedies in the eighteenth century, and between 1660 and 1720 more than sixty plays were written by women.

But old ways die hard. The patterns of conventional New Comedy are still very much with us. I understand that the makers of the film *Pretty Woman* had to change the original ending in order to make the prostitute and the magnate seem to live together happily ever after. When I asked my thirteen-year-old granddaughter how she liked the current film *Reality Bites,* she said she liked it but it was predictable. What she meant was that she understood the conventions of New Comedy and saw from the start that the woman would choose the charismatic, underemployed, dope-ridden hunk over the responsible, hardworking nerd, and that a "happy" ending would ensue from the merger.

It is not hard to understand the enduring appeal of this form. It offers the promise of harmony and order in a chaotic world. The urge to merge is unquestionably powerful, and the escape from freedom is perennially seductive. But autonomy is as important as relationship. Good marriages have blessed both individuals and society, but their traditional structure has been defined by patriarchy, and romantic comedy often seems to perpetuate the pattern. Its irresistible "happy ending" is potentially dangerous for women. It has been argued that the ultimate carrier of oppression is the psyche of the oppressed. Too many girls still fail to focus on their own lives because consciously or unconsciously they are waiting for their prince to come and determine their destinies. The Cinderella complex is still alive and well in the United States. Students often complain that Bassanio in *The Merchant of Venice* is not good enough for Portia, or that Orlando in *As You Like It* is not equal to Rosalind, or even that Viola is too good for Orsino; but they never seriously reject the mandatory "happy ending" of marriage.

In teaching Shakespeare, it may be useful to have students imagine how his plots might have been treated differently by a female playwright. The Canadian dramatist Ann-Marie MacDonald has taken up this challenge in her play *Goodnight Desdemona (Good Morning Juliet)*. Her central character imagines that both *Romeo and Juliet* and *Othello* were meant to be comedies—and certainly not New Comedies. The author plays out farcically the possibilities of a transvestite Romeo and Juliet and of a Desdemona who adopts the perquisites of a man. The play not only demolishes "tragedy," but it also rejects the generic limitations of comedy. It is funny, and it ends "happily," but it deconstructs its originals in ways that raise interesting questions.

Modern women playwrights have begun to draw new pictures. Their plays may be funny, though the humor is often black or self-deprecatory. The laughter these plays evoke is clearly tension-releasing. Serious modern plays by women often defy traditional categorization. They may end "happily" but almost never in marriage, though marriage may figure in their plots. Their authors give their women lives that are complex and not neatly resolved. These women's plays tend to be more in the vein of Chekhov's *The Cherry Orchard*, which he insisted was a comedy, than in the modes of Shakespeare. Caryl Churchill's *Cloud Nine*, Wendy Wasserstein's *The Sisters Rosenweig*, Beth Henley's *Crimes of the Heart*, and Timberlake Wertenbaker's *Our Country's Good* all share a special interest in women. But they carry women's stories far beyond the potential pleasures of courtship. We no longer hear much about virgins (one of the young women of *Reality Bites* is shown recording sexual encounter #66, although she has trouble remembering the name of her partner). Not one of these modern women's plays ends with a wedding. Their conclusions are muted, although they do share a very guarded pleasure in change, growth, and survival, which may entitle them to be thought of as having "happy endings." The important thing is that women have become major players. Some seeds of this development might just possibly be found in Shakespeare's comedies. He accepted the premises of New Comedy—that men need virginal and preferably affluent wives to ensure the purity and prosperity of their progeny and that marriage is the end of the story for women. (Men survive to be heroes of histories and tragedies.) The limitations, especially for women, are real; but Shakespeare expanded the boundaries of the form by imagining interesting female characters, thereby opening the way to patterns beyond courtship and automatic matrimony.

Twelfth Night and *Othello,* Those Extraordinary Twins

❧

Stephen Booth
UNIVERSITY OF CALIFORNIA, BERKELEY

Although this essay gets general at the end—and very, very preachy—its immediate occasion is particular and mundane: concern on the part of one of this volume's many editors that, conditioned as you might be by theme-park thinking, you will wonder at, and object to, the coupling here of plays so variously and urgently unlike one another as *Twelfth Night* and *Othello.*

By "theme-park thinking" I mean the kind of thinking that causes teachers and publishers and repertory companies to assign or publish or schedule works in groups determined by some shared topic. An obvious instance is the pairing of *Romeo and Juliet* and *West Side Story* on syllabuses, in paperbacks, and at Shakespeare festivals. *Hamlet* and *Rosencrantz and Guildenstern Are Dead* make an equally popular, equally handsome couple, and *Richard III* and Josephine Tey's novel *Daughter of Time* keep company almost as steady. The same sort of urge results in thematically chosen seasons of Shakespeare plays. For instance, Shenandoah Shakespeare Express called its 1993 repertory (*Romeo and Juliet, Antony and Cleopatra,* and *A Midsummer Night's Dream*) "a season of love," and, one year when it couldn't find a common denominator for its four chosen plays, the California Shakespeare Festival felt impelled to fake it by tagging its season "His Infinite Variety."

Theme-park thinking is, of course, not exclusive to the Shakespeare industry. Instructors in mandatory composition courses for college freshmen routinely choose readings on the basis of a common theme. I can't think of any actual examples at the moment, but the kind of thing I'm talking about would be pairing *Cyrano de Bergerac* with *Pinocchio* (works of heightened nasality), or grouping *Lady Windermere's Fan, Lady Chatterley's Lover,* and *Lad, a Dog.*

The label I give it and the flippancy of my last examples have, I trust, betrayed my distaste for theme-park thought. I will come back later to that distaste and attempt to validate it. For the moment, however, I must get on with the job I was brought in to do, namely, justifying the choice of two patently dissimilar plays as the basis for this volume—justifying the choice in exactly the terms I have been sneering at.

So.

Twelfth Night and *Othello* are plays that tell stories that appear radically different in kind and that evoke radically different responses from audiences, but in actuality—in an actuality I will later say is irrelevant—they are remarkably similar.

Some of the likenesses between *Twelfth Night* and *Othello* are ones that would not be worth a second thought if they did not occur in plays that share a deeper similarity. I want to start with some trivial, incidental points of likeness and work my way down gradually to the plays' deep thematic likeness.

To begin with the truly minimal, central deceivers in both *Twelfth Night* and *Othello* echo and play on "I am that I am," the phrase in Exodus 3:14 by which Jehovah so unsatisfactorily defines himself for Moses. During their second interview, Olivia asks the disguised Viola "his" opinion of her and thereby opens the way into an ontological cul-de-sac:

OLIVIA
    Stay. I prithee, tell me what thou think'st of me.
VIOLA
    That you do think you are not what you are.
OLIVIA
    If I think so, I think the same of you.
VIOLA
    Then think you right. I am not what I am.
          (*Twelfth Night*, 3.1.145–48)

Iago uses the same words in celebrating the difference between what he is and what he appears to be:

    For when my outward action doth demonstrate
    The native act and figure of my heart
    In complement extern, 'tis not long after
    But I will wear my heart upon my sleeve
    For daws to peck at. I am not what I am.
          (*Othello*, 1.1.67–71)

For one more petty likeness between *Twelfth Night* and *Othello*, both plays are at pains to introduce false ocular evidence into deceptions that succeed without that hard-won evidence. In *Twelfth Night*, the scene in which Feste the clown visits the imprisoned Malvolio begins with instructions from Maria to Feste: "Nay, I prithee, put on this gown and this beard; make him believe thou art Sir Topas the curate. Do it quickly" (4.2.1–3). While Feste puts on the disguise, Maria leaves the stage to fetch Sir Toby. Although she returns immediately, Maria does not speak again until the first Feste/ Malvolio interview is over. Only then does she say the second of her two speeches in the scene: "Thou mightst have done this without thy beard and gown. He sees thee not" (4.2.67–68). And in *Othello* Iago contrives to plant Desdemona's strawberry-spotted handkerchief upon Cassio and then is so typically lucky as to have Bianca bring the handkerchief onto the stage and confront Cassio with it in sight of the concealed Othello. Iago's scheme works perfectly: his charade convinces Othello that Desdemona has been false to him with Cassio. But *any* handkerchief would have served as evidence. After Cassio and Bianca exit, Othello comes forward to Iago:

OTHELLO How shall I murder him, Iago?
IAGO Did you perceive how he laughed at his vice?
OTHELLO O Iago!
IAGO And did you see the handkerchief?
OTHELLO Was that mine?
IAGO Yours, by this hand! . . . .

(4.1.188–94)

For another sort of likeness entirely between *Twelfth Night* and *Othello*, listen to the following lines:

> Why should I not, had I the heart to do it,
> Like to th' Egyptian thief at point of death,
> Kill what I love?—a savage jealousy
> That sometimes savors nobly. But hear me this:
> Since you to nonregardance cast my faith,
> And that I partly know the instrument
> That screws me from my true place in your favor,
> Live you the marble-breasted tyrant still.

I like to put those lines on spot-passage tests—*ungraded* spot-passage tests—to see what percentage of my students will guess that Othello is the speaker. Sometimes every member of a class will agree that the lines (*Twelfth Night*, 5.1.119–26; spoken by Orsino) are Othello's.

For larger evidence of kinship between *Twelfth Night* and *Othello*, consider the surprising similarity between the Toby-Andrew relationship in *Twelfth Night* and the Iago-Roderigo relationship in *Othello*. In both cases a foolish, well-to-do young man, desperately ambitious of a woman he cannot hope to have, is gulled for profit by another man. Moreover, the engineered fight into which Cassio and Roderigo are gulled and into which Montano intrudes to become its chief victim (*Othello*, 2.3) echoes the engineered fight into which Viola and Andrew are gulled and into which Antonio intrudes to become its chief victim (*Twelfth Night*, 3.4).

And the motif of following and service is common to the two plays.

But the big likeness between *Twelfth Night* and *Othello* is their common denominator in the topic of evidence, a topic I have already touched on incidentally and one that is central to both plays. The centrality of evidence to the events of the plays is obvious in Malvolio's readiness to accept the (extremely persuasive) false evidence of Maria's letter, in various characters' confidence that clothes make Viola a man and that anyone who looks just like one of the twins must be that twin, and in Othello's readiness to accept Iago's fiction on evidence insufficient to withstand any slight effort to test it. What is not so obvious is that the topic of trustworthy and untrustworthy evidence recurs incidentally and in a variety of dimensions all over both plays and gives each the kind of extra unity and thus identity that unostentatious alliteration or internal rhyme can give a line of verse.

I want to start my list of examples of concern for evidence in the two plays with an example of unreliable evidence from which a character draws a valid conclusion. When in her soliloquy in 2.2 of *Twelfth Night* Viola examines Olivia's behavior toward her and draws a conclusion from it, her evidence is no stronger than—is in fact rather weaker than—Malvolio's when he is fooled by Maria's letter. The big difference is that Viola's guess happens to be right.

> I left no ring with her. What means this lady?
> Fortune forbid my outside have not charmed her!
> She made good view of me, indeed so much
> That methought her eyes had lost her tongue,
> For she did speak in starts distractedly.
> She loves me, sure! The cunning of her passion
> Invites me in this churlish messenger.
> None of my lord's ring? Why, he sent her none!
> I am the man.
>
> (2.2.17–25)

The reading of evidence is pervasive in *Twelfth Night.* For instance, Viola's soliloquy follows immediately upon the exit speech of Malvolio, who has followed Viola to return to her the ring she never gave Olivia: "Come, sir, you peevishly threw it to her, and her will is it should be so returned. If it be worth stooping for, there it lies, in your eye; if not, be it his that finds it" (2.2.13–16). At the end of 1.5, Olivia called Malvolio onto the stage and told him to run after "that same peevish messenger, / The County's man," who, she says, "left this ring behind him, / Would I or not. Tell him I'll none of it" (1.5.307–9). Building only upon Olivia's word "peevish," Malvolio reads "left this ring behind him" as evidence of a fully imagined, wholly imaginary scene in which "Cesario" "peevishly threw the ring" to Olivia.

The following speech, the one in which Viola asks her rescuer to help her to a disguise, is a series of variations on the theme of evidence:

> There is a fair behavior in thee, captain,
> And though that nature with a beauteous wall
> Doth oft close in pollution, yet of thee
> I will believe thou hast a mind that suits
> With this thy fair and outward character.
> I prithee—and I'll pay thee bounteously—
> Conceal me what I am, and be my aid
> For such disguise as haply shall become
> The form of my intent. I'll serve this duke.
> Thou shalt present me as an eunuch to him.
> It may be worth thy pains, for I can sing
> And speak to him in many sorts of music
> That will allow me very worth his service.
> What else may hap, to time I will commit.
> Only shape thou thy silence to my wit.
>
> (1.2.50–64)

Viola begins the speech by saying that she will take the captain's outward behavior as evidence for his inner virtue, saying so in a sentence wrapped around a reminder that "a beauteous wall / Doth oft close in pollution." Then she asks the captain's help in making the evidence of her outside deceptive.

As I have implied, the topic of evidence and conclusions drawn from it occurs even in the play's minutiae. One more example is the casual reference to "the picture of 'We Three'" (2.3.17). The picture in question was common, a kind of canned practical joke: a drawing of two donkeys or of two idiots captioned "We Three." The picture and its caption invite the viewer to square the evidence of the picture of two creatures with the caption's assertion of three by concluding that he or she is the third jackass or the third fool.

Before continuing with the topic of evidence in *Twelfth Night* and *Othello,* let me first acknowledge that that topic, like any pervasive topic in a literary work, is a theme and, second, insist on the difference between the kind of attention to themes that I objected to when I talked about theme parks and a kind I recommend. When two or more works are grouped on the basis of a common theme, the theme can become the object of study rather than the individual literary works it inhabits. And, when that happens, students get confirmation of a long-held suspicion, the suspicion that they are only made to read difficult works *because* they are difficult, that a Shakespeare play is to their real purposes as penitential push-ups in army boot camp are to service in the field, that *Twelfth Night* or *Othello* or *Hamlet* is only a humbling obstacle course between them and discussion of topics more conveniently embodied in any day's news and in any number of current movies. If one is to show students valid reason for reading and/or seeing a Shakespeare play (as opposed to a readily accessible work in the students' own idiom), then one must show them how that play works, what gives a vast and various Shakespeare play its intense oneness, its identity as a thing rather than a string of narrative parts. What I am pushing is the idea of considering themes in the plays—particularly unobtrusive themes, themes that are not specifically discussed by the characters—as skeletal structures that hold a play together. In doing that, one gets closer to the play, rather than moving away from it.

I placed that digression where I did because it leads nicely into the next elements in my demonstration of the pervasiveness of evidence as a topic in *Twelfth Night* and *Othello.* A way to get students to see the skeletal structures I've been talking about is to direct their attention to elements in a play that seem out of place or useless. The technique works particularly well in exploring the thematic ribs that the topic of evidence furnishes to *Twelfth Night.* Consider the evidentiary minuet Viola and Sebastian perform at the moment of their reunion:

SEBASTIAN
    Do I stand there? I never had a brother,
    Nor can there be that deity in my nature
    Of here and everywhere. I had a sister,
    Whom the blind waves and surges have devoured.
    Of charity, what kin are you to me?
    What countryman? What name? What parentage?
VIOLA
    Of Messaline. Sebastian was my father.
    Such a Sebastian was my brother, too.
    So went he suited to his watery tomb.
    If spirits can assume both form and suit,
    You come to fright us.

SEBASTIAN   A spirit I am indeed,
  But am in that dimension grossly clad
  Which from the womb I did participate.
  Were you a woman, as the rest goes even,
  I should my tears let fall upon your cheek
  And say "Thrice welcome, drownèd Viola."
VIOLA
  My father had a mole upon his brow.
SEBASTIAN   And so had mine.
VIOLA
  And died that day when Viola from her birth
  Had numbered thirteen years.
SEBASTIAN
  O, that record is lively in my soul!
  He finishèd indeed his mortal act
  That day that made my sister thirteen years.
VIOLA
  If nothing lets to make us happy both
  But this my masculine usurped attire,
  Do not embrace me till each circumstance
  Of place, time, fortune, do cohere and jump
  That I am Viola. . . .

(5.1.237–65)

Like some critics, many directors, and most audiences, students are likely to find fault with such scrupulosity about drawing an obvious conclusion from evidence. In finding the extravagant meticulousness of Viola and Sebastian superfluous and foolish, we demonstrate our failure to learn what might be called the moral of *Twelfth Night:* "Don't let overwhelming evidence overwhelm you."

Note that I said "what *might* be called." Since *Twelfth Night* has never delivered that moral or any other, to fish a moral up would be wantonly creative. To work a workable lesson—or "point"—out of *Twelfth Night* would be to present as a fact of the play— the play we actually have—what might have been true of a play Shakespeare could have made with the materials he used to make *Twelfth Night.* If the moral of a literary work isn't apparent, then it doesn't exist. I introduce the matter of moralizing because, just as students are used to being asked to see that a play or poem or story has something "to say," they are also used to the idea that themes in literary works are what those works are "about." I want it understood that I am not saying that *Twelfth Night* and *Othello* are about evidence but that (to exchange my endoskeletal metaphor for an exoskeletal one) evidence is *about* them—wrapped *around* them—that the theme of evidence is one of the elements that gives each its identity, its integrity.

Let me now come back from that prophylactic detour to point out that the very syntax of the last five of the lines quoted above from the exchange between Viola and Sebastian is such as to invite audiences to jump to a false conclusion. These are the five lines:

  If nothing lets to make us happy both
  But this my masculine usurped attire,
  Do not embrace me till each circumstance
  Of place, time, fortune, do cohere and jump
  That I am Viola. . . .

"If nothing lets . . . but" (that is, "if nothing stands in the way except") is a familiar kind of construction, one that customarily brushes aside some negative consideration as trifling, and one that promises a succeeding imperative clause that instructs the pauser to go forward (for instance, "If nothing's keeping you from going away this weekend but finding someone to feed your goldfish, go ahead; I'll take care of the fish"). Here the imperative, "Do *not* embrace me," is exactly the opposite of the one signaled. Moreover, since the dismissive gesture appears in the context of a long and seemingly superfluous rehearsal of minor facts confirming the obvious, it presumably echoes audiences' impatience with the extreme caution of Viola and Sebastian. The "If nothing lets" / "Do not embrace me" lines are one last bit of bait in a passage that all but begs its audiences to leap to conclusions.

Othello too is woven through with variations on the theme of evidence. And it too has something that could be called, but should not be called, a moral. Here the moral would be "Do not confuse what is probable with what is true." The confusion is encapsulated in the phrase "what he found himself was apt and true" (5.2.213). When Emilia challenges Iago to contradict Othello's assertion that it was Iago who told him to suspect Desdemona of infidelity, Iago's response is "I told him what I thought, and told no more / Than what he found himself was apt and true" (5.2.212–13).

Whereas in *Twelfth Night* Viola and Sebastian appear to have learned the lesson the play doesn't teach us, in *Othello* no one involved—no one onstage and no one in the audience—learns anything. Consider Othello's arsenal. In the last scene, Othello draws his sword and runs at Iago (5.2.282). Montano immediately takes the sword from Othello and gives it to Gratiano, whom he charges to keep Othello prisoner: "Take you this weapon / Which I have here recovered from the Moor. / Come, guard the door without. Let him not pass, / But kill him rather" (286–89). Moments later Othello tells us that he has another weapon in the chamber; Shakespeare has him pause to tell us more about it than we need to know: "It is a sword of Spain, the ice brook's temper" (303). Then in an exchange with Gratiano Shakespeare makes Othello take time to furnish an endorsement for this second sword: "Behold, I have a weapon. / A better never did itself sustain / Upon a soldier's thigh" (310–12). About twenty-five lines later, after a second attempt on Iago's life, Othello is disarmed a second time. Then, when Othello proves to have one weapon more and stabs himself to death, Cassio says "This did I fear, but thought he had no weapon" (422). I have never known an audience to laugh at Cassio's misplaced confidence or even to snort derisively at the line—even though we have witnessed a painstaking demonstration of the folly of assuming that the loss of one weapon means that Othello is weaponless, and even though that demonstration comes at the end of a play that repeatedly shows us people casually interpreting evidence and casually concluding from it on the basis of probabilities.

As with *Twelfth Night,* a close look at elements apparently gratuitous to the job of dramatizing the story of Othello can help students toward seeing the architectural coherence the topic of evidence gives the play. A good instance of this kind of nonessential activity is the opening sequence of 1.3, a sequence in which the Duke of Venice and his council of senators perform a forty-four-line exercise in weighing evidence and drawing probability-based conclusions from it. The Duke and the senators have several different reports of the number of ships in the Turkish fleet (1.3.1–6). The council sees that the evidence at hand is useless as to the number of ships, but, since all reports agree that the fleet is headed for Cyprus, the council accepts that much of the evidence in the disparate accounts is trustworthy (7–14). Then a messenger comes in to contradict what they took to be their one reliable piece of intelligence: "The Turkish preparation makes for Rhodes" (18). Thereupon the councillors change the logic on which they base conclusions about the Turks. They shift from reliance on the probability that the reports are reliable when and if they are in consensus to reliance on the probability that a given kind of people will do what one's previous experience leads one to expect them to do. The Duke asks one of the senators to comment on the new report of the Turks' destination. This is the senator's analysis and the conclusion the Duke draws from it:

> This cannot be,
> By no assay of reason. 'Tis a pageant
> To keep us in false gaze. When we consider
> Th' importancy of Cyprus to the Turk,
> And let ourselves again but understand
> That, as it more concerns the Turk than Rhodes,
> So may he with more facile question bear it,
> For that it stands not in such warlike brace,
> But altogether lacks th' abilities
> That Rhodes is dressed in—if we make thought of this,
> We must not think the Turk is so unskillful
> To leave that latest which concerns him first,
> Neglecting an attempt of ease and gain
> To wake and wage a danger profitless.
> DUKE
> Nay, in all confidence, he's not for Rhodes.
>
> (1.3.22–37)

Another messenger enters immediately to announce that the fleet has changed its course and is now openly making for Cyprus (39–46).

Like Viola in *Twelfth Night* when she correctly concluded that she was the object of Olivia's affections, the senators and the Duke just happen to be right. They are lucky. They insist on the foreignness of "the Turk," and yet assume that his motives and movements can be predicted. The Duke and senators are, as I say, lucky. Others in the play are not. Their excellent logic is regularly blind to possibilities they themselves embody. Desdemona runs off with an elderly exotic *and* assumes that everyone else's behavior will be not only rational but based on premises obvious to her. Iago, as he says, knows what he is—unnatural by any standard we bring with us into the theater—and *therefore* assures us that Desdemona will act as experience has shown him *eccentric* women *ordinarily* do: "knowing what I am, I know what she shall be," he says at 4.1.87, and—earlier, in the "put money in thy purse" speech to Roderigo—"It cannot be that Desdemona should long continue her love to the Moor. . . . It was a violent commencement in her, and thou shalt see an answerable sequestration. . . .

She must change for youth. When she is sated with his body she will find the error of her choice" (1.3.384–88, 393–94). From Brabantio—who is confident that the possible actions of his daughter are limited to the probable ones—to Emilia—who, improbably enough, never says "O, *that* handkerchief" and yet speculates confidently on the probabilities of human behavior in her "all the world" speeches in 4.3 and is similarly confident about Bianca's guilt in the attempt on Cassio's life in 5.1—the characters in *Othello* rush headlong to reasonable wrong conclusions on the basis of the same sort of assumption-based logic by which the Duke's council reached a right one.

I said that narratively useless passages like the council scene in 1.3 are good places to go to show students the skeletons that support the narrative flesh of Shakespeare plays. Another good starting place is the very existence of characters like the generally superfluous clown who appears briefly at the beginning of 3.1 of *Othello* and at the beginning of 3.4. In 3.1 he does some standard clowning with the musicians. Then Cassio speaks to him:

CASSIO   Dost thou hear, mine honest friend?
CLOWN   No, I hear not your honest friend. I hear you.
CASSIO   Prithee, keep up thy quillets.

(3.1.22–24)

This too is standard clowning, but consider its kind. What the clown does in his absolutism is refuse to let context and idiom limit his interpretation of Cassio's words; the clown refuses to draw the conclusion that the meaning of Cassio's question is the obvious one. When he makes his second and last appearance, the clown does nothing at all but (1) exercise caution about inferring the obvious meaning of what he hears and (2) insist on the frailty of the human mind (note, moreover, that the exchange between Desdemona and the clown is not only one in which Desdemona's purpose is to get information but one in which reliable information and the means of getting it become actual subjects of the conversation):

DESDEMONA   Do you know, sirrah, where Lieutenant Cassio lies?
CLOWN   I dare not say he lies anywhere.
DESDEMONA   Why, man?
CLOWN   He's a soldier, and for me to say a soldier lies, 'tis stabbing.
DESDEMONA   Go to! Where lodges he?
CLOWN   To tell you where he lodges is to tell you where I lie.
DESDEMONA   Can anything be made of this?
CLOWN   I know not where he lodges; and for me to devise a lodging and say he lies here, or he lies there, were to lie in mine own throat.
DESDEMONA   Can you inquire him out, and be edified by report?
CLOWN   I will catechize the world for him—that is, make questions, and by them answer.
DESDEMONA   Seek him, bid him come hither. Tell him I have moved my lord on his behalf and hope all will be well.
CLOWN   To do this is within the compass of man's wit, and therefore I will attempt the doing it.

Clown exits.
(3.4.1–22)

I set out many paragraphs ago to demonstrate likenesses between *Twelfth Night* and *Othello.* I think I have done that. In recent paragraphs I have drifted from demonstrating the existence of an element common to the two plays into demonstrating the pervasiveness of one of them—one theme, evidence and conclusions derived from it—within the individual plays. I changed my focus in preparation for insisting once again on the radical difference in value between the two enterprises. To talk about a thematic or situational link between *Twelfth Night* and *Othello* (or any other pair of works) is to focus not on either of *them* but on a likeness accidental to the essence of each and is thus, as I said, to move away from the objects one purports to study and onto a middle ground. On the other hand, to talk about alliteration-like thematic repetitions *within* a play is to talk about the play, that *play*, not what that play talks about. One needs to avoid slipping into the sort of folly one would commit if one said or seemed to be saying that, for instance, *Twelfth Night* and *Othello* are plays *about* evidence, are disguised tracts in which Malvolio and Othello are mere furniture. But, if one avoids that particular escape route from one's putative topic, to examine the warp and woof of a Shakespeare play (or any other literary work) is to go a good way in the direction of an answer to the big questions about the works we study and teach: What is all the fuss about? Why do people read and study and teach some things and not others? If the dramatized situation in a play is what matters—if our purpose in a classroom is to discuss the kinds of things that happen in the story—why bother with the play; why not move directly to discussion of the issue or issues the play presents?

And that brings me back at last to my objection to theme-park thinking: it provides a focus for study that is not of the literary works but of something else. For instance, I don't think that any student ever truly believes that the reason he or she values the movies or television programs or other fictions he or she values above others of their kind is anything like the sorts of reasons teachers and editors' introductions to Shakespeare texts imply that they do or should. We will never dispel the all-but-universal belief that what one thinks about plays and stories and poems and what one *should* think are naturally different until we look at the objects we teach as they are (which is to say, as they seem to be) and not as awkward stepping stones to socially or morally or intellectually more dignified concerns.

As I said, I think I have demonstrated enough likenesses between *Twelfth Night* and *Othello* successfully enough to put down editorial fears that the plays will seem too different to be profitably studied in tandem. The demonstration, however, is little more than a critical parlor trick. Remember that "Those Extraordinary Twins" in my title comes from Mark Twain, who used it as the title for a farce about an imaginary circus freak. My demonstration of likenesses between two plays that do not show that likeness is an open and foolish invitation to teachers and students alike to make *Twelfth Night* and *Othello* into a purely imaginary freak—an invitation to think and talk about *Twelfth Night* and *Othello* as if they, each and together, had the identity foisted upon them by the arbitrary and alien focus of this essay. The likenesses between the plays are indeed many and deep, but they amount to nothing as compared to the truth that prompted this essay: *Twelfth Night* and *Othello* are different, urgently different.

And, being so urgently different, they are perfect candidates to cohabit a syllabus. If one thinks as I do that it is pedagogically desirable to block off any path away from one's putative object of study—that one does students harm if one leads them to think that we do, and they should, value *Twelfth Night* or *Othello* (or any of the other works that adults have loved so much and so long) as sites for considering *other things,* things other than the plays themselves—then *Twelfth Night* and *Othello,* a pair that does not of itself offer any open avenues out, are *the* perfect pair.

No Cloven Hooves

Doris Adler
HOWARD UNIVERSITY

Othello combines the traditional conflicts of the English morality play and some of the principles of classical tragedy. The themes dramatized in this complexly structured play are explored and reinforced by language and rhetoric rich in emblematic signification. The tragic history of black Othello, both classical hero brought low by hubris and an allegorical illustration of Everyman's human blindness, is echoed in the persistent repetition of the terms "black" and "white" with all of their metaphorical suggestions and contradictions. To ignore or disregard any one of these complexly intertwined strands diminishes the understanding of the rich tragic texture of *Othello*.

The classic structure of *Othello* is most apparent in its singleness and unity of plot, enhanced by the driving force of compressed time, the relative unity of place, and the absence of either "low" characters or comic material. Although Othello's error in judgment seems, at first glance, to be jealousy, both Othello and Desdemona are vulnerable initially because of their overweening pride that they are above the carnal stings necessary to perpetuate the human race. Othello announces his own godlike immunity in a moment of dramatic irony that rivals the proud blindness of Oedipus. When Desdemona pleads with the Senate to be allowed to follow Othello into battle rather than being forced to remain "a moth of peace" in Venice, Othello supports her request with the following:

> Let her have your voice.
> Vouch with me, heaven, I therefore beg it not
> To please the palate of my appetite,
> Nor to comply with heat (the young affects
> In me defunct) and proper satisfaction,
> But to be free and bounteous to her mind.
> And heaven defend your good souls that you think
> I will your serious and great business scant
> For she is with me. No, when light-winged toys
> Of feathered Cupid seel with wanton dullness
> My speculative and officed instruments,
> That my disports corrupt and taint my business,
> Let housewives make a skillet of my helm
> And all indign and base adversities
> Make head against my estimation.

(1.3.295–309)

33

No mere mortal bridegroom, his marriage yet unconsummated, and his future at the mercy of the dogs of war, Othello seeks only to be free and bounteous to her mind.

Desdemona, too, has married to live on a Platonic plane not shared by most lovers who elope in defiance of parents, tradition, and convention. Described by her father as a maiden, never bold, who has rejected the suits of the curled darlings of Venice, and by Othello as one who placed the responsibilities of managing her father's household before her own desire to hear the stories of Othello's adventures, Desdemona loved Othello for the dangers he had passed and "wished that heaven had made her such a man." This ambiguous wish is, in the main, tacitly emended in the understanding to mean that she wished heaven had made such a man *for her*. The words as stated and read in their literal construction suggest, however, that she wishes she had *been* such a man and serve as strong motive for her plea to accompany Othello to Cyprus:

> My heart's subdued
> Even to the very quality of my lord.
> I saw Othello's visage in his mind,
> And to his honors and his valiant parts
> Did I my soul and fortunes consecrate.
> So that, dear lords, if I be left behind,
> A moth of peace, and he go to the war,
> The rites for why I love him are bereft me . . .
>   (1.3.285–92)

Desdemona, like Othello, would lead the proud life of the plumed helm, but since heaven did not make her such a man, she seeks to become one with the very quality of Othello, master wearer of the plumed helm, one with his mind, his honors, his valiant parts in a marriage to be consummated by the rites of a shared war.

And so the proud pair, joined in their superiority to the "young affects" of their human mortality are ripe for the fall that begins with their kiss in Cyprus. The breathless, broken rhythm and gasping consonants as much as Othello's words are persuasive that Othello desires more than "to be generous and bountiful to her mind." Unless the line is rattled off like a jump-rope rhyme, the stops demanded by the arrangement of consonants in Othello's first response to Desdemona in Cyprus imitates the stopped breath and full throat of intense emotion:

> It gives me wonder great as my content
> To see you here before me. O my soul's joy!
>   (2.1.199–200)

The stops and breaks and hissing release of breath are even more evident in the lines

> I cannot speak enough of this content.
> It stops me here; it is too much of joy.
> And this, and this, the greatest discords be
> That e'er our hearts shall make!
>   (2.1.214–17)

The lines are equally persuasive to Iago who responds "O, you are well tuned now" (2.1.218).

If this moment is obvious as the beginning of a classic fall, it is also obvious as a deviation from the classic plot structure. The machinery that brings about the catastrophe, the diabolical plotting of Iago, is closer to the machinations of the Vice of the morality play than to the antagonist of a classical tragedy. Othello, himself, in his final meeting with Iago makes the morality-play association explicit as he realizes Iago is a "devil" and looks for his cloven hooves:

> I look down towards his feet; but that's a fable.—
> If that thou be'st a devil, I cannot kill thee.
>
> (5.2.336–37)

In these lines Othello sums up the failure of all drama—classical, morality, or contemporary—all instruction, all human reason. We, like Othello, recognize the cloven-hooved devil of state, page, or pulpit as evil to be shunned or fought, and we, like Othello, fail to see evil in the familiar people and circumstances of our lives: the parent who treats us as property, the lover who consumes and forgets, the preacher who feeds coffers and starves the poor, the politicians who promise peace and take us to war. We, like Othello, recognize the shining winged angel as the realized abstraction of good, and we, like Othello, snuff out the good in guiltless mates and strangers—sandaled sons of carpenters who heal the blind. We, like Othello, all human kind, are too tragically blind to distinguish good from evil, to know black from white, to save ourselves from our own mortality.

Before examining the use of black and white as a rhetorical method of reaffirming that man is too blind to distinguish black from white, it is imperative to look closer at the morality, or allegorical structure, of *Othello* and particularly at the role of Iago within that structure. One has only to consider the initial popularity of Marlowe's *Doctor Faustus* and Spenser's *The Faerie Queene* to recognize that the long tradition of the realized abstractions of the seven deadly sins continued as a central expectation of Shakespeare's audience. These sins, identified in medieval tradition as pride, envy, avarice, sloth, anger, gluttony, and lechery were expanded in the morality drama to include other permutations of evil. The pride of both Othello and Desdemona was probably more apparent to the audience of Shakespeare's day than it is to us. True, both Othello and Desdemona are sincere, virtuous, blind to any pride in their well-mated assumption that they are among that happy breed who are above the physical desire shared by lesser newly-wed mortals. Pride does not appear as a recognizable, imperious enslaver, and Iago has no cloven hooves.

While Pride is evident in the assumption of superiority shared by Othello and Desdemona and in Othello's rhetoric and actions, other familiar figures from the morality structure are more obvious. Othello becomes a monster of jealousy; Cassio is brought down first by "the devil drunkenness" and then by "the devil wrath" (2.3.315–16); Iago conjures an image of the demon lust that racks the minds first of Brabantio and then of Othello, and Bianca dramatizes the power of that demon in her submissive pursuit of Cassio. But Iago, himself, comes closest to impersonating one of the realized abstractions of the morality play; in motive and method Iago is a consummate realization of Despair, the sin held to be more deadly than pride despite the place generally given to pride as the most deadly of the seven sins. Of course, in a major sense of the word, despair is pride, for despair knows there is no good, no happiness, no hope. This pride in ultimate knowledge is the ultimate hubris and will brook no threat of contradiction. Despair must destroy all evidence of good to reaffirm that there is no good, all happiness to prove there is no happiness, all hope to prove there is no hope. Despair must prove wiser than all wisdom.

Iago, who names too many reasons for his hatred of Othello for any to be believed, like the figure of Despair in *The Faerie Queene,* creates deadly discontent in all those he encounters by rationally probing and enflaming their secret areas of weakness. Unlike Spenser's representation of Despair, Iago has no grisly, dull-eyed countenance to make him immediately recognizable; there are no cloven hooves. The bright bubble of happiness veers away from the obvious danger of the malcontent and is too often burst by the seemingly innocent question or comment of a seemingly disinterested friend or associate: "Are you going to wear that?" "Do you really trust him?" "I like not that."

Honest Iago leaves no bubble unburst. The smug ignorant assurance of the foolish Roderigo that he can pay an agent to acquire whatever his heart desires is such an open playground for the temptation of despair that Iago takes him to destruction and damnation in his spare time. By blatantly addressing the racial prejudice and fears that Brabantio has kept buried beneath his self-flattering hospitality to the prestigious African general, Iago allows the old father no way to salvage his image of himself as an important member of the Senate, to maintain a loving relationship with his daughter, or to continue life itself. Iago catches Cassio between his weakness for drink and the weakness of his need to be one of the boys and quickly destroys his happiness in his promotion. Having already exposed Emilia's anxiety about her adequacy as a wife by suggesting her disloyalty to him with Othello, Iago persuades her to disloyalty to Desdemona by demanding the handkerchief; he must destroy her enduring loyalty by taking her life. The constant, noble, loving nature of Othello and Desdemona, their love, and their happiness are negations of despair and must be destroyed if the knowledge of despair that there is no constancy, no nobility, no love, no happiness is to be reaffirmed. Iago knows they must be conquered; he does not know the specific area of attack until Othello and Desdemona "fall" in love in Cyprus; then he knows exactly which strings to play.

Iago's accurate knowledge of the fine points of human susceptibility is a central stroke in Shakespeare's portrayal of despair. Othello, beset both by messengers from the Senate and by Brabantio's men at the Sagittary in the first hours of his marriage, is calm, dignified, and eminently rational; Othello, aroused by the alarm bell in the first hours of his time alone with Desdemona in Cyprus when he is no longer a platonic lover, is as fiery and angry as Iago could wish him to be. Desdemona, urged by Cassio, at Iago's instigation, to plead his case on the morning after she has discovered that she has neither married Othello only for his mind and quality as a warrior nor been married only that he might be free and bounteous to her mind, is ripe to overflowing with the short-lived power of the new and pleasing bride who might well send her new husband for golden apples from the Hesperides and fully expect to make apple pie for dinner. Iago can be certain that now that Othello has discovered that his free uncircumscribed condition is lost to Desdemona in a love that has awakened all his youthful affects, he will be more than willing to believe that she affects all men in the same way that she has affected him. Caught in the passion to which he had assumed himself to be superior, Othello, in his innocent pride, will assume all lesser men to be even more susceptible. Once Othello imagines Desdemona's power to be universal, and Desdemona longs to test her individual power with Othello, Iago has both of them ready to surrender to despair. With his plan successfully initiated and his victims in his sights, Iago calls upon the "Divinity of hell" (2.3.370) to make everything seem other than it is; virtue will seem evil, evil will seem virtuous. Metaphorically, black will seem white, and white will seem black, and neither love nor reason will provide eyeglasses for man's tragic blindness.

With the union of black Othello with white Desdemona and the evident "blackness" of the white Iago, the metaphors and multiple signification of *black* and *white* are at work in the tragedy from its opening moments. There are few words that carry more complex, confounding baggage. The confusion began early in our language when Old English *blaekan*, meaning to burn or scorch, was used for the color of charcoal, the total absorption, or the total absence of light, and *blac*, a word similar in appearance and sound, was used for shining white, the total reflection or presence of light; the two words in early documents are not always distinguishable even by context. But usage worked to polarize them. The association of the words with day and night, light and darkness, ignorance and knowledge, blindness and sight, clean and dirty, good and evil, had a long history before they were used to distinguish peoples of European and African origins. In northern Europe, long before equatorial and subequatorial peoples were known to exist, the power of evil was represented as a figure of darkness, first as a black dog and later as a black demon. In early mystery and morality plays the devil, or the force of evil, was a figure dressed in black. The long, ugly history of the exploitation and enslavement of Africans and those of African descent undoubtedly encouraged the conflation of the complex connotations of *black* and *white* with the skin color of those of European ancestry and those of African ancestry.

Othello explores, inverts, and confuses these complex connotations. The greater part of the play takes place at night, in darkness. It includes a noble black hero married to one whiter than monumental alabaster, and draws on and compounds all the familiar negative uses of black, positive uses of white or fair, and then, through rhetorical and theatrical devices, confounds all the confusions already present in the terms black and white. Within the play Othello's African blackness is associated, on the one hand, with nobility, courage, and exotic adventure. On the stage he traditionally wears white. But increasingly his color is coupled, rhetorically, with animals, bestiality, criminality, literal and moral filth, sorcery, the pit of darkness, and the devil himself. White, or more often fair, with its other meaning as just or evenhanded, signifies all beauty, virtue, heavenly shows, and even, in a witty scene with deadly rhetoric, humans as opposed to nonhumans. Iago, jesting with Desdemona as they await Othello's ship, makes *black*, signifying a brunette, synonymous with *foul*, and *white* synonymous with *wight*, or person (2.1.156, 173).

All is other than it seems. Black Othello is described by the Duke as being metaphorically white. White Iago is a villain, metaphorically a black villain. Bianca, a white whore whose name means *white*, is metaphorically morally black. Only Desdemona, whiter than monumental alabaster, is both literally and metaphorically white. How logical that Othello, who has long understood that prejudice-blinded Venetians assumed that a black face meant a black soul, should be led to believe that he had wrongly assumed that Desdemona's white face revealed her white soul. Just as there are no cloven hooves, so there are no halos or wings. All mortals are too tragically blind to distinguish metaphor from reality, good from evil, black from white.

Othello combines the structural and thematic traditions of ancient classical tragedy with conventions of the English morality play and sets them forth in dramatic and rhetorical images of black and white that engage our human reason, our human fears, and, all too often, our human weaknesses. The tragedy that reveals our mortal blindness has, all too often over the centuries, been seen and read with eyes too blind to distinguish between the literal simplicity and the metaphorical complexity of *black* and *white*, too blind to recognize the primal evil of despair in the open honest face of a clever, witty man, too blind to see beyond the prevailing conventions of a particular time and place. *Othello* is a great metaphor for the tragic reality of mortal blindness.

PART TWO

Teaching Shakespeare Through Performance

·

MICHAEL TOLAYDO

EDITOR

Up on Your Feet with Shakespeare: The Wrong Way and the Right

MICHAEL TOLAYDO
ST. MARY'S COLLEGE OF MARYLAND

You have probably read or heard this before:

"Shakespeare is hard to understand!"

"They talk funny!"

"The words are archaic!"

"It is written in Old English and needs to be translated!"

"You need to be English to do it!"

"The characters talk too much!"

"The plays are too long!"

"Why not read a modernized version?"

You may have heard or read that a useful and fun approach to Shakespeare is to get students up on their feet to perform scenes from a play. You may even have tried it.

You and your students may have spent a large amount of creative effort and time making sure that all the words were pronounced correctly; that everyone understood what the lines *really* meant; that the audience could see everything; that the actors spoke loudly and moved appropriately; that the costumes, the stage properties, and setting were as splendid and as precise as you could make them. You may even have mounted a production of all or part of a play for the rest of the school. Lots of folks probably worked extremely hard and the production no doubt was well received and everyone felt very proud, and rightly so. Certainly your students had a singular understanding of their parts and of the play they were acting in.

If you have done any of the above, you were the director—perhaps with a fellow drama teacher or a few students. You had to understand what the play was about, what the actors should wear, where the actors should stand, and where they should move in order to make the story clear for the audience. You had to work on the text in order to make all these decisions; this work was at times difficult, but probably also rewarding. You had to be director, producer, researcher, and manager in order to give life to the performative words printed on the page. Would that we could do that with every play we teach!

I'd like to suggest that, with a few modifications and with a different intention, we *can* get close to that comprehensive approach with every play we teach. I am advancing a teaching strategy that puts into play the necessary tools and skills to examine more difficult and complex portions of the play and promotes *for students* self-esteem and confidence in their own ideas and opinions.

As a practicing teacher, I strongly believe that an introductory approach to all the plays we teach can best be achieved without *theatricality* but through the performance of an immediately comprehensible scene. But we must begin by eliminating the idea that you—the teacher—have to be the director, and that pronunciation, costumes, sets, lighting, movement, facial expressions, and audience are initial concerns. When the teacher acts as director, we are essentially telling our students what the lines mean, how they should act, what Shakespeare "meant," and what is right, what is wrong. We are doing most of the interpretive work. We are translating the scene for our students. We are passing on our own version of meaning. There's nothing wrong with this if we are interested in *production.* However, if we are attempting to teach; if we are interested in laying a groundwork for our students to explore a Shakespeare play— and future plays—on their own and together; if we want them to think meaningfully about what they are reading; if we want them to have individual responses to texts and to discuss differing points of view—we need to allow our students to be their own textual directors at the outset.

When I speak of performance, I am not speaking about creating a scene for stage performance, nor am I suggesting that this work involves acting skills. I am rooted in the notion that, in getting up on their feet and doing a scene in the classroom, students will discover that this exercise is a learning experience all by itself. By beginning to study a play in this way, and not necessarily beginning with the first scene of the play, the play is opened up and provides the basis for further active exploration of plot, character, structure, language, genre, or What You Will.

A scene performed and directed by students (with your guidance, of course) provides the class with firsthand experiences and insights into the play that can be used later in a variety of ways. The discoveries made during these performance sessions will connect, add, and resonate information throughout the rest of the study of the play.

This process involves questions. Questions about text are asked by the teacher and students *not* to seek definitive answers but to advance several interpretive possibilities and choices. These explications will often be challenged later as students come to grips with more of the play. What is important here is that students are accumulating a bank of knowledge about the scene and about Shakespeare's use of language. This actively places students squarely in the middle of Shakespeare's text.

To say that Shakespeare's language is easy is foolish; however, to state that "The words are archaic!" or that "It is written in Old English and needs to be translated!" or "You need to be English to do it!" is also foolish. There is dialogue in every play which is very easy for virtually all students to understand. Through performance, we can learn to tackle more complex scenes and make them engaging to teachers and students alike.

This performance process will work with students of any age—elementary school through graduate seminar. You know your own students, and you know that all classes are not the same. With your students' strengths and weaknesses in mind, feel free to augment, adjust, disregard, alter, and rearrange the following lesson plan.

Before any assignments or books are given to my students, I begin my first class with a photocopied scene. I make certain that the scene is enlarged, has no glossary or notes, and is on more than two pages. Group scenes—those with several characters—involve more students and they are usually easy to understand because they are full of exposition. I have selected the first part of Act 2, scene 1 from the New Folger edition of *Othello* and enlarged it.

I make sure that there is a copy of the scene for each class member. As I hand out the scenes, I ask that no one look at them until my signal. Naturally, many students do not pay attention to this request. When I have distributed a copy of the scene to each student, I do not ask for volunteers but rather select my readers. I want to stress here that I do not select only my actor-type students or confident readers to read the good parts, nor do I ask males to read only the male roles and females to read only female parts. We will be reading this scene several times and we want to find out what the scene is about, not who can play a particular part better. I am not casting a play, but involving students in the text and its meanings and along the way hopefully breaking down a few stereotypical presumptions. I make sure that I have a different set of readers for each page. Readers change with the page, even if a character's dialogue continues from the previous page.

Every group scene contains parts of varying length, and this is no exception. First Gentleman on page 1, Montano on page 3, and Second Gentleman on page 4 all have very few lines. Therefore you can get your students with reading difficulties into the action immediately. When we are ready, I ask my students to begin and request the rest of the class not to read along but to listen. I tell my readers that they should not worry about trying to figure out the correct pronunciation but to do the best they can and vocalize unfamiliar words the way they think they should sound. There are no Elizabethans around to tell us how words were pronounced at the time, and it really does not matter very much anyway; eventually we will collectively come to a pronunciation we feel is right for our scene. I further stress that they should try to read for sense and not worry about acting the parts; if they want to, however, that is fine with me. Lastly, we need to read loud enough so the rest of the class can hear. I want the class to eventually feel at home with the words.

After they have read through the scene, I praise the readers. I will then select a new group of readers and ask them to read the scene again. This second reading is not to get a "better" reading, but to encourage familiarity with the text. I ask the rest of the class to listen and to note what differences and new information they observe within the scene.

I begin a discussion session with a few questions. I emphasize that, for the purposes of this discussion, the answers to the questions asked are all contained within the scene and its possibilities, not through a broader knowledge of the play or through fantasy. The handout of the scene is our entire play. *Students must find lines and ideas in the text to support their views.*

Initial Discussion

1. Who are the guys on pages 1 and 2? (Possible answers: "Some sailors." "Some Gentlemen." "A lieutenant called Michael Cassio.")

2. What is a lieutenant? (Possible answers: "An officer." "Second in command of an army unit.")

3. Who are the guys on pages 3 and 4? (Possible answers: "More sailors and gentlemen." "Desdemona." "It says on page 4 'enter Desdemona, Iago, Roderigo, and Emilia.'" "Desdemona is a lady . . .")

4. What is going on here? (Any answer is acceptable as long as it can be supported from the text. Possible answers: "They are waiting for a ship." "The Turkish fleet sinks." "Michael Cassio arrives . . . another ship comes in 'A sail, a sail, a sail!'" "Desdemona and the rest arrive. . . .")

5. Are all the folks in the scene the same? What can you find that is different about some or all? Why are some of the characters called Gentleman and some have names? What about the messenger? (Find the lines in the text that support your argument.)

6. Do all these guys know each other well? (Several answers are possible, and can be relatively well supported by the text. Since the class will direct and enact this scene, the students must decide—for the purposes of this in-class enactment—which of the characters in the scene are well known to each other and why. Are all the gentlemen the same? What does their language tell us? Does Cassio know Montano as well as he knows Desdemona and Iago? After they have explored the text and come to some different conclusions about some of the less than clear relationships, ask for a hand vote to decide which the class prefers; majority rules.)

Sometimes I assign a student to write all the answers on the blackboard or a piece of paper. I then reassign parts and ask the students to read the scene through again. This time I ask students to make a note of what new information they discover and also to circle any word or phrase they don't understand.

Second Round of Discussion

1. What did you notice this time around? Any characters we missed the first time? Any new ideas about what is going on? Do you want to update any of the information we found during the earlier discussion? (Possible answers: "There is a messenger." "There is a character called Iago." "Also a Moor called Othello." "Emilia and Roderigo don't speak." "Othello is captain, or a general." "Cassio's ship is 'a noble ship of Venice.'" "There was a war and some of the characters are in the military." "Othello is married." "Emilia is also a woman . . .")

2. Any other comments about anything else that is going on in this scene? (Anything that can be supported by the text is possible.) You may wish to assign students to write down on the board or on separate sheets of paper the characteristics considered acceptable by the class for each role.

3. What words do you have circled that you don't understand? (Frequent answers: "high-wrought flood," "ruffian'd," "mortise," "segregation," "chidden," "the burning Bear," "like molestation view," "enchafed flood," "designment halts," "sufferance," "a Veronesa," "like a full soldier," "bark," "surfeited," "stand in bold cure," "paragons," "quirks," "blazoning pens," "ingener," "congregated sands," "sennights's speed," "Jove," "extincted.")

Answers to some questions about meaning can be provided by other members of the class. For the answers to questions that their peers can't answer, direct students to look up the answers after class or during class, either in a good text like the New Folger edition, or the *Oxford English Dictionary*, or C. T. Onions's *A Shakespeare Glossary*. I always provide answers to a few questions but not more than a few. I may ask, for example, "What does a 'high flood' suggest?" and then, "What do you think 'wrought' could mean?" If they do not come up with a suggestion, I may ask, "Does anyone know what 'to wrench' means?" "Who knows astrology? What is the Bear? What do sailors use the stars for?"

Depending on the nature of your class, you may wish to read the scene one more time with another set of readers, or with previous readers speaking different roles if you have a small group, and ask a few more questions. I will sometimes include a fast read-through involving each class member. We will form a circle, and beginning with one student begin to read the scene. As soon as a reader comes to a question mark, a period, a colon, a semicolon, or an exclamation point—commas do *not* count—the next person in the circle picks up the line. We want this reading to be smooth and even, and for it to make sense.

We are now ready for the class to put the scene "on its feet." I select a new cast to act out the parts—this can be anyone who wants to read who hasn't yet had a turn, along with second-round readers to complete the cast. *The remainder of the class will direct the scene. No one is uninvolved.* The operating principle here is that there are many different workable ways to stage this scene—not one correct way. Before actual performance work, we need to consider these questions:

1. Where does this scene take place? (Frequent answers: "by the seaside," "on a dock," "in a lighthouse.") The cast and directors need to check the text to make sure the location "fits." We should realize very soon that it is unadvisable to put the scene directly by the sea because they cannot see the sails and the Gentleman and Messenger inform Montano about the events and Montano says, on page 2, "Let's to the sea-side, ho!" Where else could the scene take place during the storm? Once a location has been agreed upon for this production, what does it look like? What period is it in? Elizabethan? Modern? If Elizabethan, what does the place have in it? Use chairs and desks and anything else in the room to create the space you want.

2. Entrances and exits—Who should come onstage from where? With whom? Why? Does the text give you a clue?

3. Who's the most important person in the scene? Who *thinks* he's the most important person in the scene? Does this change during the scene? If there are military characters, does rank come into play? How do you act it out to show this?

4. How does the cast enact the decisions the class agreed to earlier—about whether all these guys know each other well?

After getting advice from the directors, the cast acts out the scene once. After this first run-through, cast and directors discuss what worked and what changes they would make in the next enactment. The same cast, or a newly selected one, plays the scene again incorporating suggested changes.

Before the end of class, ask for comments on the process of getting a scene on its feet. Is it as complicated as they would have though? Why? Why not? Point out the advantages of working this way with a group—many creative viewpoints and many minds working on the same questions. You may wish to assign groups to present the scene at a later class using some of the other locations and characteristics mentioned earlier. This introductory session may take two class periods, and you can go back to or assign this process at any time during the semester.

The students—without the aid of notes, translation, or "helpful" explanatory material from the teacher—have come to understand what's happening in a scene from a Shakespeare play by working through the process of getting the scene from the page into performance. During this process students have acquired important tools and experience: they have spoken Shakespearean language, acted out parts, engaged in literary analysis, and begun to establish a collaborative and energetic relationship with the playwright.

OTHELLO

ACT 2, SCENE 1

MONTANO
What from the cape can you discern at sea?
FIRST GENTLEMAN
Nothing at all. It is a high-wrought flood.
I cannot 'twixt the heaven and the main
Descry a sail.
MONTANO
Methinks the wind hath spoke aloud at land.
A fuller blast ne'er shook our battlements.
If it hath ruffianed so upon the sea,
What ribs of oak, when mountains melt on them,
Can hold the mortise? What shall we hear of this?
SECOND GENTLEMAN
A segregation of the Turkish fleet.
For do but stand upon the foaming shore,
The chidden billow seems to pelt the clouds,
The wind-shaked surge, with high and monstrous mane,
Seems to cast water on the burning Bear
And quench the guards of th' ever-fixèd pole.
I never did like molestation view
On the enchafèd flood.
MONTANO   If that the Turkish fleet
Be not ensheltered and embayed, they are drowned.
It is impossible to bear it out.
THIRD GENTLEMAN   News, lads! Our wars are done.
The desperate tempest hath so banged the Turks
That their designment halts. A noble ship of Venice
Hath seen a grievous wrack and sufferance
On most part of their fleet.
MONTANO
How? Is this true?
THIRD GENTLEMAN   The ship is here put in,
A Veronesa. Michael Cassio,
Lieutenant to the warlike Moor Othello,
Is come on shore; the Moor himself at sea,
And is in full commission here for Cyprus.
MONTANO
I am glad on 't. 'Tis a worthy governor.
THIRD GENTLEMAN
But this same Cassio, though he speak of comfort
Touching the Turkish loss, yet he looks sadly
And prays the Moor be safe, for they were parted
With foul and violent tempest.

MONTANO   Pray heaven he be;
  For I have served him, and the man commands
  Like a full soldier. Let's to the seaside ho!
  As well to see the vessel that's come in
  As to throw out our eyes for brave Othello,
  Even till we make the main and th' aerial blue
  An indistinct regard.
THIRD GENTLEMAN   Come, let's do so;
  For every minute is expectancy
  Of more arrivance.
CASSIO
  Thanks, you the valiant of this warlike isle,
  That so approve the Moor! O, let the heavens
  Give him defense against the elements,
  For I have lost him on a dangerous sea.
MONTANO   Is he well shipped?
CASSIO
  His bark is stoutly timbered, and his pilot
  Of very expert and approved allowance;
  Therefore my hopes, not surfeited to death,
  Stand in bold cure.

Voices cry within. "A sail, a sail, a sail!"

CASSIO   What noise?
MESSENGER
  The town is empty; on the brow o' th' sea
  Stand ranks of people, and they cry "A sail!"
CASSIO
  My hopes do shape him for the Governor.

[A shot.]

SECOND GENTLEMAN
  They do discharge their shot of courtesy.
  Our friends, at least.
CASSIO   I pray you, sir, go forth,
  And give us truth who 'tis that is arrived.
SECOND GENTLEMAN   I shall.
MONTANO
  But, good lieutenant, is your general wived?
CASSIO
  Most fortunately. He hath achieved a maid
  That paragons description and wild fame,
  One that excels the quirks of blazoning pens,
  And in th' essential vesture of creation
  Does tire the ingener.

How now? Who has put in?

SECOND GENTLEMAN
  'Tis one Iago, ancient to the General.

CASSIO
  'Has had most favorable and happy speed!
  Tempests themselves, high seas, and howling winds,
  The guttered rocks and congregated sands
  (Traitors ensteeped to clog the guiltless keel),
  As having sense of beauty, do omit
  Their mortal natures, letting go safely by
  The divine Desdemona.
MONTANO   What is she?
CASSIO
  She that I spake of, our great captain's captain,
  Left in the conduct of the bold Iago,
  Whose footing here anticipates our thoughts
  A sennight's speed. Great Jove, Othello guard,
  And swell his sail with thine own powerful breath,
  That he may bless this bay with his tall ship,
  Make love's quick pants in Desdemona's arms,
  Give renewed fire to our extinct spirits,
  And bring all Cyprus comfort!
                              O, behold,
  The riches of the ship is come on shore!
  You men of Cyprus, let her have your knees.
  Hail to thee, lady, and the grace of heaven,
  Before, behind thee, and on every hand
  Enwheel thee round.
DESDEMONA   I thank you, valiant Cassio.
  What tidings can you tell of my lord?
CASSIO
  He is not yet arrived, nor know I aught
  But that he's well and will be shortly here.
DESDEMONA
  O, but I fear—How lost you company?
CASSIO
  The great contention of sea and skies
  Parted our fellowship
                    Within "A sail, a sail!"   [*A shot.*]
                    But hark, a sail!
SECOND GENTLEMAN
  They give their greeting to the citadel.
  This likewise is a friend.
CASSIO   See for the news.
  Good ancient, you are welcome. Welcome, mistress.
  Let it not gall your patience, good Iago,
  That I extend my manners. 'Tis my breeding
  That gives me this bold show of courtesy.

"A Touch, a Touch, I Do Confess": Sword Fighting in the Classroom

Michael Tolaydo
St. Mary's College of Maryland

I suggested in my previous essay that "a scene performed and directed by students (with your guidance, of course) provides the class with firsthand experiences and insights into the play that can be used later in a variety of ways."

One aspect of classroom performance that can generate this kind of firsthand insight is stage combat. Using a couple of very basic and *SAFE* techniques, students have the opportunity both to get up on their feet and "do," to further experience how plastic the text is and how decisions about movement and style can help to define character. I stress, once again, that the choices we, the class, make must be textually supported. This unit can be held outside if the weather permits or in the gymnasium or on the tennis courts.

I ask my class to come to the next one, or two, sessions in clothes they can roll around in. It is possible to complete the combat part of this class in an hour with a smallish class, but I prefer to use two class periods. Although what follows seems long in written form, it actually moves very quickly once you begin. I tell my students that we—males and females—are going to do some stage combat and I ask that they read all of Act 3, scene 4, of *Twelfth Night*. We are going to present this scene and perform the comic fight involving Viola, Sir Andrew Aguecheek, Sir Toby Belch, and Antonio. In my experience very few students avoid this reading assignment. Prior to teaching this unit, I show the fight sequence from *The Princess Bride* and Franco Zeffirelli's *Romeo and Juliet*. I inform my students that in the 1800s some actors would attach flints to their blades to make them spark and that when electricity was available, a famous actor/director named Henry Irving wired his swords in order to create a shower of sparks during contact. I don't know if anyone was electrocuted, but there is a record that rubber insulation was soon put onto the sword handles. My students always enjoy this, and we discuss how good the filmed fights are, how clear they are, how they dramatically build to several climaxes, and how they are believable because they are carefully choreographed and rehearsed sequences, like a dance.

I bring to class three-feet by one-quarter-inch wooden dowels. Any hardware store will have a supply. One-quarter-inch width is just right. A thinner dowel can break and splinter and a thicker one has no give and is dangerous. Holding the dowels, which most of my students want to grab right away, I begin with a little history.

The English sword weighed twelve-plus pounds and was primarily a hacking weapon. In 1540 Henry VIII had granted Letters Patent to the London Masters of Defence, and they were granted permission to teach the use of the traditional sword and buckler (a small shield). According to Holinshed, virtually every person over eighteen carried at minimum a dagger. The nobility and their servants all had swords or rapiers. Hardly anyone traveled without a sword or rapier, and even the clergy carried daggers. Most haberdashers sold bucklers. The use and knowledge of weapons was widespread.

The word "rapier" is thought to have come from the Spanish *espada ropera*, which means "costume sword." By the beginning of the sixteenth century, the rapier became a gentleman's sword worn for protection and denoting rank. Later the rapier came to be accepted as a fencing sword used by anyone so inclined. It was the first two-edged sword that could be used as a thrusting and cutting weapon. European dueling codes soon developed, and gentlemen were schooled by Masters of the Fence. Fencing masters from Italy, where the art is thought to have originated—though some historians credit Spain—excelled as teachers and were much sought after.

It was an accepted standard that an English gentleman, in order to be properly educated, needed to travel abroad. Many of these young men returned to England with direct knowledge, or at least with anecdotal knowledge, of the Italians' scientific and systematic development of the rapier as a thrusting weapon.

About thirty-five years after Henry VIII's Letters of Patent, Rocco Bonetti, an Italian, bought a building from the playwright John Lyly in which to teach the technique of the rapier. He was soon followed by other Italian masters. A disagreement between the practice of "cutting at your opponent" favored by the English sword-and-buckler school and the "thrusting" Italian rapier method soon evolved. A biased view favoring the English system of defense is promoted in George Silver's *Paradoxes of Defence*, published in 1599. We see examples of these different schools of thought in *Romeo and Juliet*. Sampson and Gregory carry swords and bucklers while Tybalt asks for his rapier and fights with Mercutio and Romeo, who also wield rapiers. Most of Shakespeare's audiences were fully cognizant of the moves and "arts of defence" practiced by the actors on the theater stages of London.

In 1605 James I gave the Master of Defence the power to legally govern the teaching of fencing. (However, in his 1613 *Edict and severe censure against private combats and Combatants*, James tried to ban private dueling.) A guild of Masters of the Noble Science of Defence was established, and one could qualify as scholar, free scholar, provost, or master by "playing a prize." Much like our karate competitions, the Elizabethans held "prize fights" which, while serious in intent, developed into popular spectator entertainments. In the same way that the theater found it very difficult to gain authorization from the city fathers to perform within the London city limits, the masters "playing a prize" also had to move to Blackfriars and beyond. They joined the banished actors and dancers.

Virtually any time an Elizabethan playwright chose to use combat in a play, he did so to mark a climax or to highlight a dramatic moment. The fencers often used the theaters for their "prize fights." We know that the Theatre (owned by the Burbages, Shakespeare's partners, before they were forced to move across the river and build the first Globe) and the Curtain were used in this way. According to G. B. Harrison, some of the afternoon audience for *Romeo and Juliet*, first performed at the Theatre, would probably have attended "prize fights" there on the previous day. Shakespeare, Middleton, Dekker, Marston, and Ben Jonson all wrote about weapons and include fights in some of their plays, suggesting that they had a working knowledge of them. In fact, Jonson was sent to prison for killing actor Gabriel Spencer in a duel in 1598. Richard Tarlton, one of the most famous actors in Shakespeare's and Burbage's company, was a Master of Defence, achieving this rank in 1587.

After I've given them some background (which can also be done by means of a handout) and aware of the fact that I'm still holding the dowels, that students have a lot of energy, and that their natural instincts are to grab them and start bashing away with them, I realize that we need to dissipate some of this energy. At the same time I want to incorporate the idea that, in order to fight onstage, we need to look good and look like we know what we are doing. We need to know how to move with a rapier. I ask, "If you have a rapier in your hand and your opponent has one too, how much of your body do you want to leave open to attack?" Most students will agree that they need to show as little as possible. So they must face their opponent sideways, looking over their shoulder. If right-handed, a student looks over her right shoulder, presenting an opponent a view of her right side. Left-handers reverse the move. In actuality, the most comfortable position is to face one's partner at about a three-quarters position. In order to move forward and backward fluidly, without losing balance, the student should spread his legs slightly and sit down in the body, so that he can move forward and backward quickly, without hopping up and down as if on a trotting horse. It doesn't look good (I demonstrate), and it is hard to attack and defend yourself, if you are hopping about like a rabbit. I line all my students up against the gym wall, tell them to turn sideways, right-handed students turning left and left-handed students turning right, and ask them to look over their shoulder at me, making a T with their feet. The leading foot should face me and the back foot should be at a right angle to the body. (See Fig. 1.) I then ask the students to take a comfortable step forward, leaving the back foot in place. To help them recognize this as the balanced position, I ask them to imagine a weighted string in front of their nose, noticing that it would divide the body in half. They should now have equal weight on both feet. To maintain

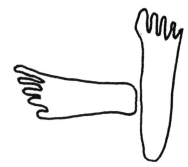

FIGURE 1

this balanced stance while advancing, they must lift the front foot, take a comfortable step forward, and slide the back foot to where the front foot was before. To move backward, they apply the same principle, sliding the front foot to where the back foot was before they moved. Unless the knees are slightly bent, this movement is awkward and causes a hopping gait. The knees must be bent to move forward and backward on a straight line, keeping the body sideways to a partner. This is the neutral position. (See Fig. 2.)

FIGURE 2

In order to naturalize this movement, and to control the energy level, I have them race from one side of the gym, or field, to the other. I always emphasize that they need to look good and to move like fighters who know what they are doing, the smoother the better. "If you want to look 'cool,' you can let your nonsword hand trail behind you, or place it on your back hip, and take a handkerchief or hold it in your trailing hand level with your head." (See Figs. 3, 4, 5.)

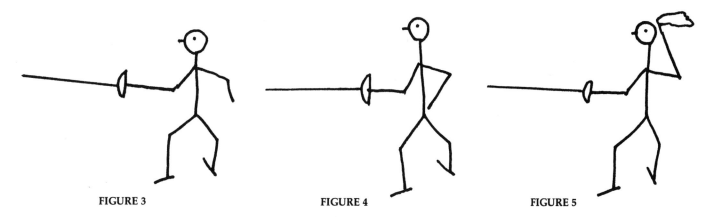

FIGURE 3   **FIGURE 4**   **FIGURE 5**

I still have not handed out my dowels. The races are fun, and I keep them at it while encouraging attention to the correct form as the class moves backward and forward. For the last race before I give out dowels, I divide the class and have one half go in a line to the other end of the gym. The first group races forward, touches the their partners at the other end, who then race backward. Hopping, running, and such are subject to disqualification. By the end of this fundamental movement session, I have a lot of tired students. I return to these activities intermittently, always stressing the need to look good and to move in this manner naturally. Whenever the class becomes a little too rambunctious, we work on movement to disperse excess energy.

My main concern is always *safety*. I have never had a student who has been hurt, and I believe that one of the reasons for this is that I continually return to basics during these sessions. I make sure each set of combatants always has a monitor and that everyone rotates. What I mean by this is that I break the class up into threes. One student acts as a monitor and, after a given amount of time, he switches with one of the combatants. We repeat this again so that all three students get to fight and monitor each other and all experience working together. Monitors are instructed to make sure that their team looks good and that they work safely. They are responsible. You know your class and who hangs out with whom. I make a point of partnering students who don't usually interact beyond the classroom.

I am now ready to hand out the dowels, and I give two to each threesome. I designate one student *A* and the other *B*. With the monitors on the side, I tell each pair of fighters to face each other and begin: "Everyone, keep your swords facing to the floor, and *A*s find a distance where, in the balanced position, you can hold your sword at arm's length in front of you without quite touching your partner. In other words, to touch them, you would have to take a step forward. *A*s and *B*s, look in each other's eyes. *B*s, keeping your eyes locked onto your partner, wave your arms about slowly. *A*s, can you see all of *B*s body and all the movement?" The reply will always be yes. "This," I tell them, "is your guarantee of safety! If you are always looking into your partner's eyes, you can see every movement he or she makes. Even though you know where each cut is going to go, it is choreographed; by looking in your partner's eyes, you can see everything and therefore avoid any accidents. If you are watching the point of attack, you can't see anything else. Monitors, it will be your job to make sure that the moves don't get too frantic and that both fighters keep eye contact. I want to hear you yelling, 'EYES' and 'SLOW DOWN.' If you feel that you are losing control at any time, yell 'STOP.' Anyone who does not listen to the monitor will have to leave the class." I make sure the class understands that I am deadly serious about this before I resume.

I continue, "We can learn a lot and have a great time, but if people act recklessly, they are endangering others as well as themselves." There are always one or two students who will not heed this warning, and after they have been thrown out once, they rarely prove troublesome again.

The fighters have to maintain the arm's-length position. Not everyone takes equal steps, so each team should practice keeping this distance. With swords held down, I have the monitors work on this until the students seem comfortable. *A*s move forward while *B*s move back and so on. I may incorporate a race here, working on movement and distance, having the *A*s advance and their *B* partners back up and then reverse it. After everyone has practiced for a while, we are ready to begin using the weapons.

The usual way to hold a sword is to have a thumb lying on top with the index finger curled underneath. You do not want to hold it stiffly. You want to allow the wrist to be flexible. There is no weight put onto the weapon when cutting; the action is accomplished through the movement of the whole body in order to make the move look good. All cuts should involve the entire body. You want to try to make large arcs as you move the sword. This exaggeration gives the impression of force and allows the audience to follow the blade. Sport fencing, unlike stage combat, is not dramatic because the movements are simply too quick to follow.

I now demonstrate the target areas of the body. (See Fig. 6.) The body divides into five specific points of attack and defense: the right and left knee, the right and left upper arm in line with the upper chest, and the center of the head. (You may wish to add thighs, waist, and the neck areas later.) I have assigned a number to each of these five attack and defense areas; some fight choreographers use letters; but there is no set method of labeling these points. The important thing is that everyone knows which system is being used.

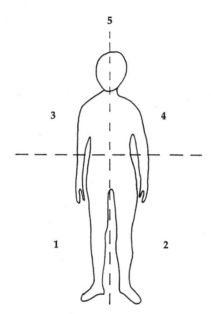

FIGURE 6

With As facing their partners, they take one step forward for each blow and then return to the neutral position before they perform the next. They proceed in sequence from targets 1 through 5. Keeping eye contact, As lightly touch their opponents' right knee, left knee, right arm (chest height), left arm, and top of the head. It is important to maintain eye contact with your partner and to work with an aim toward accuracy. The Bs, swords down, stand still. We want to make the angle of the cut as wide as possible and to aim it so that it looks like blows 1 and 2 would cut the knee off, and blows 3 and 4 the arm off, and 5 would split the body in half. Once the monitor is satisfied that the As know this, look "cool," and are comfortable with it, they switch with the As. The Bs then work on the same cuts. Then they switch and the new As (the first monitors) have their turn. I find that this is the most efficient rotation pattern.

Some stage-fight choreographers believe that it is safer to aim the cut a little apart from the body. This can lead to inexact placement of blows. Through experience I have found that when the defenders know that the point of attack is a target on their bodies, they are able to consistently place their swords in the same place. There should be no real weight in the blow; the body is doing most of the work. Not only does this look better, but it's safer for both parties.

After we are satisfied with the cuts, we work on the parries—defensive positions. Even though the fight is choreographed and the fighters have learned the sequences, the time it takes to parry is less than the time involved in making a cut. This time difference works as a natural safety factor, and with some practice, students, striving for realism, can time their parries so that they do not telegraph where the blows are going.

"In order to parry cut 1, from a neutral position where your sword would be pointing forward, you break your wrist inward so that your sword is close to you and protecting the right side of your right knee at a ninety-degree angle to the floor." (See Fig. 7.)

"In order to parry cut 2, from a neutral position where your sword would be pointing forward, you break your wrist inward so that your sword is close to you and protecting the left side of your right knee at a ninety-degree angle to the floor." (See Fig. 8.)

"In order to parry cut 3, from a neutral position where your sword would be pointing forward, you bring the sword point upward parallel to your body and hook your sword elbow as far as you can behind your back so that your sword—pointing straight up—is close to you and protecting all of the upper right side of your body." (See Fig. 9.)

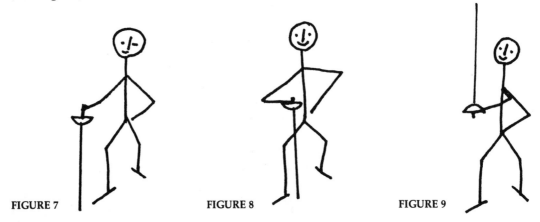

FIGURE 7   FIGURE 8   FIGURE 9

"In order to parry cut 4, from a neutral position where your sword would be pointing forward, you move the sword across your body to the left and bring the point upward toward the ceiling. Your forearm should remain parallel to the floor, making an L with your sword, which is close to you and protecting the upper left side of your body." (See Fig. 10.)

"In order to parry cut 5, from a neutral position where your sword would be pointing forward, you bring your sword up so that the blade is parallel to the floor. The sword is held above the head and forward from the face. The sword handle should be to the right of your head, and your fingernails will be pointing toward your opponent." (See Fig. 11. See Fig. 12 for a variation, where the handle is to the left of the head and the fingernails point in the opposite direction.)

FIGURE 10   FIGURE 11   FIGURE 12

Taking one step backward for each parry and returning to the neutral position before they perform the next, the *A*s move through the sequence 1 through 5. Once the monitor is satisfied that the *A*s know the moves and are comfortable moving with them, the group rotates in order to give everyone an opportunity to practice.

We now have a sequence of cuts and parries and are ready to add movement. Reminding everyone about the safety concerns—go slowly, accuracy, eye contact—with *A*s attacking and *B*s parrying and monitors in charge, we slowly go through the sequence from 1 to 5, with both *A*s and *B*s in motion. Each cut requires a step forward with a corresponding step backward for the parry. We do not return to neutral after each blow.

Once all the students have practiced safely cutting and parrying, we are ready to create a stage fight. Obviously, a sequence of cuts 1 through 5 can be rearranged so that *A*s and *B*s attack and defend in different sequences. The sequences can be mixed up and varied but must be planned and learned by both partners and the monitor. Your students will come up with a lot of imaginative configurations, and if you have time, you may want to suggest that, with a monitor, they work up a sequence to show. The whole class can watch each group's sequence, commenting on believability and safety. I impress upon my students that if the fight looks unsafe, we worry about the performers' safety and forget about the character.

Getting back to *Twelfth Night*, I have my students go through the process outlined in "Up on Your Feet with Shakespeare: The Wrong Way and the Right," either in groups, on their own, or in class. For *Twelfth Night* we concentrate on Act 3, scene 4, and especially pages 127–31 in the New Folger edition. Here are a few examples of some of the many questions we could ask and explore: "Both Sir Andrew and Viola are afraid; how are they different?" "Would Sir Andrew know how to hold a sword? Would Viola?" "Is Sir Toby a good fighter? Is Antonio?" "How can we show a difference between all these characters and the way they move and fight?"

This is a very basic approach to stage combat, and there is a lot more that we could work on. Your students will be very creative and probably know a lot about this already. If you have the time, getting hold of a fight choreographer who can come in and give a class on slaps, punches, falls, rolls, hand-to-hand fighting, and sword and dagger is relatively cheap and in many communities easy to do. I often have my students work in slow motion, especially in group scenes. This works very well for the first scene of *Romeo and Juliet,* where the brawl can accommodate a variety of styles.

If you are concerned about the safety of using dowels, you may want to put a piece of foam rubber on the ends. I always collect the dowels at the end of the session and make sure that I keep them. In some instances I allow students to take them out and work alone. I require, however, that a monitor always be part of the group and present at every rehearsal.

Stipulating that they have to justify their character choices textually, I assign groups to present to their peers a scene that includes a fight. I may have more than one group present the same scene. I don't believe that every scene in the play needs to be covered in the classroom, and this could be an example of my students coming to grips with a scene for the first time, on their own. They began *Twelfth Night* on their feet (probably all or part of Act 2, scene 3,) and have some experience using performance for analysis. I may ask them to keep a journal, or present some written notes recording the rehearsal process. I am not interested in the final result so much as I am in the discussions, the vocabulary research, and all the textual reasons leading up to their performance choices. This exercise continues to enhance my students' ability to speak Shakespeare's language, to act out parts, to engage in literary analysis of the scene, and to continue to establish a collaborative and energetic relationship with the playwright.

PART THREE

In the Classroom

·

N<small>ANCY</small> G<small>OODWIN</small>

E<small>DITOR</small>

Twelfth Night

•

MARTHA HARRIS

EDITOR

Dear Colleague,

QUESTION: Why should middle-school or high-school teachers spend their Shakespeare chip on *Twelfth Night?*

ANSWER: It's great comedy. Students will laugh at

- moonstruck lovers
- gender jokes
- mismatched couples
- practical jokes
- fops and fools
- goofy costumes
- comic revenge
- wacky sword fights

ANOTHER ANSWER: The poetry is pleasing—from the opening speech ("If music be the food of love, play on . . .") to the last song ("With a hey ho, the wind and the rain . . ."), the language sings.

QUESTION: Well, then, what's up with this *Twelfth Night* unit?

ANSWER: The idea is to help seventh-through-twelfth-grade students experience Illyria, a place where, according to director Michael Tolaydo, you can find parking places right in front of the building and where when you kiss somebody, hair does not get in your mouth. It's also a place where, according to Kenneth Branagh's Renaissance Theatre Company production, a winter mood can blow in, where clowns can be sad and aristocrats lonely. This unit is meant for teachers who are willing to hold off on overworked analysis and let Shakespeare teach Shakespeare. To concentrate on the text and let whatever madness happens happen.

QUESTION: So, how do you let Shakespeare teach Shakespeare?

ANSWER: You let students get close to Shakespeare's words through:

- **Performance.** Students read the whole play—together, out loud. Most of the time they read standing up with scripts in their hands. Moving. Acting out the words. But each day's activity is different, so they experience many ways to read out loud: choral readings, small-group readings, rehearsal-hall readings, and so on. Built into the many types of out-loud readings are activities to help students learn about such things as cutting scripts, paraphrasing, stage moving, and looking for action clues in the language.

- **Reflection.** After classroom performances, students will, as homework, reread the scene and reflect on the words and ideas in the scenes by answering CQ's— contemplation questions.

QUESTION: How much time does this unit take?

ANSWER: No matter if your class is very young and new to Shakespeare, or if the students are very capable readers and quite familiar with Shakespeare's works, or if curriculum constraints prevent you from spending from four to six weeks on one play, you can use this unit to your best advantage.

- **If this is your class's first adventure with Shakespeare.** Start with small activities from *Shakespeare Set Free: Teaching* Romeo and Juliet, Macbeth, *and* A Midsummer Night's Dream—tossing lines on page 45 and the insults on page 125. These get students up and moving and get them comfortable with Shakespeare's language before plunging into acting a scene in Lesson 1. Also, for those with no Shakespeare experience, the *Twelfth Night* Sampler approach, described below, might be a better approach than attempting to read the entire play, start to finish.

- **If you have only one or two weeks to spare for a Shakespeare unit.** Look at the Acting Company Activity, page 125. Preselect the scenes as suggested in the lesson. Have the whole class read a synopsis of the play. Then see the key scenes in action as presented by the class acting companies. Or appoint one group as the Narrator Group. They could read a synopsis and prepare a running story of the play, splicing in the acting of scenes by other groups. Or try a *Twelfth Night* Sampler. The following six lessons provide about two weeks' worth of activities, and introduce the students to most of the major characters and plot lines in the play:

Lesson 3: Discovering Illyria
Lesson 6: Performing 1.4 and 1.5
Lesson 8: Role Playing and Performing 2.3
Lesson 10: Close Reading 2.4
Lesson 11: Performing 2.5
Lesson 14: Performing 3.1, 3.2, and 3.3
Lesson 15: Sight Gags
Lesson 16: Sword Fighting
Lesson 17: Video Wrap-up
Lesson 19: Acting Companies

Again, a play synopsis would be helpful for the students to read so they would know how all of these scenes tie together.

• **If your students can read large chunks of the play on their own.** Students who are able to read the play on their own, as homework, will certainly get more enjoyment out of the play if they also have a chance to bring the scenes to life in the classroom. The following sequence of lessons could be used for this type of class:

Week One: Students read Acts 1 and 2 on their own and do the classroom activities in lessons 3, 6, 7, 8, and 10.

Week Two: Students read Acts 3, 4, and 5 on their own and do the classroom activities in lessons 11, 13, 16, and 18.

QUESTION: What about a final exam?

ANSWER: There is no final test with pencil and paper. Instead, students present a festival of *Twelfth Night* scenes.

Enjoy this excursion to Illyria.

Martha L. Harris

Your colleague,
Martha Harris
North Community High School
Minneapolis, Minn.

UNIT CALENDAR FOR
Twelfth Night

🕊 1	🕊 2	🕊 3	🕊 4	🕊 5
LESSON 1 Meeting Shakespeare's Words and Finding Meaning Text: 2.2	LESSON 2 Evoking Twelfth Night Folly	LESSON 3 Discovering Illyria Text: 1.1, 1.2	LESSON 4 Designing Movement Text: 1.3	LESSON 5 Demonstrating Blocking Text: 1.3
🕊 6	🕊 7	🕊 8	🕊 9	🕊 10
LESSON 6 Performing 1.4 and 1.5 Text: 1.4, 1.5	LESSON 6 Performing 1.4 and 1.5 *(cont.)* Text: 1.4, 1.5	LESSON 7 Explicating "Willow Cabin" Text: 1.5.271–279	LESSON 8 Role Playing and Performing 2.3 Text: 2.1, 2.2, 2.3	LESSON 9 Concentrating on Character
🕊 11	🕊 12	🕊 13	🕊 14	🕊 15
LESSON 10 Close Reading 2.4 Text: 2.4	LESSON 11 Performing 2.5 Text: 2.5	LESSON 12 2.5 on Video Text: 2.5	LESSON 13 Cutting and Rehearsing 3.1, 3.2, and 3.3 Text: 3.1, 3.2, 3.3	LESSON 14 Performing 3.1, 3.2, and 3.3 Text: 3.1, 3.2, 3.3
🕊 16	🕊 17	🕊 18	🕊 19	🕊 20
LESSON 15 Sight Gags Text: 3.4.1-204	LESSON 16 Sword Fighting Text: 3.4.205-415, 4.1.1-70	LESSON 16 Sword Fighting *(cont.)* Text: 3.4.205-415, 4.1.1-70	LESSON 16 Sword Fighting *(cont.)* Text: 3.4.205-415, 4.1.1-70	LESSON 17 Video Wrap-up Text: 4.2, 4.3, 5.1
🕊 21	🕊 22	🕊 23	🕊 24	🕊 25
LESSON 17 Video Wrap-up *(cont.)* Text: 4.2, 4.3, 5.1	LESSON 18 A Closer Look at Character	LESSON 18 A Closer Look at Character *(cont.)*	LESSON 19 Acting Companies	LESSON 19 Acting Companies *(cont.)*
🕊 26	🕊 27			
LESSON 19 Acting Companies *(cont.)*	LESSON 19 Festival Day			

LESSON **1** **"The Churlish Messenger"**

Meeting Shakespeare's Words and Finding Meaning

❧

PLAY SECTION COVERED IN THIS LESSON

2.2 Malvolio delivers Olivia's ring to Viola, who begins to realize that Olivia is smitten with her.

LINES: Malvolio, 12; Viola, 28

❧

WHAT'S ON FOR TODAY AND WHY

Because it is a fast, powerful way to break the language barrier between contemporary English and the Early Modern English spoken in Elizabethan England, students will begin *Twelfth Night* with acting. Before fear and dread have a chance to set in, they will be on their feet exclaiming about "moderate pace," "the cunning of her passion," and "thriftless sighs."

Act 2, scene 2 (2.2) is short, it contains enough information to help students perceive relationships among some of the characters, and it provides a chance to become familiar with a scene they will meet later as an old friend.

Your best preparation for this lesson is to read Michael Tolaydo's article "Up on Your Feet with Shakespeare: The Wrong Way and the Right" on page 41. Photocopy 2.2—in larger type and with no notes, as he suggests—so that students' first encounter with Shakespeare's words will be as a short, manageable script.

WHAT TO DO

1. Acting Circle

Have students put their chairs in a circle. Tell them that they are actors just reporting for the first day of rehearsal. Pass out a one-page script of 2.2.

Going around the circle, have students in turn read to a major punctuation mark—period, semicolon, colon, question mark, exclamation point.

Tell students to watch for words they're not familiar with as they follow the reading. After the reading, ask students to point out words they don't know. Ask if others can explain the words. If you like, throw in *brief* explanations of Elizabethan-isms ("thou," "art"), but for the most part let the students help each other.

Read the scene again, this time with one Malvolio and three Violas, who split her long speech in lines 17–41 ("I left no ring" to "for me t'untie"). Ask: What's going on here? Who are these two people? Look at the language. What clues do you get about them and about the action?

Change casts and try another round, this time telling students to look for more clues about what's happening in this little scene. As students read, encourage them to use their voices to convey some sort of mood or emotion as they say their lines. Again, more questions: What are these two people talking about? What's the deal with this ring? Who is Countess Olivia? Is there anything odd about Viola? Why does Malvolio call her "sir"? (Don't tell the students she's dressed as a man; let them discover this as the lesson unfolds.)

2. Acting the Scene

Now get the first part of the scene (up to Viola's soliloquy) on its feet. Designate an acting space in your classroom. Ask a new pair of students to take the roles of Malvolio and Viola, and send them with scripts in hand to the makeshift stage. As the actors read their parts, have the remaining students suggest movements appropriate to the text. Important: use a real ring, and don't let students get away with minimal movement. Make them decide where Malvolio and Viola enter, how they walk, when they turn, and so forth.

To get used to the idea that there are many "right" ways to do a scene, change casts and suggest that they try these variations:

- **The Chase.** Malvolio chases Viola all around the room as he reads his lines.
- **Hot Potato.** Malvolio and Viola keep tossing the ring back and forth like a hot potato as they say their lines.
- **Take It.** Malvolio keeps trying to give the ring to Viola, or deposit it on her person in some way, but he can't get rid of it.

3. The Soliloquy: Theme and Variation

When you think you've milked the dialogue for all it's worth, return to the acting circle and look at Viola's soliloquy. Have the whole class read it together, OUT LOUD. They may think this is weird, but that's OK. The ear knows things about Shakespeare's language that the eye can't guess. Again try some variations: Have the males and females alternate reading lines. Have single voices read the words in parentheses. Overemphasize the iambic rhythms (DisGUISE, I SEE thou ART a WICKedNESS whereIN the PREGnant ENeMY does MUCH). Have the appropriate sides of the room or rows read different lines.

After reading the soliloquy several times, gather more information: What does this add to our understanding of what was going on with the ring? Of Viola? By now, if not before, students will catch on that Viola is posing as a man.

4. Closer Reading

Have students look more closely at these lines: "How easy is it for the proper false / In women's waxen hearts to set their forms!" Ask: What is the image that you see when you hear these words? How much truth is in this statement? Is it only true for women? What is ironic about Viola saying this line in this particular situation?

Ask: What is different about the arrangement of the words on the page in the dialogue section and in Viola's monologue? Most will notice that the former is prose, the latter poetry. You might take a few minutes at this point to talk about iambic pentameter, but don't belabor it. Now is not the time to focus on poetic terminology.

5. Preview

Complete the day's activity by telling the students a little bit more about *Twelfth Night*. If you like, use Handout 1: "A Guide, or, What You Will," a summary in verse composed by Lucy Bell Sellers, a teacher in Germantown, Pennsylvania.

HOW DID IT GO?

No matter how they pronounced the words, no matter how ineptly they acted, if students used their own brains and Shakespeare's language to re-create Viola and Malvolio and this bit of ancient comedy, you have won the day.

HANDOUT 1

A GUIDE, OR, WHAT YOU WILL

by Lucy Bell Sellers

Twelfth Night's plot is hard to follow,
(Not to mention hard to swallow),
Thus, we thoughtfully provide
For your enlightenment, a Guide.

A set of twins were almost drowned
In shipwreck, but were later found,
Though neither knew his twin was saved;
The play's about how they behaved.

The girl, one Viola by name,
In boyish clothing straightway came
To wait upon the local lord,
Whose habit was, when he felt bored,
To wallow deep in songs and verse—
Which was exceedingly perverse,
Since she for whom his love was deep—
Olivia—thought him a creep.

Olivia had her problems too.
Her brother's death made her so blue
She'd sworn off seeing men at all
And snubbed them when they came to call.

The Duke, who wouldn't take her "no,"
Dispatched his Viola to go,
(Disguised still, you ought to know,
And answ'ring to "Cesario").

Now Viola in manly clothing,
Inspired anything but loathing.
Imagine, then, her inward stir
To have the lady fall for her!
While she (we say without rebuke)
Had fallen madly for the Duke.

So far so good, though we have not
As yet begun the other plot,
Which now we'll undertake at once:
Sir Toby Belch was not a dunce,
But though Olivia's uncle, he
Was into drunken revelry,
To pay for which, he (being broke)
Brought around a wealthy bloke,
Sir Andrew A., to woo the niece,
While Toby skinned him of his fleece.

Now learn, because this isn't trivia,
The dour steward to Olivia,
Malvolio, both prim and proud,
Was out to get the Toby crowd.
For partying, he gave them hell,
Sir T., Sir A., and M. as well.
Maria, sep'rate from their riot,
Had only tried to keep them quiet.
Thus, sore at being scolded so,
She plotted 'gainst Malvolio
To make him seem a perfect ass.
What subsequently came to pass
Seems suddenly beyond our scope—
And so, farewell, we'll let you cope.

2 "More Matter for a May Morning"

Evoking Twelfth Night Folly

WHAT'S ON FOR TODAY AND WHY

If things go well today, two important messages will reach the students' brains. First, they will learn the essential spirit of Twelfth Night traditions.

Second, they will learn that you expect them to pay attention to the play as they work their way through it, to reflect on it in a regular and disciplined manner, and to demonstrate their reflections by one of two methods: log or act test.

For years, I prescribed logs for all my students, but that didn't work very well. Some students just didn't keep up with the work on a daily basis but crammed it all in at the last when it was due—that is, if they did it at all—making the exercise seem pointless. This year I tried something different. I gave students two choices:

- **Keep a Log.** After every section you read or perform, summarize it, record your personal thoughts about it, and find a memorable line and new vocabulary word from it. Do your log in the style of Handout 2: *"Twelfth Night* Log."
- **Take an Act Test.** At the end of each act, take the test in Handout 3, which includes summarizing the act and explicating quotes. Do this as a take-home test. Allow about two hours for each test. Turn in your papers at the end of each act.

Both of these choices require ongoing reflection and absorption of information during the reading of the play, so each met my goal, and the results were much more satisfactory. The students who did the logs did a wonderful, thorough job with them, and I wasn't bothered with the shoddy, pointless logs of the past.

So now is the time for a major decision. How will students show you that they are thinking about the people and events of *Twelfth Night?* No matter what choice they make, as they work through the unit, everyone should reread the section of the play that they worked on in class and do the contemplation questions (CQs) that are scattered throughout the unit because they address specific issues associated with their lessons and give students common ground for debate. Handout 4: "Contemplation Questions" shows the whole array. Give the handout to your students, or keep the list for your own use, as you like.

Decide how students are to organize the CQs. Will they keep them in a notebook and turn them in at specified times? Will they do them on notebook paper, index cards, photocopied forms? Arrive at the best method for you and your class.

WHAT TO DO

1. Talking About "What If"

Organize the class into small groups. Give each group a card with one of the following "What If" situations written on it. Yes, they are goofy and childish, but that is the point.

- What if all the students became teachers and all the teachers became students?
- What if there were three people with this situation: Person *A* loves Person *B* who loves Person *C* who loves Person *A*?
- What if everyone woke up one morning and found they had turned into the opposite sex?
- What if everyone in this room looked exactly alike?

Give each group ten minutes to brainstorm a list of things that would happen if their "What If" situation took place.

2. "What If" Skits

Give the groups ten more minutes to devise short skits portraying one of their "What If" ideas. Have each group present its skit for the class.

After the skits, tell the class that they've just done a Twelfth Night activity and explain the Elizabethan Twelfth Night custom. Corresponding to the religious holiday commemorating the visit of the Magi to the newborn Christ Child, the secular holiday Twelfth Night was called "Feast of Fools." Somewhat like our Halloween combined with our April Fools' Day, Twelfth Night was a time for pranks and disguises, playful games and folly. In the introduction to the New Folger edition of *Twelfth Night*, Barbara A. Mowat and Paul Werstine explain that Twelfth Night is the twelfth night after Christmas, the last night of the extended Christmas season, and ". . . thus it marks the boundary between games and disguisings and the business of the workaday world."

In *The Riverside Shakespeare*, Anne Barton explains that Twelfth Night is a "period of holiday abandon in which the normal rules and order of life were suspended or else deliberately inverted, in which serious issues and events mingled perplexingly with revelry and apparent madness" (404). This, Barton explains, is "the atmosphere in Illyria: a country where everyone (except, perhaps, Feste) is very much in earnest, but also a little insane."

3. Reflections

Establish how students will demonstrate their reflections on *Twelfth Night* as they move through the unit. Explain the procedure whereby students work in logs or take act tests.

Also explain that each time they work on a section of the play in class you expect them to reread it and think about it that night. Tell them that throughout the unit they will answer CQs—contemplation questions. Arrive at an orderly method for doing this—in a notebook, a portfolio, whatever pleases you and your students.

Give the first CQ: Are there any holidays that, in your experience, are connected with carefree fun and merrymaking? What are they? Tell about a holiday, or a time, when you were inordinately silly.

HOW DID IT GO?

The quality of the skits and the responses to them will indicate the extent to which students will relax into the Twelfth Night mode. If you have students who consider themselves too mature for such foolishness, assure them that this unit might be light-hearted but it is not intellectually inferior. It will stimulate their minds as well as their sense of playfulness.

You might want to think ahead to how you will respond to and/or evaluate logs and act tests. Will you put grades on this work? Will you note the progress students make from the first sections to the last? Will you use the logs as the foundation for a longer paper or project? What can you do to deepen the students' experience with *Twelfth Night* through reflection?

HANDOUT 2

TWELFTH NIGHT LOG

Act _____, Scene _____, Lines _____ to _____

SUMMARY AND SIGNIFICANCE	PERSONAL THOUGHTS AND CONNECTIONS
A MEMORABLE LINE	A NEW VOCABULARY WORD

❧

HANDOUT 3

ACT TESTS

First, summarize the act.

Second, for each of the following quotes, answer the following questions:

1. Who said this speech?
2. To whom was this speech directed?
3. Where in the play is this speech? Give line numbers.
4. What is happening at the time this speech is spoken?
5. Phrase by phrase, how would you put this speech in your own language?
6. What suggestions do you have for the actor who says this speech?

ACT 1

- O, she that hath a heart of that fine frame
  To pay this debt of love but to a brother,
  How will she love when the rich golden shaft
  Hath killed the flock of all affections else
  That live in her; when liver, brain, and heart,
  These sovereign thrones, are all supplied, and filled
  Her sweet perfections with one self king!

- And to comfort you with chance,
  Assure yourself, after our ship did split,
  When you and those poor number saved with you
  Hung on our driving boat, I saw your brother,
  Most provident in peril, bind himself
  (Courage and hope both teaching him the practice)
  To a strong mast that lived upon the sea,
  Where, like Arion on the dolphin's back,
  I saw him hold acquaintance with the waves
  So long as I could see.

- What is *"pourquoi"*? Do, or not do? I would I had bestowed that time in the tongues that I have in fencing, dancing, and bearbaiting. O, had I but followed the arts!

·   —Cesario,
Thou know'st no less but all. I have unclasped
To thee the book even of my secret soul.
Therefore, good youth, address thy gait unto her.
Be not denied access. Stand at her doors
And tell them, there thy fixèd foot shall grow
Till thou have audience.

· Your lord does know my mind. I cannot love him.
Yet I suppose him virtuous, know him noble,
Of great estate, of fresh and stainless youth;
In voices well divulged, free, learned, and valiant,
And in dimension and the shape of nature
A gracious person. But yet I cannot love him.
He might have took his answer long ago.

ACT 2

· You must know of me, then, Antonio, my name is Sebastian, which I called Roderigo. My father was that Sebastian of Messaline whom I know you have heard of. He left behind him myself and a sister, both born in an hour. If the heavens had been pleased, would we had so ended! But you, sir, altered that, for some hour before you took me from the breach of the sea was my sister drowned.

· How will this fadge? My master loves her dearly,
And I, poor monster, fond as much on him,
And she, mistaken, seems to dote on me.
What will become of this? As I am man,
My state is desperate for my master's love.
As I am woman (now, alas the day!),
What thriftless sighs shall poor Olivia breathe!
O Time, thou must untangle this, not I.
It is too hard a knot for me t' untie.

· My masters, are you mad? Or what are you? Have you no wit, manners, nor honesty but to gabble like tinkers at this time of night? Do you make an ale-house of my lady's house, that you squeak out your coziers' catches without any mitigation or remorse of voice? Is there no respect of place, persons, nor time in you?

· Say that some lady, as perhaps there is,
Hath for your love as great a pang of heart
As you have for Olivia. You cannot love her;
You tell her so. Must she not then be answered?

- I will be proud, I will read politic authors, I will baffle Sir Toby, I will wash off gross acquaintance, I will be point-devise the very man. I do not now fool myself, to let imagination jade me; for every reason excites to this, that my lady loves me.

ACT 3

- By innocence I swear, and by my youth,
  I have one heart, one bosom, and one truth,
  And that no woman has, nor never none
  Shall mistress be of it, save I alone.
  And so adieu, good madam. Nevermore
  Will my master's tears to you deplore.

- For Andrew, if he were opened and you find so much blood in his liver as will clog the foot of a flea, I'll eat the rest of th' anatomy.

-              Hold, sir, here's my purse.
  In the south suburbs, at the Elephant,
  Is best to lodge. I will bespeak our diet
  Whiles you beguile the time and feed your knowledge
  With viewing of the town. There shall you have me.

- Come, we'll have him in a dark room and bound. My niece is already in the belief that he's mad. We may carry it thus, for our pleasure and his penance, till our very pastime, tired out of breath, prompt us to have mercy on him, at which time we will bring the device to the bar and crown thee for a finder of madmen.

- Therefore, this letter, being so excellently ignorant, will breed no terror in the youth. He will find it comes from a clodpoll. But, sir, I will deliver his challenge by word of mouth, set upon Aguecheek a notable report of valor, and drive the gentleman (as I know his youth will aptly receive it) into a most hideous opinion of his rage, skill, fury, and impetuosity. This will so fright them both that they will kill one another by the look, like cockatrices.

- Methinks his words do from such passion fly
  That he believes himself; so do not I.
  Prove true, imagination, O, prove true,
  That I, dear brother, be now ta'en for you!

ACT 4

- No, I do not know you, nor I am not sent to you by my lady to bid you come speak with her, nor your name is not Master Cesario, nor this is not my nose neither. Nothing that is so is so.

· What relish is in this? How runs the steam?
  Or I am mad, or else this is a dream.
  Let fancy still my sense in Lethe steep;
  If it be thus to dream, still let me sleep!

· I say this house is as dark as ignorance, though ignorance were as dark as hell. And I say there was never man thus abused. I am no more mad than you are.

· To him in thine own voice, and bring me word how thou find'st him. I would we were well rid of this knavery. If he may be conveniently delivered, I would he were, for I am now so far in offense with my niece that I cannot pursue with any safety this sport the upshot. Come by and by to my chamber.

ACT 5

·   A witchcraft drew me hither.
  That most ingrateful boy there by your side
  From the rude sea's enraged and foamy mouth
  Did I redeem; a wrack past hope he was.
  His life I gave him and did thereto add
  My love, without retention or restraint,
  All his in dedication. For his sake
  Did I expose myself, pure for his love,
  Into the danger of this adverse town . . .

·   But hear me this:
  Since you to nonregardance cast my faith,
  And that I partly know the instrument
  That screws me from my true place in your favor,
  Live you the marble-breasted tyrant still.
  But this your minion, whom I know you love,
  And whom, by heaven I swear, I tender dearly,
  Him will I tear out of that cruel eye
  Where he sits crownèd in his master's spite.—
  Come, boy, with me. My thoughts are ripe in mischief.
  I'll sacrifice the lamb that I do love
  To spite a raven's heart within a dove.

· O thou dissembling cub! What wilt thou be
  When time hath sowed a grizzle on thy case!
  Or will not else thy craft so quickly grow
  That thine own trip shall be thine overthrow?
  Farewell, and take her, but direct thy feet
  Where thou and I henceforth may never meet.

· Do I stand there? I never had a brother,
  Nor can there be that deity in my nature
  Of here and everywhere. I had a sister,
  Whom the blind waves and surges have devoured.
  Of charity, what kin are you to me?
  What countryman? What name? What parentage?

· Your master quits you; and for your service done him,
  So much against the mettle of your sex,
  So far beneath your soft and tender breeding,
  And since you called me "master" for so long,
  Here is my hand. You shall from this time be
  Your master's mistress.

·   Madam, you have done me wrong,
  Notorious wrong.

· Why, "some are born great, some achieve greatness, and some have greatness thrown upon them."
  I was one, sir, in this interlude, one Sir Topas, sir, but that's all one.

❧

HANDOUT 4

CONTEMPLATION QUESTIONS

- **LESSON 2**

  Are there any holidays that, in your experience, are connected with carefree fun and merry-making? What are they? Tell about a holiday, or a time, when you were inordinately silly.

- **LESSON 3**

  Sketch or describe in words your first impressions of Orsino, Olivia, and Viola. If you like, sketch or describe your preliminary ideas about a set for a *Twelfth Night* production.

- **LESSON 5**

  Find and comment on four lines from the scenes you've read so far: a line that has beauty in it, a line with a good joke, a line that sounds modern, a line that appeals to you for any reason.

- **LESSON 6**

  Review 1.5 and focus on Feste. How long do you think he has been in Olivia's household? Is he a carefree fool with no troubles? Does he have a brain? If you were a director, whom would you cast for Feste? How would you costume him or her? Can you find some clues in the script that suggest action for Feste? If you were a director, what would you want the Fool to be doing physically in this scene?

- **LESSON 7**

  Write the three pieces of information from today's lesson you consider the most memorable.

- **LESSON 8**

  Are you more of a Toby or more of a Malvolio when it comes to getting rowdy?
  Look again at Feste's song in this scene. Does it seem in keeping with the mood of the scene? Do the words reflect what's going on? How?
  Find what you consider a pretty good joke in this scene. What's funny about it to you?

- **LESSON 9**

  Draw a diagram or chart that shows the characters and their relationships to each other. Or, do a storyboard of the plot so far.

• LESSON 10

Think again about the views of love you met in 2.4. Do you think there's a difference in the way men love and the way women love? Do either Viola or Orsino express views similar to your own? Or do you have a position on this question different from both of these characters? Find a line in this scene that you like or that strikes you in some way and comment on it.

• LESSON 12

Have you ever played a practical joke on someone, or been the victim of a practical joke? Write about your experience, making parallels between what happened to you and what's happening to Malvolio.

Make a list of all the epithets that are used for characters in this scene (e.g., rascally sheep-biter; overweening rogue).

• LESSON 14

Find lines that show how Viola and Orsino express love, and reflect on how their method of expressing love defines their personalities. Also express an opinion on whether or not Feste knows that Cesario is a female.

• LESSON 15

Choose what you consider the four choicest lines, copy them, and tell why they are great.

• LESSON 16

Look at Antonio's speech in 3.4.384–89 ("But O, how vile an idol proves this god!" to "empty trunks o'erflourished by the devil"). Paraphrase it, comment on it, and give some examples of what he is talking about.

• LESSON 17

If you were commissioned to design and direct a production of *Twelfth Night*, where would you set it? What would your Illyria look like? What would be your take on each character? What costumes, music, and special effects would you want?

How would you get each character off the stage in 5.1? Think about where they are going and how they feel. Do they stop and shake hands with other characters? Do they slink off or run off? This will be the last time the audience will see them. What impression do you want to leave?

LESSON **3** **"What Country, Friends, Is This?"**

Discovering Illyria

ﻬ

PLAY SECTIONS COVERED IN THIS LESSON

1.1 Orsino, wracked with love for the lady Olivia, learns that she refuses to see him.

LINES: Orsino, 31; Curio, 2; Valentine, 9; other lords, 0

1.2 The shipwrecked Viola arrives on shore with the Captain. Learning that her brother has probably drowned in the wreck, she decides to disguise herself as a boy and seek employment as a page with Duke Orsino.

LINES: Viola, 35; Captain, 32

ﻬ

WHAT'S ON FOR TODAY AND WHY

Continuing the on-their-feet activities of the previous two lessons, the students will perform a "walk-through" reading of the first two scenes. Plunging students into the play with all five senses will help their brains begin to make creative and critical connections with Shakespeare's marvelous language.

As in the *Othello* unit, your actors will benefit greatly from the use of hats—festive, fancy, madcap, any old hats you can get your hands on. There are so many characters to keep straight, and each one is a distinct personality easily matched to a signature hat. Let the students decide which hat suits which character, and let actors use them throughout the unit.

WHAT TO DO

1. Vocal Exercise

Ask each student to say the line "If music be the food of love, play on." Try for a wide variety of vocal inflections. ("*If* music be the food of love . . . ," "If *music* be the food of love . . . ," and so on.) Make sure each student says the line.

Talk about the line: how is music the food of love?

2. Performing 1.1

As in the Acting Circle on page 65, do a read-around of 1.1 with each student taking a sentence. Ask: Who does Orsino seem to be? What's his problem? How do his companions regard him? Choose hats for Orsino, Curio, and Valentine.

After reading the scene two or three times, have three students move to the designated acting space. Using the text and the rest of the class as directors, improvise a set with furniture and props at hand. Ask: What kind of music do you imagine playing during this scene? Are the musicians on stage? Where?

Have the actors read the scene on their feet, scripts in hand, moving all the while. Let various students take turns as director, adding movement to the scene as you go. Again, ask for lots of movement—

> TEACHER: Now, we're not rocks. We move. We gesture.
> GERALD: We puke.
> JIMMY: Do we have to?
> SUE ANN: Can we trade parts?
> TEACHER: Robert, start with the Duke's part. Melissa, will you start off as the director? Imagine this is the Duke's palace. Now look at the script. What room in the palace are we in? What furniture is there? What is the Duke doing as the scene opens? Where should he be?

3. Performing 1.2

Cast 1.2, choose hats for Viola and the captain, and proceed as above.

4. Discussion

Ask: Viola says to the captain in 1.2 ". . . though that nature with a beauteous wall / Doth oft close in pollution." What does she mean? What are examples of nature closing pollution in a wall of beauty?

Ask students to find a line from either of these two scenes that strikes them in some way and comment on it.

5. Oral Evaluation

> TEACHER: Show me with your fingers. On a scale of 1–10, 10 being the highest, how well do you comprehend these two scenes?
> JIMMY: 5
> SUE ANN: 2
> MELISSA: This is incredibly simple to understand.
> TEACHER: I must tell you the truth. This is my third time reading *Twelfth Night*, and my comprehension level is an 8. Do not worry if you don't understand every word or every phrase. You're doing great.

6. CQ

Ask students to reread 1.1 and 1.2 then sketch or describe in words their first impressions of Orsino, Olivia, and Viola. Ask those who want to, to sketch or describe their preliminary ideas about a set for a *Twelfth Night* production.

HOW DID IT GO?   The oral evaluation told all.

LESSON 4   **"My Very Walk Should Be a Jig"**

Designing Movement

PLAY SECTION COVERED IN THIS LESSON

1.3 After a night of carousing, Sir Toby Belch brings Sir Andrew Aguecheek to meet his niece Olivia. They encounter Maria, Olivia's lady-in-waiting, who scoffs at Toby's scheme to have Sir Andrew court Olivia.

LINES: Toby, 60; Maria, 31; Andrew, 46

WHAT'S ON FOR TODAY AND WHY

As Mowat and Werstine point out in the introduction to the New Folger *Twelfth Night*, many of Shakespeare's stage directions are internal—written right into the dialogue. To alert students to the actions that might accompany the words in the script, they will comb through 1.3 looking for clues to stage action and imagine further action not mentioned in the text.

Some advance preparation is necessary for this activity. The class will be working in groups of four or five. Each group will need the following:

- one piece of construction paper (ah! the empty stage)
- one handful of pawns such as buttons, earrings, or small objects—Parchesi game board pieces work nicely (oh! the characters)
- one script for making notes about stage movement (ugh! more work!)

This is a fairly long scene with much action culminating in Andrew's comic dance, so I suggest dividing it into smaller sections for your class. For maximum enjoyment, encourage students to keep their heads in the game and be adventurous in building in the movements. Since most external stage directions ("Enter Sir Andrew" or "He offers his hand") were added by editors long after Shakespeare put pen to paper, give students a photocopied script with the external stage directions removed.

WHAT TO DO

1. Read-Through

Quickly assign parts for 1.3 and read aloud so students can become familiar with the overall pattern. Or listen to a recording of the scene. Talk about the scene briefly. Ask: What's happening? Who are Toby, Maria, and Andrew? Where do they seem to be? How are they connected to Olivia? Where have you heard of her before? Aim not for in-depth analysis, but for a general grasp of the characters and the scene. Decide on hats for characters who have none assigned yet.

Ask students for the names of three current dances, and have them use those names in place of "galliard," "coranto," and "sink-a-pace."

2. Looking for Action Clues

Organize the class into groups of four or five. Give each group its paper, pawns, and script. Assign each group a section of the scene. A simple way to do this is to divide the scene in thirds: Maria and Toby, lines 1–43; Andrew, Toby, and Maria, lines 44–79; Andrew and Toby, lines 80–139.

First have each group visualize where this scene is taking place. A kitchen? Outside in a garden? Where? What furniture and props are onstage to be used by characters? Tell each group to sketch out their ideas on their construction paper as if it were a blueprint or floor plan.

Next, tell them to read aloud their section of the scene, stopping after *each speech* to decide what gestures or movements the character makes as he or she says the words. Have them comb the speech carefully for clues about action and use the pawns and blueprint to help them visualize movement around the stage.

If they want, let students stand in for characters and move their own selves around as they visualize what the characters are doing. Remind them to have the characters use their eyes, their faces, posture, gestures—all of this counts as movement—and to make good use of the furniture and props on stage. If anything, have them err on the side of going too far with movement. Tell them to ham it up; this should be a busy, active scene, not a static one with characters standing around.

Finally, instruct the groups to appoint a recorder whose job it is to get their decisions about movement written on the script.

EXAMPLE [1.3.1–6]

SCRIPT	*MOVEMENT*
TOBY: What a plague means my niece to take the death of her brother thus? I am sure care's an enemy to life.	He sits down at a table, eating from a bag of sunflower seeds, leaving the seeds on the table. Shakes his head, showing disgust at his niece's behavior.
MARIA: By my troth, Sir Toby, you must come in earlier o' nights. Your cousin, my lady, takes great exception to your ill hours.	She comes over to wipe the seeds into a wastebasket. Wags her finger under Toby's nose on "great exception."

HOW DID IT GO?

Did students learn to "suit the word to the action, the action to the word"? If so, they have picked up one of the important lessons of this unit. If, in your opinion, they did not make enough progress with adding movement, talk about ways to add movement when the groups demonstrate their plans in Lesson 5.

LESSON **5** **"What Is Thy Excellence in a Galliard, Knight?"**

Demonstrating Blocking

❧ _____

PLAY SECTION COVERED IN THIS LESSON

1.3 After a night of carousing, Sir Toby Belch brings Sir Andrew Aguecheek to meet his niece Olivia. They encounter Maria, Olivia's lady-in-waiting, who scoffs at Toby's scheme to have Sir Andrew court Olivia.

LINES: Toby, 60; Maria, 31; Andrew, 48

❧ _____

WHAT'S ON FOR TODAY AND WHY

Movement is a challenge for students. For one thing, it calls for energy. For another, it calls for exploration into the new. But because it is so important to successful performances, stay on the acting groups to do more not less in the way of movement. In today's demonstrations of stage movement (this is also called "blocking"), coax from students as much physicality as possible.

WHAT TO DO

1. Show and Tell

Tell students to pair with another group. Exchange blocking plans, and try to walk through the scene using the other group's plan. Usually a few glorious omissions are uncovered. A character may be left onstage directionless, or someone might appear to speak to an unknown party.

2. Discussion

Ask: Were there big differences between groups in how you visualized the scene? Did these differences happen because you understood the words of the text differently? Did you discover any "built in" stage directions in the text—clues about what the characters must be doing as they say their words? What were the most obvious?

3. Performance

If time permits, choose a blocking plan and enact it, this time with human actors.

4. Discussion

You have now met Orsino, Curio, Valentine, Viola, Captain, Maria, Toby, Sir Andrew, and (briefly) Malvolio. Ask: What do these characters look like in your mind? Do you know anyone who reminds you of any of them?

Ask students to think in particular about Sir Andrew. Ask: How many references can you find to Andrew's looks, talents, or favorite pastimes?

5. CQ

Ask students to find and comment on four lines from the scenes they've read so far: a line that has beauty in it, a line with a good joke, a line that sounds modern, a line that appeals to them for any reason.

HOW DID IT GO?

By watching and listening to the groups, especially as they show their blocking ideas to each other, you can find out how much sense students are making out of Shakespeare's language. The impromptu performance will reveal the extent to which students are learning to suit the action to the word.

LESSON **6** **"But We Will Draw the Curtain and Show You the Picture"**

Performing 1.4 and 1.5

PLAY SECTIONS COVERED IN THIS LESSON

1.4 At the Duke's court, Orsino treats Viola as a trusted page and buddy, but Viola reveals to the audience that she would rather be his wife.

LINES: Valentine, 5; Viola, 14; Orsino, 27; Curio, 0; Attendants, 0

1.5.30–97 The Fool and Olivia trade witticisms.

LINES: Fool, 37; Olivia, 20; Malvolio, 11

1.5.98–163 Toby comes home drunk and reports that there is a young gentleman at the gate. Malvolio checks him out, and Olivia agrees to see him.

LINES: Maria, 5; Olivia, 23; Toby, 6; Malvolio, 22

1.5.164–251 The "boy" Viola (now called Cesario) calls on Olivia to offer Orsino's compliments.

LINES: Olivia, 42; Viola, 45; Maria, 1

1.5.252–318 Cesario's protestations grow more dramatic, and Olivia reveals that she is interested—not in Orsino but in his page. As a ploy to ensure Cesario's return, Olivia sends Malvolio to give Cesario a ring and say he left it at her villa.

LINES: Viola, 26; Olivia, 40; Malvolio, 2

WHAT'S ON FOR TODAY AND WHY

In short segments, students will tackle 1.4 and 1.5 on their own. Informed by the scene work they have done before, they will work in small cooperative groups to prepare and present performances. Because they are fairly uneventful, skip the first twenty-nine lines of 1.5. If you wish, summarize them for the class. Introduce the character of Feste and give an example of his comic material.

Even though you have been working with performance methods for several days, it is a good idea to write on the board the steps you expect the actors to follow:

1) Read the scene round robin, changing readers at major punctuation marks.

2) Talk about what's going on in the scene and work out any spots where you don't understand the language.
3) Read again. Talk some more.
4) Cast.
5) Get on your feet and work out the movement.
6) Put it together and rehearse again.

This lesson will take two days.

WHAT TO DO

1. Scene Assignments

Organize students into five groups. Give each group one of the scene sections listed above. Make sure that everyone in the group has a specific job: actor, director, master/mistress of ceremonies (explains the scene to the class before and after presentation).

Review the procedure for scene preparation you have written on the board. Set clear expectations. Tell students that they will rehearse today and perform tomorrow.

2. Rehearsal

Give student groups time to prepare their scenes. This will no doubt take one full class period. Help the students with lines just enough to enable them to understand the scene. Don't overkill by trying to explain everything to them.

3. Day 2: Performances

Have each group present its scene to the class. Set the scene. Give each group a frothy introduction. Encourage applause. Make sure that each group conveys the essential information in its scene to the rest of the class. If they fail to do this in their performance, ask questions so everybody knows what's going on in every scene.

4. Discussion

Ask: Why do you think Olivia so quickly gets interested in "Cesario," especially when she's been refusing the attentions of the Count? How does this reflect on her supposed mourning? Have you ever had someone show an interest in you when you really didn't want them to? How did you handle it?

Ask: Let's take the scenes one by one. Can you think of any additional action that would enhance the comedy? What about costumes, music, set—how could these add to the comic effect?

Ask: In these scenes, how many compliments can you find? Pick one or two and try reading them various ways—experiment with pauses, voice inflection, and tone. What works?

5. Homework

As always, read the sections we worked on in class. For this lesson, please read all of 1.5.

6. CQ

Ask students to review 1.5, focus on Feste, and answer these questions:

· How long do you think he has been in Olivia's household?
· Is Feste a carefree fool with no troubles?
· Does he have a brain?
· If you were a director, who would you cast for Feste? How would you costume him or her?
· Can you find some clues in the script that suggest action for Feste? If you were a director, what would you want the Fool to be doing physically in this scene?

HOW DID IT GO?

Since students saw parts of the play instead of reading it directly, the post-performance discussion, homework, and CQ will be the best indicators of their level of understanding.

LESSON 7 "Loyal Cantons of Contemnèd Love"

Explicating "Willow Cabin"

ஃ————————

PLAY SECTION COVERED IN THIS LESSON

1.5.271–79 Viola's "Willow Cabin" speech

LINES: Viola, 9

ஃ

WHAT'S ON FOR TODAY AND WHY

To acquire a more conscious perception of the richness and complexity of Shakespeare's language, students will analyze the "Willow Cabin" speech, paying attention to the connections and the resonances of the words.

This is a change—from broad action to small words—but one plane locks with the other.

WHAT TO DO

1. Choral Reading

Have the class read the "Willow Cabin" speech ("Make me a willow cabin at your gate" through "But you should pity me") together out loud, choral-reading style. Read it several times, using different sound combinations—high voices on one line, low voices on the next; repetitions of the last word of every line; one person per phrase or sentence; overemphasis of the iambic pentameter rhythm or any other choral-sound variation you can invent. Just read it enough times to let the words really sink in.

2. Paraphrase

Organize the class into groups of three. Provide each person with a duplicated copy of the speech and encourage students to mark it up as they comb through the words. Have dictionaries or C. T. Onions's *A Shakespeare Glossary* available.

Tell students: Figure out exactly what Viola is saying in this speech. Be as accurate as possible, but put the speech in your own words. Look up every word whose meaning you're the least bit unsure of. Do some words have more than one meaning? Make sure everyone in your group understands the meaning of each word as it is used in the passage.

When they have worked out definitions and connotations, tell students to *write out* a paraphrased version, one paper per group. Give them fifteen minutes to complete all the work in this section.

3. Attitude

Interrupt and ask students to determine Viola's attitude toward this speech. Unpeel the layers: Viola's attitude toward Orsino, Viola's attitude toward Olivia, Viola's attitude toward Orsino's courtship of Olivia. Finally, arrive at Viola's attitude toward the speech. Ask students to consider all these—and more—and add to their papers a few comments about how Viola's attitude would affect her delivery of this speech.

4. Poetic Patterns

Ask students to read the passage aloud once more. Have them listen for repetitions of and connections between sounds. Use your own judgment about whether to use poetic terminology, but direct the students to listen for rhyme, assonance, alliteration, synonyms, or whatever connections their ears and brains pick up. (Examples: cantons/contemned; sing/babbling/cry; Olivia/O.) There is no one right answer to this exercise. Encourage exploration.

5. Reports

After students have had time to study the passage and work together in small groups, reassemble as a class. Have each group read its paraphrase. Discuss differences and likenesses between groups' findings. Then ask them to report what they found out about tone and sound connections.

Ask the big question: What effect do the sound devices have on you? On your understanding of the passage?

6. Senses

On the board or on big sheets of newsprint, write these categories: "Sight," "Sound," "Taste," "Smell," "Touch." Have the class list under each category words from the passage that relate to these various senses. Examples:

Sight	*Touch*
willow	reverberate
gate	air
house	
hills	

When the lists are complete, stand back and take a look with the students. Are there any patterns? Does anything interesting emerge?

7. Further Exploration

Ask students to consider the passage in some other ways: If this passage were a piece of music, what would it be? What clothes would it wear? If this passage were a banquet, what food would be on the table? What colors are in this passage? In all cases, have students point to words that bring forth their associations.

8. Microcosm to Macrocosm

Discuss: What do these words have to do with Viola? With the play as a whole?

9. CQ

Ask students to write the three pieces of information from today's lesson they consider the most memorable.

10. Act Test

If you have offered the act-test option, it is now time to give the Act 1 exam. Do it as a take-home test or arrange the schedule so you can fit it into class time.

HOW DID IT GO?

Did the words in this passage come to life for the students? Were they able to hear and see things they passed over before? Did Shakespeare's language give them pleasure? If you can say even a partial yes to these questions, hallow your name to the reverberate hills.

LESSON **8** **"A Common Recreation"**

Role Playing and Performing 2.3

☙

PLAY SECTIONS COVERED IN THIS LESSON

2.1 Unknown to Viola, her twin brother, Sebastian, and the sailor Antonio arrive on Illyria.

LINES: Antonio, 13; Sebastian, 34

2.2 Malvolio delivers Olivia's ring to Viola, who begins to realize that Olivia is smitten with her.

LINES: Malvolio, 13; Viola, 28

2.3 Maria tries to quiet the late night carousing of Toby, Sir Andrew, and Feste. Malvolio orders them to behave or he will kick them out. In retaliation, the revelers plan a trick to humiliate him.

LINES: Toby, 55; Andrew, 46; Fool, 30; Maria, 35; Malvolio, 20

☙

WHAT'S ON FOR TODAY AND WHY

One way into Shakespeare's language is to make a connection between Elizabethan situations and present-day ones. Today students will role-play the events of 2.3 then perform the scene.

WHAT TO DO

1. Review 2.1 and 2.2

Ask several students to read the summaries of 2.1 they wrote in their logs. Then have them look over 2.2, the scene they enacted the first day of this unit. Elicit comments and summaries.

2. The Party: Contemporary Version

Ask for five to seven volunteers to do some role-playing in front of the class. Act as narrator, set up the following situation, and let the actors run with it:

• **The scene:** Aunt Jane's party room
• **The people:**
Cousin Joe—a great party-er who's staying temporarily with Aunt Jane
Joe's "buds"—two to four people
Cousin Rhonda—friendly with Cousin Joe and his pals

Cousin Micky—not friendly with Cousin Joe or anyone else

Gender is of no importance in these roles. Switch names at will.

• **The situation:** (This is where the first two or three or four students begin their role-play.) Cousin Joe and pals are having a great time, getting louder and louder as they party.

Pretty soon, Cousin Rhonda comes in, saying they should pipe down, but they are having too much fun for that.

Then Cousin Micky comes in and really gets mad at everybody, threatening to get them all in trouble with Aunt Jane.

Let the students figure out ways to end the scene. One ending to suggest if they don't come up with it themselves is that Cousin Micky finally storms out of the room and the rest of the people laugh at him and continue to party.

3. The Party: Shakespeare's Version

After the role playing, turn to 2.3. Cast and read through line 124 ("Go shake your ears!"). Discuss.

> TEACHER: OK, anything familiar in this scene?
> LAURIE: The people still talk funny.
> JOE: It's a party scene. Like the one we were doing.
> LAURIE: What's a "catch"?

Talk about parallels in the scene and the role-playing activity. Ask: If the revelers were going to play a trick on Malvolio to get back at him, what would be good? Gather ideas for a few minutes; then recast and have students read the rest of the scene.

4. The Full Effect

Try the scene again, on its feet. Have onlookers give directorial suggestions. Go all out with songs and movement.

5. CQ

Ask students:

• Are you more of a Toby or more of a Malvolio when it comes to getting rowdy?
• Look again at the Fool's song in this scene. Does it seem in keeping with the mood of the scene? Do the words reflect what's going on? How?
• Find what you consider a pretty good joke in this scene. What's funny about it to you?

HOW DID IT GO? If you haven't already, take up the CQs and listen to what the students are saying about this unit. If needed, make adjustments to the pace, the assignments, the classroom activities.

LESSON **9** # "I Will Boldly Publish Her"

Concentrating on Character

WHAT'S ON FOR TODAY AND WHY

One of the pleasures of *Twelfth Night* is getting to see Shakespeare's genius at creating characters. Although he uses stock ones like the unrequited lover, the cranky old man, the lovable drunk, the fop, and more, Shakespeare gives characters everyday tics and foibles that bring them right off the page. Even with the small part like Antonio, the audience meets a distinct and approachable person.

To help students distinguish the characters, and to give them an opportunity to spend more time with them, they will do a series of character exercises. To prepare for these, photocopy Handouts 5 and 6.

WHAT TO DO

1. Personality Traits

Organize students into ten groups of two or three members each. Assign each group a character: Orsino, Viola, Toby, Maria, Andrew, Feste, Olivia, Malvolio, Antonio, Sebastian.

Give them Handout 5: "Personality Traits." Tell them to comb Act 1 and Act 2.1–3 for lines or phrases said by or about their character that reveal something about her or his personality. Be a demon about exact citation.

> FAWNDA: I don't get this worksheet.
> TEACHER: OK. What character does your group have?
> FAWNDA: Orsino.
> TEACHER: What can you say about Orsino's personality?
> FAWNDA: He's lovesick. Always moaning about this woman he can't have.
> TEACHER: Perfect. Have your scribe write down "lovesick" in the first blank under "personality trait." Now, find a line or phrase that proves you're right.
> FAWNDA: It's all over the place. Right at the first of the play he says, "O, when my eyes did see Olivia first, methought she purged the air of pestilence. That instant was I turned into a hart, and my desires, like fell and cruel hounds, e'er since pursue me."
> TEACHER: Superb. Have your scribe copy that line into the quote column. Add the line numbers, and you're on your way.
> FAWNDA: Line numbers! That's so much trouble!
> TEACHER: Careful citation—the mark of a successful scholar.

2. Profiles

Give each committee a copy of Handout 6: "Character Profile." Have each group appoint a scribe, and instruct the scribe to write the committee's answers in penmanship suitable for publication.

Tell students to hold in their minds all the information they gathered doing the Personality Traits exercise and complete Handout 6. Allow about ten minutes for this.

3. Improvisations

Reassemble the whole class and have each group of students give a "rundown" of their character. Invite responses and questions from the rest of the class.

Then call for group members to play their characters in the following improvisations:

- Malvolio and Maria go to the food market.
- Orsino and Viola get caught in a rainstorm and take refuge in a very small cave.
- Same situation. This time it's Sir Andrew and Olivia.
- Toby comes in late to church after a night of carousing. Malvolio is the preacher.
- Sebastian and Viola, neither knowing the other is alive, meet accidentally. Viola is still dressed as Cesario.
- Antonio runs into Viola dressed as a man and mistakes her for Sebastian.

4. Posters

Give each group a large piece of white paper and ask them as homework to draw or find a picture of their character and design a poster around it. Have them incorporate the profile (Handout 6) and trait sheet (Handout 5).

5. CQ

This is a good time to think about the whole play up to this point. Ask students to draw a diagram or chart that shows the characters and their relationships to each other. Or do a storyboard of the plot so far.

HOW DID IT GO?

Did understanding and appreciation of characters improve during this lesson? Are students reading with their imaginations turned on? Are they seeing how the characters affect each other? If so, you accomplished the work of Lesson 9.

HANDOUT 5

PERSONALITY TRAITS

In your group, talk about personality traits. Does your character show courage, tenderness, deceit, greed, trust, naïveté, leadership, sorrow, vengeance, lust, justice, or what? Pick the top three personality traits for your character. Then comb the play for lines to prove these traits. Try to find more than one quote to prove each trait. List the trait, quotes, and line numbers in the chart below.

PERSONALITY TRAIT	QUOTES FROM *TWELFTH NIGHT* TO PROVE IT	LINE NUMBERS
1.	1.	
	2.	
	3.	
2.	1.	
	2.	
	3.	
3.	1.	
	2.	
	3.	

&

HANDOUT 6

CHARACTER PROFILE

Complete this chart for the character you were assigned. Assume that your character is alive now. Have fun. Be playful, but at the same time be true to your character.

NAME:

AGE:

OCCUPATION:

PHYSICAL DESCRIPTION—

    HEIGHT:

    WEIGHT:

    HAIR:

    EYES:

FAVORITE STYLE OF CLOTHING:

FAVORITE HANGOUT:

FAVORITE BOOK:

FAVORITE SONG:

FAVORITE PERSON:

FAVORITE CAR:

FAVORITE THING TO DO ON SATURDAY AFTERNOON:

GREATEST ACHIEVEMENT:

TOP FIVE THINGS ON THIS PERSON'S MIND:

    1.

    2.

    3.

    4.

    5.

&

LESSON **10** **"Light Airs and Recollected Terms"**

Close Reading 2.4

❧

PLAY SECTIONS COVERED IN THIS LESSON

2.4.1–87 In what he assumes is a man-to-man talk about women, Orsino expresses his lovesick state and gets Cesario to tell him about "his" love for one of Orsino's age and complexion.

LINES: Orsino, 47; Curio, 5; Viola, 8; Fool, 27

2.4.88–137 Continuing in the man-to-man vein, Viola and Orsino debate the trueness of womanly hearts, and Viola tells of a woman who loved as strong as any man but hid her love.

LINES: Orsino, 26; Viola, 24

❧

WHAT'S ON FOR TODAY AND WHY

Building on their sensitivity to the nuances of language they developed in the close reading of the "Willow Cabin" speech, students will work as a class to do a close reading of the first section of 2.4 and in small groups to do the last section. Use the hum in the classroom to judge how far to take these activities. If, as students get on the word level, ideas begin to click for them, keep the work going, even if you have to continue to a second day. If not, lead them as far as you can, but stop short of standing in front of the class and suggesting "right" answers or telling students what Shakespeare meant when he wrote this act. *No one* knows "what Shakespeare meant."

To prepare for today's work, photocopy Handout 7: "Close Reading 2.4."

WHAT TO DO

1. Character Posters

Have students display the character posters and profiles from Lesson 9. Accompany this display with brief presentations from each character group so that all students know all characters.

2. Close Reading 2.4.1–87

Read lines 1–87 (from "Give me some music" to "Let all the rest give place"). Or, for variety, play a recording of these lines, having the class follow the text as they listen.

Discuss the action of this section: the differences in moods between Viola and Orsino, the irony in Viola's speeches, Orsino's attitude about the nature of women. Each time a student answers a question, have her point to a line from the text to prove her point.

Zoom in on lines 34–45 ("Too old, by heaven" to "doth fall that very hour"). Ask students to look in this passage for comparisons—people comparisons (between women and men) and poetical comparisons (between women and roses). Ask: How does the one comparison affect the other?

Ask students to read the passage again, this time looking for words and a category. Are there words that leap off the page and want to group themselves in a category like "vegetables," "colors," "weapons," or whatever? If they seem muddled by this game, suggest the category of "time" and ask students to find all the words that would fit. They may find other categories as well, so give them free rein to experiment.

Ask students to read the passage once again, this time to look for anything notable about how Shakespeare put the words together—word order, word patterns, prevailing sounds, patterns of any kind.

Have a small discussion to clarify the term "dramatic irony"—the two-tiered thinking that occurs when the audience knows something that one or more of the characters do not. Ask students: How does this term apply to this passage? To 2.4.1–87? To the play so far?

3. Close Reading 2.4.88–137

Break students into small groups. Instruct groups to read 2.4.88–137 ("Once more, Cesario" to "My love can give no place, bide no denay") for general meaning. Then, using Handout 7: "Close Reading 2.4," have the groups choose either Orsino or Viola, and study his or her words for close reading. It might be fun to try same-sex groups, females focusing on Viola's lines, males on Orsino's, or vice versa.

Again, the point is to put students in close contact with *Twelfth Night* language and let Shakespeare teach Shakespeare. So there are no right answers.

To give you an idea of what students might find, here are some responses from those who have worked this handout before:

• **Comparisons.** Shakespeare compares Viola, a woman concealing love, to a bud with a worm inside—both are eaten away from the inside (2.4.123–24); Orsino compares passion to appetite—while women's appetite is small, his is as large as the sea (2.4.105–10).

- **Word Categories.** In 2.4.89–95 Orsino's group of students notice the category "treasure" and fit in "prizes," "fortune," "bestowed," and "gems." In 2.4.122–30, Viola's group notice the category "sadness" and fill it with "pined," "melancholy," and "grief."
- **Dramatic Irony.** In Viola's line "Say that some lady, as perhaps there is" (2.4.99) students pick up on the fact that the audience knows Viola's talking about herself but Orsino doesn't. Likewise, Orsino's group can point out that when he asks in 2.4.115 "What dost thou know?" that the audience and Viola know a great deal more about what's going on than Orsino does.
- **Personal References.** Students point out that Viola talks about herself through references to hypothetical others—"My father had a daughter" (2.4.118)—and hides herself in clever narrative while Orsino characterizes himself in bombastic exaggerations—his appetite is "as hungry as the sea" (2.4.110), his love is "more noble than the world" (2.4.90).

4. Reports

After small groups have had time to study the language and work Handout 7, call the Orsino and Viola groups together to hash out what they discovered. Then give several thoughtful minutes to this question: What does language reveal about personality? End this session by reading the last two lines of 2.4—

> To her in haste. Give her this jewel. Say
> My love can give no place, bide no denay.

Ask: What action caps the long discussion of 2.4? Compare this action to the ideas Orsino put forth in this act. Does this comparison invite irony? Compare the action to Viola's ideas—does this invite irony? Do any words or sounds or images in these last two lines chime with or underscore words or images you encountered earlier in 2.4?

5. CQ

Ask students to think again about the views of love they met in 2.4 and to answer these questions:

- Do you think there's a difference in the way men love and the way women love?
- Do either Viola or Orsino express views similar to your own? Or do you have a position on this question different from both of these characters?

Then ask them to find a line in this scene that they like or that strikes them in some way and comment on it.

HOW DID IT GO?

The vibrations in the voices during small-group work and class discussion will show how far students were able to delve into the intricacies of language for this lesson.

HANDOUT 7

CLOSE READING 2.4

Do a close reading of the Viola–Orsino dialogue from 2.4.88–137 ("Once more, Cesario" to "My love can give no place, bide no denay"). Concentrate on either Viola's or Orsino's lines. Get on the word level and notice how your character uses language. Search the script for the devices and word tricks listed in the chart below. When you find them, record them on the chart. Quote lines and give line numbers to verify your findings.

TASK	FINDINGS	LINE NUMBERS
Search for **COMPARISONS** your character uses. Choose several that particularly chime with your character's personality. Summarize them or quote them.		
Find a passage that is thick with words that suggest a certain **CATEGORY**. Name the category and list the words that fit in it.		
Look for lines with a strong sense of **DRAMATIC IRONY**, lines where the audience knows more than one of the characters.		
Consider how your character refers to himself or herself. What style of **SELF CHARACTERIZATION** do you see?		

LESSON **11**

"If You Will Then See the Fruits of the Sport"

Performing 2.5

ﬢ

PLAY SECTION COVERED IN THIS LESSON

2.5 Malvolio falls for Maria's trick. With Fabian, Toby, and Andrew watching from behind the boxtree, Malvolio finds the letter Maria forged, believes it to be to him from Olivia, and makes plans to make startling alterations to his appearance.

LINES: Toby, 41; Fabian, 31; Andrew, 13; Maria, 18; Malvolio, 109

ﬢ

WHAT'S ON FOR TODAY AND WHY

This scene is not very funny on the page, and yet onstage it is one of the highlights of the play. Acting the scene out is the only way to let students in on the joke.

It is a long scene, with many long speeches by Malvolio. To break it up, and to help students see the humor, they will first do what Malvolio does, find Maria's letter. Then they will perform the scene.

To prepare for this lesson, photocopy Handout 8.

WHAT TO DO

1. Gulling the Students

Before students get to class, plant Handout 8: "Maria's Letter," perhaps scented liberally with exotic perfume, in a prominent place. Pretend to find the letter and begin to read it to the class.

After a short while, stop and ask students if they know what this is. When they guess, gives them copies of the handout and together pore over Maria's letter to figure out her scheme as best you can.

2. Gulling Malvolio: Section 1

Briefly talk about Fabian, the new character students will meet in this scene. Appoint one student, maybe one who needs bonus points, to follow Fabian for a few lessons and do a poster about him.

Assign parts and ask students to read the first thirty-two lines of the scene (to "Slight, I could so beat the rogue"). Stop and talk about how the class wants to arrange the stage for this scene. Of utmost importance is where to put Malvolio in relationship to the boxtree and the people behind it. Use classroom furniture to approximate your design.

Ask five students to enter the acting space and take the parts of Toby, Fabian, Andrew, Maria, and Malvolio.

Have the rest of the class discuss how to block the scene, using the five volunteers as silent actors. Move these silent actors around in different ways, trying out different blocking ideas. Helpful questions: where are the conspirators? (Clue: "boxtree.") Where does Maria come from? Who places the letter? Where? Where do the conspirators hide? How do they hide? Do they stay put or dart around from hedge to hedge? How does Malvolio enter? How does the audience know that Malvolio doesn't see or hear the conspirators?

Then have these five or, better yet, five new volunteers read the same lines again, with the blocking ideas.

3. Gulling Malvolio: Section 2

Proceed as above with lines 33–87 ("Peace, I say" through "O, peace, and the spirit of humors intimate reading aloud to him"). Be playful with the movement. Keep pressing for suggestions so students can help each other visualize the antics of the characters. Unless you are working with very advanced actors, make this a slapstick scene rather than subtle comedy. Encourage double-takes, lots of head-bobbing and mugging. Keep asking: How can you make this funnier? But draw the line at letting the funny bits overtake rather than underscore the comedy Shakespeare wrote.

When you get to the part where Malvolio fantasizes about first Olivia then Toby, try having dream figures act out the fantasy—Malvolio in his branched velvet gown, Olivia on the daybed, Malvolio extending his hand to a subservient Toby. If this works, keep it. If not, throw it out.

Ask students: Why does Malvolio's fantasy make Toby so mad? How can he show how mad he is? How can you heighten the moment when Malvolio finds the letter?

4. Gulling Malvolio: Section 3

With expertise and momentum building, complete the scene, again interrupting when necessary to ask questions about what actors are doing and why they are doing it. In the footnote about "C-U-T" in the New Folger edition, the editors warn us about taking the bawdy reference too seriously, but the scene will be funnier for some students if they know that "cut," along with the phrase "and thus makes she her great P's," could have obscene connotations.

The problem in staging this scene is how to break up the long passages of the letter. Have students coach the actor playing Malvolio to experiment with pauses, facial expressions, and movement.

HOW DID IT GO?   To what extent did students use their voices and their bodies to make the comedy of this scene happen? If all went well, there was much laughter and students found pleasure in doing the scene. If not, don't despair—there's more comedy coming up.

HANDOUT 8

MARIA'S LETTER

Jove knows I love,
But who?
Lips, do not move;
No man must know.
I may command where I adore,
But silence, like a Lucrece knife,
With bloodless stroke my heart doth gore;
M.O.A.I. doth sway my life.

If this fall into thy hand, revolve. In my stars I am above thee, but be not afraid of greatness. Some are born great, some achieve greatness, and some have greatness thrust upon 'em.

Thy fates open their hands. Let thy blood and spirit embrace them. And, to inure thyself to what thou art like to be, cast thy humble slough and appear fresh. Be opposite with a kinsman, surly with servants. Let thy tongue tang arguments of state. Put thyself into the trick of singularity. She thus advises thee that sighs for thee.

Remember who commended thy yellow stockings and wished to see thee ever cross-gartered.

I say, remember. Go to, thou art made, if thou desir'st to be so. If no, let me see thee a steward still, the fellow of servants, and not worthy to touch Fortune's fingers.

Farewell. She that would alter services with thee.

The Fortunate-Unhappy

Postscript____
Thou canst not choose but know who I am. If thou entertain'st my love, let it appear in thy smiling; thy smiles become thee well. Therefore in my presence still smile, dear my sweet, I prithee.

LESSON **12** # "This Simulation Is Not as the Former"

2.5 on Video

ɜ🐌 _____

PLAY SECTION COVERED IN THIS LESSON

2.5 Malvolio falls for Maria's trick. With Fabian, Toby, and Andrew watching from behind the hedge, Malvolio finds the letter Maria forged, believes it to be to him from Olivia, and makes plans to make startling alterations to his appearance.

LINES: Toby, 41; Fabian, 31; Andrew, 13; Maria, 18; Malvolio, 109

ɜ🐌 _____

WHAT'S ON FOR TODAY AND WHY

At this writing, there are not many versions of *Twelfth Night* available on video. The BBC Shakespeare Series production directed by John Gorrie presents an ordered Elizabethan Illyria with a mature Maria and salty British accomplices. Some folks think it's not very *funny*. It is available through The Writing Company (1-800-421-4246).

The Renaissance Theatre Company version directed by Kenneth Branagh presents a winterscape where Maria's prank seems a ploy to bring gaiety to a sad, world-weary Toby. This videotape is available through Films for the Humanities (1-800-257-5126).

The boxtree scene is a highlight of both productions, and because students enjoy and appreciate seeing scenes they have acted then done by professionals, 2.5 is a great choice for video analysis. Seeing both of these productions back to back will show students the range of possibilities that directors have in staging Shakespeare.

If a videotape is beyond your budget, skip this lesson. If your school can afford just one videotape, adapt this lesson. Your students will find video analysis one of the best activities in the unit. If you can manage both videotapes, cue them up to 2.5.

WHAT TO DO

1. 2.5 on Video

Show the BBC version of the boxtree scene. Suppress comments, but ask students to jot down brief notes for discussion later. Show the Renaissance Company version of 2.5. Again, hold off oral comments, but have the students get their reactions to the scene in writing.

2. Discussion

Let the comments pour forth. Having done the scene so recently, students will have a great deal to say about the staging, blocking, vocal inflections, costumes, comedy bits, and directorial decisions of this scene. Emphasize that there is no one "correct" way to do a scene, that Shakespeare's script accommodates and survives different interpretations.

3. Thrusting Greatness upon Them

If you are a teacher who sees value in going beyond the fringe for the cause of infusing Shakespearean language into the vocabulary of your students, try this ploy. If antics repel you, stop reading and go directly to section 4, CQ.

Offer up for attention this one line from Maria's letter: "Some are born great, some achieve greatness, and some have greatness thrust upon them."

Invite several students to speak the line, stressing different words and using different vocal styles. Ask students to react to the line. They will probably comment that it is the sort of phony line a motivational speaker or a salesman might use.

But it is fun to say. So make a vow that each person in the room—teacher included—will, during the course of this day, say the line to some unsuspecting person.

Furthermore, vow that you will say the line with a perfectly straight face and offer no explanations no matter how hard your audience presses you. If you like, set up a visual cue to trigger comments. Tie a ribbon or put a sticker on students and tell them if anybody asks them about it to reply with "Some are born great, some achieve greatness, and some have greatness thrust upon them."

4. CQ

Ask students to answer these questions:

- Have you ever played a practical joke on someone, or been the victim of a practical joke? Write about your experience, making parallels between what happened to you and what's happening to Malvolio.
- Make a list of all the epithets that are used for characters in this scene (e.g., "rascally sheep-biter," "overweening rogue").

5. Act Test

If you are offering this option, administer the test for Act 2.

HOW DID IT GO?

Students' attention to the video clips will show how their imaginations are creating *Twelfth Night* as they read it. If they argue that the BBC

Maria is too old or that the Renaissance Company Sir Andrew is too subdued, this tells you how Maria and Sir Andrew are in the students' brains.

If they delight in the wildly varying range of *Twelfth Night* productions rather than complain that a director didn't get it right, commend yourself.

If in the future a student says to you, "Last year Ernie and Shannon came into Home Ec class with these blue ribbons tied on their wrists, and when we asked them about it, they said, 'Some are born great, some achieve greatness, and some have greatness thrust upon them'— do we get to do that?", order champagne. And then shiver to think about how powerful language has to be to stay with a student that long.

LESSON **13**   **"Corrupter of Words"**

Cutting and Rehearsing 3.1, 3.2, and 3.3

𝔞

PLAY SECTIONS COVERED IN THIS LESSON

3.1.1–69 Viola and Feste trade witticisms.

LINES: Viola, 30; Fool, 39

3.1.70–172 Olivia strengthens her flirtation with Cesario.

LINES: Viola, 36; Toby, 5; Andrew, 6; Olivia, 56; Maria, 0

3.2 Sir Andrew begins to catch on that he has no chance with Olivia. Toby, afraid that Andrew will leave and thus end his means of paying bar bills, convinces Sir Andrew that Olivia would like him better if he would challenge Cesario to a duel. Maria brings news that Malvolio is strutting about cross-gartered and smiling.

LINES: Andrew, 11; Toby, 32; Fabian, 24; Maria, 15

3.3 Antonio explains to Sebastian that because of an incident that happened in a sea fight with Illyria he must not be seen by officials on the island. He gives Sebastian his money to use for sight-seeing then heads for the Elephant, an inn.

LINES: Sebastian, 20; Antonio, 34

𝔞

WHAT'S ON FOR TODAY AND WHY

Cutting a scene calls for students to choose the lines that best convey the story line and characters' objectives and to eliminate the lines that are the least essential. It's a tough task. Students will change their minds many times. Therefore, copy 3.1, 3.2, and 3.3 so students won't ruin their books with erasures and scratchouts. Make a transparency of 3.1.1–70 (through "Save you gentleman").

Plan to model the cutting procedure on the first part of 3.1 then to let students cut the remaining material in small groups.

After cutting their scene, students will perform it for the other two groups.

WHAT TO DO

1. Model Cutting

Ask: Did you notice that the video productions we saw did not use every word of 2.5? Is it okay to cut lines from the legendary Shakespeare? When do you think it would be good to cut, and when would it be bad?

Arrive at a simple working guideline—leave words that advance story, character, and essential information; cut words that work against these things.

Put up the transparency of 3.1.1–70. Tell students that this is a street scene where Viola encounters Feste. Some of the jokes they crack are funny today. Some aren't. Ask for two volunteers who will read the scene all the way through one time. Go back to the beginning and decide what material will stay, what will go. Adhere to the guideline, but be aggressive. Get rid of one-third to one-half of the scene. At the same time, be smooth. Don't leave jagged transitions. Mark on the transparency as students make suggestions, but be prepared to erase and redo as students change their minds. In other words, have a glass of water and paper towels handy.

When the scene is cut, have two volunteers read it aloud. If you have done a good job, students will be amazed by the increased clarity.

2. Cutting in Small Groups

Arrange students in three small groups. Assign the first the remainder of 3.1, the second 3.2, and the third 3.3. Explain that these three scenes are short and succinct as they stand, but even so each could stand some cutting. Write on the board the cutting procedure:

- Read the scene one time through.
- Talk about the story line.
- Look for material to cut—words, phrases, sentences that do not advance the story line or character objectives.
- Read the cut scene.

Give students about fifteen minutes to cut their scenes.

3. Preparing Performances

Once the scenes are cut, have students cast and perform them. Explain that the most important job of each group is to present the events of their scene to the rest of the class, who have not read the scene and know nothing about it.

Remind students the sign of a good scene:

- actors who are all telling the same story
- well-rehearsed lines
- movement
- characters with distinguishable voices and styles

Give them the remainder of the period to prepare.

4. Homework

Tell students: Read your scene three times—twice to yourself and once aloud.

HOW DID IT GO? Ordinarily two great things happen with cutting—students turn out to be remarkably adept at it, and they look at the language a hundred times more closely than they do in a simple reading. If this did not happen in your classroom today, pick a scene later in the play and try cutting again.

Don't let students treat cutting as a one-time activity. Practice and confidence in the art of cutting should be extremely helpful to them in preparing future scenes.

LESSON 14 "Taste Your Legs, Sir, Put Them to Motion"

Performing 3.1, 3.2, and 3.3

❧

PLAY SECTIONS COVERED IN THIS LESSON

3.1.70–172 Olivia strengthens her flirtation with Cesario.

LINES: Viola, 36; Toby, 5; Andrew, 6; Olivia, 56; Maria, 0

3.2 Sir Andrew begins to catch on that he has no chance with Olivia. Toby, afraid that Andrew will leave and thus end his means of paying bar bills, convinces Sir Andrew that Olivia would like him better if he would challenge Cesario to a duel. Maria brings news that Malvolio is strutting about cross-gartered and smiling.

LINES: Andrew, 11; Toby, 32; Fabian, 24; Maria, 15

3.3 Antonio explains to Sebastian that because of an incident that happened in a sea fight with Illyria he must not be seen by officials on the island. He gives Sebastian his money to use for sight-seeing then heads for the Elephant, an inn.

LINES: Sebastian, 20; Antonio, 34

❧

WHAT'S ON FOR TODAY AND WHY

Well-cut, rollicking performances are on the bill today, so set a festive mood and lead the applause.

WHAT TO DO

1. Performances

See the performances of 3.1, 3.2, and 3.3. After each, give members of the audience a chance to ask the cast questions.

2. Comprehension

Ask students to write a three-minute summary of each of the three scenes.

3. Reflection

Give students an opportunity to show how much they know about their scene by having them answer questions in writing. Read the questions aloud one by one, pausing to let students answer. Ask:

· Who in your scene takes a specific action to demonstrate his or her love for someone else? What is that action?

· Who in your scene takes a risk or "sticks his neck out" in some way?

· What happens in this scene that will likely cause some problems or complications later in the play?

4. Discussion

Take the three questions one by one and discuss them. To refine the discussion, point out this exchange in 3.1.145–46:

OLIVIA   I prithee tell me what thou think'st of me.
VIOLA   That you do think you are not what you are.

Give some thought to Viola's line. What does it mean? What does it mean in connection with Olivia? What does it mean in connection with you?

Ask students to look through the three scenes and find at least three different lines where one character in some way declares love or caring for another. Write the findings on the board. Ask: How does the way a person declares love define his personality?

FAWNDA: I got this one. Olivia says to Cesario, "By maidenhood, honor, truth, and everything, I love thee so." That girl uses so many fancy words she trips herself up. *By maidenhood.* Get it? *Maidenhood?* She says "maidenhood," but she has no idea Cesario is a maid too.

JIMMY: I don't know if this is love or not, but when Maria rushes in, Toby lights up and calls her "the youngest wren of mine." Is that some sort of endearment? What if he called her his oldest wren, what would that mean?

TEACHER: There's no footnote, and I don't know the answer, but take a guess. Is there anything endearing about wrens?

GERALD: Well, maybe birds in general. Lovey dovey. Birds and bees.

FAWNDA: Are you saying there's something lovey dovey between Toby and Maria? Aren't they old?

SUE ANN: If you ask me, the person who shows the most love for another human is Antonio. Look, he gave Sebastian all his money. That's a lotta trust.

TEACHER: When he gives him the money, what are his exact words?

SUE ANN: Not much. "Hold, sir, here's my purse." Like giving him money is as natural as rain. Then he immediately changes the subject, says he's heading for the Elephant to get them a room.

FAWNDA: Wait a minute. How many rooms?

TEACHER: Let's go back to the main question. How does the way Olivia declares love define her personality? How does the way Toby declares love—or whatever endearment he feels—for Maria define his personality? How does the way Antonio declares love for Sebastian define his personality?

5. CQ

Ask students to find lines that show how Viola and Orsino express love, and to reflect on how their methods of expressing love define their personalities. Also ask them to express an opinion on whether Feste knows that Cesario is a female.

HOW DID IT GO?

Do students understand all three scenes? Their summaries and answers to the reflection questions will show you how carefully they listened to other students' performances.

LESSON 15 "Yellow in My Legs"

Sight Gags

PLAY SECTIONS COVERED IN THIS LESSON

3.4.1–69 Olivia encounters Malvolio in his cross-gartered yellow stockings.

LINES: Olivia, 32; Maria, 8; Malvolio, 26; Servant, 3

3.4.70–150 Toby, Fabian, and Maria taunt Malvolio and plan to shut him up in a dark room.

LINES: Malvolio, 31; Toby, 25; Fabian, 8; Maria, 17

3.4.151–204 Andrew reads his note challenging Cesario to a duel. It is meant to be menacing but sounds weak and foppish. Toby sends him out to combat.

LINES: Fabian, 9; Andrew, 4; Toby, 38; Maria, 3

🔊 _____

WHAT'S ON FOR TODAY AND WHY

3.4 is a long scene made up of several short comic episodes. To highlight the humor, break up the scene and augment reading with role-playing and sight gags. To get the full effect of the cross-gartered Malvolio, bring some yellow socks to class, ugly knee socks if possible. Also bring ample lengths of ribbon.

WHAT TO DO

1. Cross-Gartering Malvolio

Ask students to imagine that someone moved to town and that somehow we turned into depraved citizens and wanted to play a cruel trick on him. He gives us the perfect opportunity when he asks us what the cool guys wear to school. We think of the most hideous fashion possible and tell him to wear it. What would that be?

Students, of course, will recognize that this is the very trick Maria, Toby, and Fabian played on Malvolio.

Negotiate with a student you consider to be a good sport. Ask him to agree to demonstrate cross-gartering. Put him on a table or desk so the class can see his legs. Ask him to roll up his pants legs and put on yellow stockings. Ask another student to cross-garter him. The picture on page 112 in the New Folger edition shows the real thing—with the ribbon crisscrossing at the knee and tied in a complicated knot. You can also use the technique seen in many stage productions: start at the toes and crisscross the ribbon all the way to the knee and tie it in a bow.

Now ask the cross-gartered Malvolio to choose three students to join him and act 3.1.1–69. Before they begin, ask: Before he ever enters the stage, what is Malvolio's attitude? What is he thinking? What does he want? What does he think other people think of him? Besides the yellow stockings, what other major change has he accomplished?

Give your Malvolio bonus points or take up a collection for him if he will wear his yellow stockings to his next class and remember the comments people make.

2. Toby Subdues the Madman

By now Malvolio is acting nutty, being strange and surly. To get into character, take a few minutes to role-play the following situation: Two or three friends have heard that someone they know is "acting crazy" and is in need of help immediately. What happens when the friends arrive and try to deal with this wild-acting person?

Cast and act 3.4.70–150 ("O ho, do you come near me now?" to "But see, but see"). Encourage the readers to ham it up.

3. Andrew's Challenge

To help students see how weak Andrew's challenge is, ask them to role-play a dashing hero issuing a challenge to a duel to another dashing hero. Then have them play the same scene with both of the "heroes" as wimps.

Now put scripts in their hands and ask them to read and act out 3.4.151–204 ("More matter for a May morning" to "like cockatrices").

4. CQ

Ask students to choose what they consider the four choicest lines, copy them, and tell why they are great.

HOW DID IT GO?

Judge today's lesson by the laughter quotient. If students laughed, they got the joke. Not bad, considering that the jokes were written 400 years ago.

LESSON 16 "Rapier, Scabbard, and All"

Sword Fighting

ॐ _____

PLAY SECTIONS COVERED IN THIS LESSON

3.4.205–415 The comic duel

LINES: Fabian, 20; Toby, 68; Olivia, 14; Viola, 52; Andrew, 13; First Officer, 7; Second Officer, 4; Antonio, 34

4.1.1–70 Sebastian encounters first Feste, who mistakes him for Cesario, then Olivia, who declares her love for him.

LINES: Fool, 18; Sebastian, 18; Andrew, 6; Toby, 9; Olivia, 19

ॐ _____

WHAT'S ON FOR TODAY AND WHY

Just as the yellow stockings helped to set up the sight gag of Malvolio cross-gartered, so will sword fighting help to set up the comedy in the duel between Viola and Andrew. So invest in some half-inch dowel rods and teach your students how to sword fight. Michael Tolaydo will teach you *and* the students. It's easy and safe if you are strict about following the rules. Go slow. Be careful. Allow three days for this lesson.

WHAT TO DO

1. Olivia Tries Again with Cesario

Quickly read 3.4.205–26 ("Here he comes" to "bear my soul to hell"). Ask: Is there a parallel between Olivia and Malvolio? Is she acting the fool too?

Consider these lines of Olivia's about the "youth" Cesario: 'How shall I feast him? What bestow on him? For youth is bought more oft than begged or borrowed." What do you make of those lines? Do you agree with her judgment about what attracts "youth"?

2. Role-Playing the Duel

Ask for four volunteers to do some role-playing. Now that they are familiar with the characters and action of *Twelfth Night*, this role-playing can be based directly on the play characters. Narrate the events that are about to occur in this scene and have your volunteers improvise action and dialogue. Give Viola and Andrew rolled-up newspaper to use for swords.

First, Toby takes "Cesario" (Viola) aside and tells her how angry and fierce Andrew is. (Students improvise action and dialogue.) Likewise, Fabian takes Andrew aside and describes Cesario's impressive combat skills. Cesario and Andrew show great fear and trembling at the prospect of the impending duel.

The two duelers meet. Andrew draws his sword. Viola draws her sword. They are terrified and inept but make a feeble attempt to fight.

3. Walkers and Talkers

Now appoint four students to read from 3.4.227 ("Gentleman, God save thee") to 3.4.325 ("I do assure you, 'tis against my will") while the four new role-players mime the actions that go along with the words. Have the mimers use big gestures and plenty of movement.

4. Day 2: Sword Fighting

Use Michael Tolaydo's instructions on page 50 to teach students how to sword fight with dowel rods. Go slowly. This should take a day all by itself.

5. Day 3: The Scene with Swords

Organize students into groups of four. Ask each group to design a sword fight for 3.4.227–83 ("Gentlemen, God save thee" to "I care not who knows so much of my mettle"). As they plan the sword fight, have them consider the lines the actors will be saying as they wield their swords. Then group each team with a second and use the "walkers and talkers" method above to practice matching the words with action.

If time permits, ask one of the groups to perform for the rest of the class.

6. Predictions

Remind students that Antonio and Sebastian are loose on Illyria. Ask: Think about Antonio. Where does he think Viola is? If he came upon Viola dressed as a man, who might he think she was? How would Antonio react if he came upon his friend being attacked with a sword? What kind of comic effect could this create?

7. CQ

Ask students to look at Antonio's speech in 3.4.384–89 ("But O, how vile an idol proves this god!" to "empty trunks o'erflourished by the devil"). Tell them to paraphrase it, comment on it, and give some of their own examples of what he is talking about.

8. Act Test

Yes, it's time to do this chore again.

HOW DID IT GO?

Are you seeing significant advances in the way students operate with Shakespeare's language? Are they picking up the lines faster and saying them as if they know what they're talking about? Do they notice and appreciate the subtle humor of a line like "More matter for a May morning" as well as the blatant yellow stockings?

LESSON 17 "Here to Unfold What Thou Dost Know"

Video Wrap-up

WHAT'S ON FOR TODAY AND WHY

Students have pushed a great deal of *Twelfth Night* over their teeth. They know how to paraphrase, rehearse, cut, and block scenes. Soon they will put these skills to use and end the unit by performing scenes in a classroom festival. At this point in the play, however, they are racing for the border. They want to know how all this mess gets cleared up. So my favorite thing to do is to show a videotape of Acts 4 and 5, discuss the resolution of the plot, do some more contemplative questions, and build students up for their major *Twelfth Night* assignment, acting companies. This strategy takes two days.

If you are teaching this unit without a videotape, the best alternative is to divide Acts 4 and 5 into smaller sections and have groups of students perform them. This will take three to four days. Here is a suggestion for scene division:

___

4.2 Feste disguises himself as a priest and visits Malvolio in his dark room.
Four actors (but Maria's part is very short and could be read by another student)

LINES: Maria, 5; Toby, 12; Malvolio, 44; Fool, 72

4.3 This short scene is a love duet between Sebastian and Olivia. Olivia proposes. Sebastian accepts.
Two actors

LINES: Sebastian, 24; Olivia, 13

5.1.1–95 ("Now, as thou lovest me" through "Both day and night did we keep company.") Antonio explains to Orsino that he has spent the last three months in the company of the man Orsino knows as Cesario.
Five actors

LINES: Fabian, 4; Fool, 28; Orsino, 27; Viola, 5; First Officer, 6; Antonio 25

5.1.96–218 ("Here comes the countess" to "Get him to bed, and let his hurt be looked to.") Olivia joins the scene and mistakes Cesario for Sebastian. When Cesario claims that he is not betrothed to her, Olivia sends for a priest to verify her story.
Seven actors (Feste has a very small part that could be read by another student if necessary)

LINES: Orsino, 38; Olivia, 32; Viola, 15; Priest, 9; Andrew, 20; Toby, 6; Fool, 2

5.1.219–94 ("I am sorry, madam" thorough "He is much distract.") Viola and Sebastian meet and recognize each other.
Five actors

LINES: Sebastian, 32; Orsino, 9; Antonio, 4; Olivia, 5; Viola, 26

5.1.295–419 ("A most extracting frenzy" through "fancy's queen")
Five actors

LINES: Olivia, 31; Fool, 23; Fabian, 23; Orsino, 18; Malvolio, 19

᠊᠊᠊᠊᠊᠊᠊᠊᠊᠊᠊᠊᠊

No matter which choice you make, follow up with discussion and CQ.

WHAT TO DO

1. Predictions

Ask students to think for a moment about all the people in Illyria, and how they are tangled up with one another's problems. Ask: What's going to happen with Sebastian? With Cesario? With Malvolio? With Olivia? With Orsino? With Feste?

2. Preparing the Way for the Dark Room

Talk about Malvolio. When we saw him last, he had made a complete fool of himself with Olivia and she told Maria to look after him. Then we heard Toby announce that they would have him in a dark room and bound. Ask: What will Toby and the pranksters do to Malvolio? How far will they take the joke? What would be too far?

3. Acts 4 and 5 on Video

Show the videotape. This will take about thirty minutes.

4. Discussion

As always, ask questions:

· Who has changed since the beginning of the play? How? Why? Can you find lines that back up your opinion?
· How do you explain the Duke's sudden love of Viola, especially after the way she tricked him, when all during the play he expressed his love for Olivia? Can you find lines to back up your opinion?
· Can you find the lines that explain the final results of the Toby–Maria relationship?
· Which of the lovers gives the best final love speech, in your opinion? Why?
· From what you learned in *Twelfth Night*, what would we see if you looked in on each of the characters in ten years?
· Does this play give a happy ending to everyone? Who's happy and who's not? Who's connected and who's not?
· What about the romances? How do Olivia and Sebastian get together?

How do Viola and Orsino link up? Is this a satisfying conclusion? Could it be any other way?

5. Feste's Song

Have everyone turn to the Fool's song at the end of the play. Chant it. Sing it. Do what Shakespeare's company probably would have done and set it to any tune you like. Sing and dance to it. If you have a guitar player or other musician, sing it with a musical accompaniment.

Ask: If this play were done on a big stage, what different choices could be made for the staging of Feste's last song? In some productions, the director leaves Feste on stage alone for this number. In one Dallas performance, Viola opened a trunk during Feste's song, exited briefly, then came on dressed in her "women's weeds" and danced with the Duke. What possibilities can you think of?

Ask students to look at the text of Feste's song. What does it have to do with events in the play?

6. CQ

Ask students to reflect on *Twelfth Night* as a whole and answer these questions:

- If you were commissioned to design and direct a production of *Twelfth Night,* where would you set it? What would your Illyria look like? What would be your take on each character? What costumes, music, and special effects would you want?
- How would you get each character off the stage in 5.1? Think about where they are going and how they feel. Do they stop and shake hands with other characters? Do they slink off or run off? This will be the last time the audience will see them. What impressions do you want to leave?

7. Act Test

Combine tests for Acts 4 and 5 into one assignment and administer them at this time.

HOW DID IT GO?

Did students follow the action of *Twelfth Night?* Did they see growth in the characters? Did the words suggest actions and feelings? How much of the play is lodged in their heads? What do the logs and act tests reveal?

LESSON # 18 "You Shall Know More Hereafter"

A Closer Look at Character

WHAT'S ON FOR TODAY AND WHY

For many days now students have been surrounded by character posters, and scene by scene they have observed the *Twelfth Night* characters in various combinations and situations. Furthermore, they have *been* one or more of the characters in classroom performances. While all this information is still fresh in their minds, they will study one of the characters in a more focused way and develop a character-analysis paper.

The purpose of this paper is to bring all the knowledge they have gathered through their eyes, ears, bodies, and imaginations into their minds at once and to use it to draw conclusions. If you prefer, students could stop with the oral arguments, but even so students will want to be aggressive about finding lines from the text to back up their opinions.

This lesson will take two days.

WHAT TO DO

1. Preliminary Answers

Ask students to choose one of these characters for serious study: Orsino, Olivia, Viola, Sebastian, Toby, Maria, Andrew, Feste, Malvolio, Antonio. They may want to work on the character they studied in Lesson 9, or they may have warmed up to a different Illyrian.

Have them begin by looking again at their character's poster and leafing through their logs and CQs with their character in mind. Then give preliminary answers to these questions:

- In the course of the play, does your character change?
- What was the most significant moment for your character in the entire play?
- What scene best shows your character's personality? What speech in that scene? What line in that speech? What word in that line?

2. Free Writing

Ask students to free write about their character's personality, to get on paper their thoughts about what kind of person their character is. If they have trouble getting started, tell them to write down three words that describe the character then expand on each.

Give them lots of silence and plenty of time, at least ten minutes, for this writing. When they are finished, if more than one student has written about the same character, get them together and have them read their papers to each other.

3. Textual Evidence

Have them draw from their writing and from their answers to the preliminary questions a list of conclusions about their character, at least two or three. For example, a student working on Olivia might conclude that she is a smart lady but "asleep at the wheel" at the beginning of the play, or that she seems to be a very modern woman in many respects, or that she has many traits in common with Maria.

Have students write each conclusion at the top of a page of paper. Send them off to the *Twelfth Night* text to find lines said by or about their character that prove the conclusions. Tell them to copy down the lines on the appropriate page and *remember to note line numbers.* They will start the search for textual evidence in class and continue it for homework. As they work, circulate and check to see that each student is setting off in the right direction.

Ask each student to use her findings and prepare an oral argument, a presentation in which she will voice her conclusions about her character and defend these conclusions with the evidence she gathered.

4. Day 2: Presentation

Hear the oral arguments. Encourage others to agree or disagree with the presenter's conclusions. These presentations will take a full period.

5. Paper

Tell students to tie all this work up in a character-analysis paper, which will include an explanation of their conclusions about their character, their ideas about changes that the character goes through, and their judgment of the most important moment in the play for the character. You may also suggest additional points to include such as a physical description, thoughts about what actor to cast, a comparison of the character to another person in the play. Stress the importance of backing up all opinions with textual references.

Set the due date, length, and manuscript specifications as you like.

HOW DID IT GO?

If students have understood their characters in a more complex way, and if they have backed up their ideas about the characters with textual evidence, they've done their job. You will have your own criteria for evaluating the student papers. Here is a scoring guide you could use if you like:

Character Analysis Paper

1. Writer shows a mature understanding of the character. _____ (40 points)
2. Writer backs up ideas about the character with specific textual references. _____ (20 points)
3. Writer shows skillful organization of ideas. _____ (10 points)
4. Writer fully develops all ideas and all paragraphs in the paper. _____ (10 points)
5. Writer uses mechanical, manuscript, and spelling conventions appropriate to skill level. _____ (10 points)
6. Writer reaches the audience. _____ (10 points)

LESSON 19   "Why, Everything Adheres Together"

Acting Companies

WHAT'S ON FOR TODAY AND WHY

Throughout the unit, students have done acting activities. Their ability is up, and so, we hope, is their enthusiasm. What better ending to *Twelfth Night* than a festival of scenes that will demand from them all the skills they have so far, plus just a little bit more?

Students will go through the same procedure for performance as with the last scenes, but they will memorize lines and do more in the way of costumes and set.

It would be nice if each student could play the character he just researched, but life in school is not as well ordered as life in Illyria, so organize as best you can. The idea is to form acting companies that will have several days to prepare a scene or part of a scene from *Twelfth Night*. Choosing groups calls for political acumen. You may have your own preferred system—drawing straws, letting students choose their own groups, counting off by fives, and so on.

I always let students form their own groups, with the absolute limit of six to a group, abandoning entirely the educational ideal of cooperative groups carefully balanced by race, ability, gender, and politics. I do this because I want the students to have fun with the final activity, which they seem freer to do when they work with people they are comfortable with. Plus, I don't want to have to run interference during this activity with personality conflicts, pouting, or people who can't work together. If you prefer, use your divine powers to create the groups yourself. One wise teacher I know allows students twenty-four hours to trade teacher-orchestrated groups in order to give students a sense of control.

Memorization is wonderful. Much of the pleasure of Shakespeare is the pleasure of his language. The task of memorizing "plants" this language inside the students, and helps them feel the rhythms and understand the sentences in a valuable way. You decide if it is right for your students. Often, students are more willing and able to memorize than teachers realize. Even students with low reading or writing skills can dig in and memorize lines and feel better for it. Some teachers build in memorization as a requirement. I dangle the carrot of extra-credit points.

WHAT TO DO

1. Forming Acting Companies

First order of business is to organize acting companies. Limit them to no more than six in a group.

2. Making the Assignment

Explain that each acting company will present a ten-minute scene from *Twelfth Night*—their choice. Explain also that for this scene they will use rudimentary costumes, sets, and props. Tell them that to receive full benefit, they should memorize their lines, and if they do you will give extra credit.

Distribute Handout 9: "Directions for Acting Companies." Review the suggestions for scenes. Remind students that they can cut their scenes and that they can divide or combine parts to make sure that the integrity of the scene is kept and that everyone has a speaking part.

If you plan to use the performance evaluation, as described below, distribute Handout 10 at this time.

Find places for the companies to work. If you like, and if they are available, let them use other spaces in the building—hallways, stairwells, empty classrooms, cafeterias, or gym lobbies. If you are stuck with using the classroom only, announce the boundaries.

3. Clarifying the Assignment

Answer questions.

FAWNDA: What's the big deal about doing scenes? That's all we've done with this play. Do scenes. Do scenes. Do scenes. Now for the big climax—we're going to do scenes.

TEACHER: Yes, you're on to it. If this were a writing unit, we'd write. If this were a fractions unit, we'd do math problems. But this is a *Twelfth Night* unit, and *Twelfth Night* is a play, so we'll do scenes. But did you notice how skillful you've become in performing scenes? Now you can cast, read, solve problems with the language, cut, block, sword fight—you're ready for final scenes.

JIMMY: How much does this count?

TEACHER: Like a unit test.

GERALD: How many days do we get to work on it?

TEACHER: Counting today, you get three days to rehearse and one day to perform.

MELISSA: I don't have any money to spend on costumes.

TEACHER: Absolutely do not spend money on costumes. Look around your house, or your friends' houses, for something to use. You may decide to do your scene in modern dress, or to all wear black, or to get the wrestling tights for the men. Be creative, but operate on a zero budget.

SUE ANN: My uncle is a director. Could he help us?

TEACHER: You can take suggestions from anyone you like, but in the end this will be your production.

SUE ANN: Could we do this on video?

TEACHER: I have seen Shakespeare scenes done on video, in claymation, on horseback, by all male casts wearing kimonos. You have complete creative license, but there is one rule—present a ten-minute scene on festival day.

4. Getting Started

Send acting companies to their corners to start to work.

5. Rehearsal

While students rehearse, the teacher can read logs, grade act tests, do inventories, or rectify attendance records. But all the while keep one ear on the work of the companies. If by the midpoint of Day Two students are not on their feet planning movement, prod them.

6. Festival

By performance day, spirits will be running high. Students will be laughing at the costumes they drag in, and they'll be sparked up by the words they have memorized. Let this day be festive. Do whatever is in your character to call forth an air of celebration. Play music. Dress up. Light candles. Speak in Italian. Print programs. Invite distinguished guests. Serve refreshments during intermission. Wear academic cap and gown or Elizabethan dress.

7. Evaluation

There are many sound methods for evaluating acting company scenes. Some teachers maintain that the doing is all. They find it a great motivator to make the activity "all or nothing"—100 points (or an A, or whatever system you use) if the students participate in the performance and 0 points if they do not. Period. They argue that this activity is not the place to judge quality of acting or other subjective components, that what you're after is encouraging and rewarding involvement.

I use the performance evaluation in Handout 10, and I give it to the students at the same time as "Directions for Acting Companies" so students will know from the start how they will be graded.

Some teachers let students have input in evaluation. They ask each company to evaluate its members as to whether or not they fulfilled the responsibilities agreed upon. Whatever your expectation and/or criteria are, make them clear in the beginning.

HOW DID IT GO?

As Feste says in 4.2, "That that is, is. " The real test of this unit will come long after the students leave your class. It is true, they have absorbed a certain amount of *Twelfth Night* into their brains. But who knows where in their brains, or how much information, or how long the *Twelfth Night* information will stay? What I hope is that the Shakespeare material will enrich their language and give them pleasure, that in the long hereafter they will remember that they *were* Feste or Antonio or Toby, and that they will recall some of the words they said and feelings they felt.

In a more practical scope, I count the unit successful if students made the journey to Illyria and back and landed on their feet with new tales to tell and treasures to show.

ご

HANDOUT 9

DIRECTIONS FOR ACTING COMPANIES

Your group is to prepare and present to the rest of the class a scene from *Twelfth Night*. How are you supposed to do this, you ask? Read on . . .

1. Choose a Company Name

First things first. Give yourselves a name—something distinctive.

2. Choose the Scene to Do

The end product will be a ten-minute scene from *Twelfth Night*, but as you select keep in mind that you can cut. You can choose any scene you like, but if you want suggestions, here are some possibilities:

ご _____

1.3 After a night of carousing, Sir Toby Belch brings Sir Andrew Aguecheek to meet his niece Olivia. They encounter Maria, Olivia's lady-in-waiting, who scoffs at Toby's scheme to have Sir Andrew court Olivia.

LINES: Toby, 60; Maria, 31; Andrew, 48

1.5.164–251 The "boy" Viola (now called Cesario) calls on Olivia to offer Orsino's compliments.

LINES: Olivia, 42; Viola, 45; Maria, 1

2.3 Maria tries to quiet the late-night carousing of Toby, Sir Andrew, and Feste. Malvolio orders them to behave or he will kick them out. In retaliation, the revelers plan a trick to humiliate him.

LINES: Toby, 55; Andrew, 46; Fool, 30; Maria, 35; Malvolio, 21

2.4 In what he assumes is a man-to-man talk about women, Orsino expresses his lovesick state and gets Cesario to tell him about "his" love for one of Orsino's age and complexion. Viola and Orsino debate the trueness of womanly hearts, and Viola tells of a woman who loved as strong as any man but hid her love.

LINES: Orsino, 73; Viola, 32; Curio, 5; Fool, 27

2.5 Malvolio falls for Maria's trick. With Fabian, Toby, and Andrew watching from behind the boxtree, Malvolio finds the letter Maria forged, believes it to be to him from Olivia, and makes plans to make startling alterations to his appearance.

LINES: Toby, 41; Fabian, 31; Andrew, 13; Maria, 18; Malvolio, 109

3.4.1–204 Malvolio wears crossed garters; Toby and Fabian plan to cart him off as a madman.

LINES: Olivia, 32; Maria, 28; Malvolio, 57; Servant, 3; Toby, 63; Fabian, 17; Andrew, 4

3.4.205–416 The duel of Andrew, Viola, Sebastian, and Toby.

LINES: Fabian, 10; Toby, 58; Olivia, 14; Viola, 52; Andrew, 13; First Officer, 7; Second Officer, 4; Antonio, 34

5.1 Cut a scene from the madcap action of Act 5.

ɞ _____

3. Cast

Read through the scene together and decide on parts. If the number of people in your scene is different from the number of people in your group, do not quit. You can (1) double-cast some of the roles, (2) have people read more than one role, (3) combine two roles into one, (4) come up with your own creative solution to this interesting problem. Everyone in your group must say at least one line onstage.

4. Choose a Director

The director's job is to plan the blocking, give suggestions to the actors about gestures, vocal expressions, and other movements, and generally keep the group moving along.

5. Prepare the Scene

Read through the scene again and start working on understanding it. As you did in class with other scenes, read around the circle, underlining words you do not understand. Find out what they mean. Find out what the scene is about. Read again, and start cutting. Don't be afraid to cut whole sections, or parts of speeches.

6. Rehearse

YOU CANNOT SIT AT YOUR DESK TO DO THIS; YOU MUST BE UP ON YOUR FEET PUTTING MOVEMENT TO THE WORDS. Memorize your lines, and get busy bringing this scene to life.

7. Get Fancy

Make your own decisions about costumes, props, and scenery. You can be as elaborate or as simple as you wish.

8. Nail Down Responsibilities

Make a list of who will do what for performance day.
Example:
Jimmy—bring tape player, his own costume, and Melissa's hat.
Kathy—call Gerald, bring costume and Jason's sword

9. Rehearse Some More

10. Show Us Your Scene

Be ready to show your scene to the class on _____, the day of our Great Classroom Shakespeare Festival.

ɞ

🔖

HANDOUT 10

PERFORMANCE EVALUATION

ACTING COMPANY NAME:

SCENE PERFORMED:

CHARACTER	PLAYED BY	COMMENTS

POINTS POSSIBLE	TO WHAT EXTENT DOES THE PERFORMANCE SHOW:	POINTS AWARDED
15	CAREFUL READING AND REHEARSAL	
15	UNDERSTANDING OF CHARACTERS	
15	UNDERSTANDING OF PLOT	
20	UNDERSTANDING OF LANGUAGE	
15	ABILITY TO USE LANGUAGE TO PORTRAY CHARACTERS	
10	WELL-PLANNED MOVEMENTS	
10	WELL-PLANNED USE OF PROPS AND COSTUMES	
(+ 20 BONUS)	MEMORIZED LINES	
(BONUS)	SOMETHING EXTRA	
100 TOTAL (+ BONUS)		

COMMENTS:

🔖

Othello

•

LOUISA FOULKE NEWLIN AND
MARY WINSLOW POOLE
EDITORS

Dear Colleagues,

Make no mistake: *Othello* works as well in the classroom as it does in the theater. It's a dynamite play to teach. Students get hooked early and stay with it to the end.

For many, its hero is more sympathetic than Macbeth, Lear, or Hamlet. And, having no real subplot, *Othello* is easier to follow than *King Lear*; it has fewer minor characters and superfluous scenes than *Hamlet* and it moves so swiftly that students are unlikely to complain, as they often do about Denmark during the first two, long acts, that there is "no action."

The play engages their emotions, too. This painfully modern-seeming story of a noble black general, tricked and tempted into being his worst self by an evil man he mistakenly trusts, has the power to shake certain students to their depths. Although teachers sometimes believe that the emotions the play explores are too adult for many high-school students to understand, most students know more about sexual jealousy as a potentially tragic force than we like to think. Few, however, can articulate that understanding well; *Othello* gives them words for what they know but can't express.

This is not to say that all the sailing will be clear. There is a higher percentage of strong language in *Othello* than in *Hamlet, Macbeth,* or even *King Lear,* language which some schools object to having said out loud in a classroom. Some students may be uncomfortable with the complex racial issues raised by the play, and you may have to devote time to creating a climate in which students can trust each other enough to speak honestly about them. Handling the sexual matters requires sensitivity and fore-thought—before the lessons dealing with domestic violence, for example, you have to imagine how your students might respond to them and how you will respond back. All of this forethought is well worth it, however, as in certain ways *Othello* speaks much more directly to the human condition than the other great Shakespearean trage-dies and has, therefore, more to teach us about ourselves.

It is a real asset that a study of *Othello* offers opportunities to confront issues of race and violence, including domestic violence, which are all too alive today: students can discuss difficult subjects, subjects that need to be confronted and thrashed out, on the neutral-seeming territory of a sixteenth-century play. Those who have suffered from the effects of racism, either directly or indirectly, can appreciate Shakespeare's extraordinary achievement in making his Moor a respected general and military hero in a historical period when his country as a whole was strongly prejudiced against both foreigners in general and the color black in particular.

Ironically, the stage history of the play reflects an ongoing racism. Because the sight of a genuine black man playing the husband of a white woman was disturbing to some white audiences, the part of Othello was played by white actors in America until 1942, when Paul Robeson played the role on Broadway. The great nineteenth-century American black actor Ira Aldridge, briefly associated with New York's short-lived African Shakespeare Company, played Othello numerous times to great acclaim—but in Europe, where he went to live at seventeen because its environment was more hospitable to his career than that of his homeland.

The part of Iago has usually been played by a white actor; the viciousness of Iago's inexplicable hatred of Othello would seem to belong to a white man. But when André Braugher, a young black actor, took the role (in the Shakespeare Theatre's 1990 production in Washington, D.C.) opposite Avery Brooks's Othello, he brought another dimension to the play altogether.

It would be a mistake to ignore the element of race that affects Othello's relationship with Desdemona and that informs Iago's largely irrational hatred for his superior. (Be sure to read "Unfinished Business: An African-American Teacher Talks Race and *Othello*," beginning on page 215.) It would be an even greater mistake to present *Othello* **exclusively** as a tragedy of race relations. *Othello* is about much more than the marriage of a white woman to a black man. It is about two people from different worlds who are in love and who marry without parental blessing, and about a love relationship between an older man and a younger woman. It's about a husband who, believing he is doing the right thing, murders his wife. It's about the successful struggle of evil to corrupt good, and about good misplacing its trust and recognizing evil too late. Some nineteenth-century critics interpreted the Moor's murder of his wife as the reversion, under stress, to an inherently savage nature; it is crucial for students to see that *Othello*, like *Hamlet*, is essentially about a worthy and noble person who makes a tragic and irrevocable mistake that leads him to an ignoble, base course of action—and that Othello is, as truly as any other, a tragic hero.

Ideally, teacher and students will discover the play together. The teacher's role is *not* to explain everything, but to allow students to experience for themselves the complexity and ambiguity of this wonderful, terrible, beautiful play.

We are big on questions. We believe that questions are provocative and that they may often uncover deeper meanings in a scene or truths about a character that simply do not occur to students who are discovering a play for the first time. Questions don't squelch students' own ideas; on the contrary, they stimulate students to look more closely, to respond more imaginatively. And, certainly, questions about actors' or directors' choices are fundamental to experiencing the play as a work for the stage. The best questions, of course, are those that do not have "an answer."

This teaching plan is designed for students who have already studied at least one other play by Shakespeare and who therefore already possess some information about Elizabethan stage conventions, such as the aside and the soliloquy, and have developed some strategies for understanding the language. Most lessons are designed for a forty-five-minute period; a few take more than a day. You are encouraged to adapt any or all to your own classroom situation. If you have twenty days available, or fifteen, or even ten, pick and choose. Shorten assignments. Use more videotape than suggested, or less; make use of summary if you need to vault over some sections. A professional director cuts the script—so can you. Most of the activities approach the text as a script. Begin to collect a few hats and capes and props. Make a little performance space in your classroom.

If students come to understand the text as a dramatic script with multiple possible interpretations, never existing fully until performed; if the play's powerful language and imagery is given a chance to take root in their imaginations, then they will "own" the text on their own terms. They will keep on asking questions about it and trying out contradictory responses long after the study is over. Probably, they will never forget it.

We are indebted to our colleagues in the Teaching Shakespeare Institute of the Folger Shakespeare Library for their insightful and imaginative contributions to this unit: to Donna Denizé, Washington, D.C.; John Scott, Hampton, Virginia; and Martha Harris, Minneapolis, Minnesota. This unit plan is very much a collaborative effort, not the least of whose informants are the many students in diverse classrooms who have helped to mold and breathe life into the activities that follow.

Louisa Foulke Newlin
High School Shakespeare Institute
Folger Shakespeare Library

Mary Winslow Poole
Washington International School
Washington, D.C.

UNIT CALENDAR FOR
Othello

❧ 1	❧ 2	❧ 3	❧ 4	❧ 5
LESSON 1 An Introduction to *Othello*	LESSON 2 The Acting Circle Text: 1.1.74–160	LESSON 3 Dramaturgy and the Hat Trick Text: 1.1–73, 1.1.161–206	LESSON 4 Rehearsing 1.2 Text: 1.2	LESSON 5 Performing 1.2 Text: 1.2
❧ 6	❧ 7	❧ 8	❧ 9	❧ 10
LESSON 6 The Senate on Video Text: 1.3.1–342	LESSON 7 Discussing the Senate Scene Text: 1.3.1–342	LESSON 8 Searching the Text for Words and Images	LESSON 9 Close Reading and Iago's Bestiary Text: 1.3.343–447	LESSON 10 Play vs. Opera Text: 2.1
❧ 11	❧ 12	❧ 13	❧ 14	❧ 15
LESSON 11 Actors' Objectives Text: 2.1.1–233	LESSON 12 Iago's Many Voices Text: 2.1.234–334	LESSON 13 Introduction to Blocking Text: 2.2, 2.3.1–39	LESSON 14 The Drinking Scene Text: 2.3.40–284	LESSON 15 2.3 on Video The Paraphrase Game Text: 2.3
❧ 16	❧ 17	❧ 18	❧ 19	❧ 20
LESSON 16 Text and Subtext Text: 3.3.1–99	LESSON 17 The Temptation Scene in Relay Text: 3.3.37–546	LESSON 18 The Politics of Casting Text: 3.4.23–231	LESSON 19 Passing the Handkerchief Text: 3.4	LESSON 20 Othello's Fall Text: 4.1
❧ 21	❧ 22	❧ 23	❧ 24	❧ 25
LESSON 21 The Willow Scene Text: 4.2.1–198, 4.3.11–117	LESSON 22 Final Casting Call and the Director's Promptbook Text: 5.1, 5.2	LESSON 22 Final Casting Call and the Director's Promptbook (*cont.*)	LESSON 22 Final Casting Call and the Director's Promptbook (*cont.*)	LESSON 23 Acting Company Performance
❧ 26	❧ 27			
LESSON 24 Shakespeare as Verbal Opera	LESSON 25 Drawing Conclusions about the Play			

<table>
<tr><td>LESSON</td><td>1</td><td></td></tr>
</table>

"Who Can Control His Fate?"

An Introduction to *Othello*

Brief improvised role-play will offer students opportunity to experience the central triangle of *Othello* and to connect the emotions of Othello, Desdemona, and Iago to their own. Telling the story will arouse their curiosity, and a play map will help them visualize the issues and people they will meet in the play.

To invite students to respond personally and imaginatively to the action and language of the play as it unfolds, and to enable the teacher to measure how thoroughly and accurately students are reading, acting, and understanding the play, throughout the unit students will write frequently in logs.

The word "log" is used, rather than "journal," because one meaning of log is, specifically, the record of a journey—the study of a Shakespearean text is an intellectual and emotional journey. The unit contains specific log-writing assignments, but ideally, students make other, non-assigned entries: personal reactions and observations, new vocabulary worth "saving," comments on character, action, language.

WHAT TO DO

1. Role-Play

Clear a space in the classroom and ask students to act out the following situations, improvising lines and movement. Change actors frequently.

- Two men are talking. One, whom we will call the lover, has a girlfriend. The other, whom we will call the friend, tries to plant seeds of doubt in the lover about the girlfriend's loyalty.
- Two men are talking. This time the friend tries to convince the lover that his girlfriend has eyes for a particular man.

Pause and draw a triangle on the board. Ask the class to invent names for the three—the lover, his girlfriend, and the friend who is trying to make him jealous. Continue with another improvisation:

- A confrontation between the lover and his girlfriend. Believing her unfaithful, he is angry but won't say why. She is innocent and bewildered by his anger. Discuss the reasons people are jealous, and if a male might believe another male rather than his girlfriend. How does someone who is innocent *prove* it? How will the girlfriend react?

Ask the class to decide if the lover would use physical force on the girlfriend. If so, how much?

Go to the diagram on the board. Cross out the names the class has given and write "Othello," "Desdemona," and "Iago." Tell the students that they will see these same events unfold in *Othello*, but in Shakespeare's script they will see more jealousy and intrigue.

2. Play Map

Using Handout 1: "Play Map" as a guide, draw on the board a diagram showing the relationships of the major characters of the play.

As you introduce the characters, tell enough of the story to intrigue the class. Each teacher has a different storytelling style. A way that works for some is to let the students get comfortable, sit on window seats or on the floor, as if listening to a good ghost story. Using your blackboard diagram at intervals, tell the basic plot as a cracking good tale that builds to the point at which Othello, in the last scene of the play, moves silently with a candle to his wife's bedside . . . Then when suspense is at its height, ask for guesses about the story's ending.

Even if some students already know the ending, you can make the point that Shakespeare did not invent this plot and that what is crucial is the *way* he dramatized it; the class will be looking at the play as a successful dramatic script.

3. Homework

Ask students to buy or designate a bound notebook to use for a log. Give them Handout 2: "Keeping a Log." Review it with them and set expectations. Tell them when to write, how much to write, and when you will read their writing.

Free Writing: For their first log entry, ask students to take the improvisation they just did and weave a story around it. But there will be three complications:

1) The lover is black and the girlfriend is white.
2) There is a significant difference in social background between the two.
3) Of what ethnic origin is the friend?

HOW DID IT GO?

If either the role-playing or the storytelling, or both, have generated enthusiasm, you are off to a good start.

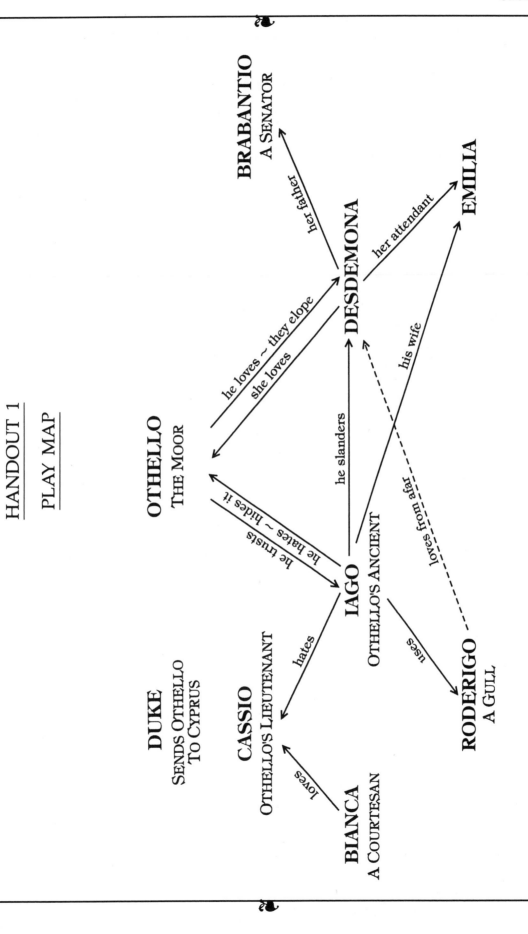

HANDOUT 1

PLAY MAP

BRABANTIO
A SENATOR

her father

DESDEMONA

her attendant

EMILIA

he loves ~ they elope

she loves

his wife

OTHELLO
THE MOOR

he slanders

he trusts

he hates ~ hides it

loves from afar

IAGO
OTHELLO'S ANCIENT

DUKE
SENDS OTHELLO
TO CYPRUS

hates

uses

CASSIO
OTHELLO'S LIEUTENANT

RODERIGO
A GULL

loves

BIANCA
A COURTESAN

❧

HANDOUT 2

KEEPING A LOG

A *log* is the record of a journey, and your log—which you will keep in a bound notebook of your own choosing—will be the record of your own "journey" through *Othello.* Each person's journey will be different. You will have specific assignments for your log, but we encourage you to add to these, to show what interests *you* about the trip. *Date each entry, and make a note of the act and scene to which your entry refers.*

Below is a list of things you might include in the log.

- *Questions* you have about the play as you read . . . and possible answers.

- A sentence commenting on the importance of a particular *scene.*

- A *line or two* that you particularly enjoyed and comments about the lines.

- Personal *impressions* of characters, and personal reactions to ideas or subjects that come up as you read.

- Notes on a *character* you performed or are going to perform. How does she feel about what is happening? What sort of person is he, and how can you tell? What do other characters say about her? What does his own use of language show about him? Write down a few phrases that you think show something about her personality or are characteristic of the way he expresses himself.

- *Words* you find interesting or amusing or would like to add to your own vocabulary. Some of these may be words still in current use and some archaic that you enjoy because of the way they sound, like "pottle" (tankard, mug) in Iago's "potations pottle-deep," or "zounds."

- Ideas you associate with certain *words that recur*—such as "chaste," "strumpet," "monster," "unnatural."

- Comments on the importance of a *recurring word* such as "honest" or *groups of related words* like "magic" and "witchcraft" or *types of words* like "beasts."

- The I-have-a-better-idea option. You can always substitute a subject of your own choosing—related to the play, of course—for the one assigned.

❧

LESSON **2** **"Zounds, Sir, You're Robbed"**

The Acting Circle

☙ _____

PLAY SECTION COVERED IN THIS LESSON

1.1.74–160 Iago gets Roderigo, who has been unsuccessfully wooing Desdemona, to awake Brabantio and tell him his daughter has eloped.

LINES: Iago, 32; Roderigo, 30; Brabantio, 25

☙ _____

WHAT'S ON FOR TODAY AND WHY

To propel the class into the main action of *Othello*, to give everyone a chance to speak Shakespearean lines in a non-threatening context, and to help students look to language for information about situation and character, students will perform a short scene as if they were actors reporting for the first day of rehearsals.

For this scene, make photocopies of Handout 3. (Handout 3 is a shortened version of 1.1.74–160, cut so that it can be done with ease in a class period.) These are more like actors' scripts and appear less daunting than a book. (If students get their copies of the whole play at the beginning of class, they may be too busy looking at the cover illustration or counting the number of pages to become actively involved in the proceedings.)

Use the technique described by Michael Tolaydo in "Up on Your Feet with Shakespeare" on page 41.

WHAT TO DO

1. Log Sharing

Ask volunteers to read aloud the log entries they wrote for homework and discuss them.

2. Acting Circle

Explain to the class that throughout this unit they will approach *Othello* as actors, that they will perform many of the scenes, but not all of them, in ad hoc acting companies.

Ask them to imagine that they have reported to the rehearsal hall for their first day of work. To get into the play at hand, they will do a short scene.

Pass out photocopies of Handout 3. Have students sit in a circle and read round-robin. Each reads a complete thought, stopping at the period, question mark, exclamation mark, or semicolon.

After reading the section round-robin once (twice, if there is time), go through another round of reading the section, this time part-by-part rather than sentence-by-sentence. Everyone is still involved, but instead of reading only a sentence, each reads the character's whole speech. During this reading, encourage students to make notes on their scripts, circle unfamiliar words, jot down questions.

3. Questions and Discussion

Talk about what is going on. Give students a chance to ask questions about anything at all, making it clear that actors, before starting to rehearse any Shakespearean play, have many questions about the text and that no one should feel embarrassed about asking anything, and that, furthermore, there is no such thing as a stupid question.

After student questions, you might stimulate further discussion by asking one or two of the following:

- Who are Roderigo and Iago? What kind of people are they? What does each seem to want from the other? Who's in control? What has just happened? Who is Brabantio? What sort of person do you think the Moor is? What about Brabantio's daughter—how do you picture her? Why is it that neither Othello nor Desdemona is mentioned by name in this scene?
- What sort of language does Iago use to tell Brabantio of his daughter's elopement? On what sort of fears and prejudices is Iago playing?

4. Finding Voices for the Characters

Following the brief discussion, ask three students to read the roles of Iago, Roderigo, and Brabantio for part of the scene, three more to read the middle section, three others to read the last section. Students will begin to hear the voices of the play, which will help them to imagine the action when they read silently.

Discuss the differences between the readings. How did these differences affect your impression of the character?

5. Acting the Scene

Ask for volunteers to get on their feet and act the scene. Ask the rest of the class to take the part of directors, suggesting movement, inflection, interpretation.

Be generous in your praise of their work.

6. Homework

Distribute the full scripts—copies of *Othello*. Ask students to read through Act 1, scene 1. After reviewing Handout 2: "Keeping a Log," ask students to make a long entry and to answer at least two of the following questions in their logs:

1. Why do Iago, Roderigo, and Brabantio hate the man they are discussing?
2. What reasons does Iago give for continuing to follow his master?
3. What kind of person do you expect the man they discuss to be? How do you imagine him? Count the number of times the word "Moor" is used in 1.1. Can you draw any conclusions?

HOW DID IT GO?

Students have had a taste of the play's language and have a basic plot outline on which to build. If they understand how they are to use the logs and are eager to keep going, you are off and running.

🙞

HANDOUT 3

A SLIGHTLY CUT SCRIPT FOR 1.1.74–160

IAGO   Call up her father
Rouse him. Make after him, poison his delight,
Proclaim him in the streets; incense his kinsmen,
Plague him with flies.

RODERIGO   Here is her father's house. I'll call aloud.
What ho, Brabantio! Signior Brabantio, ho!

IAGO   Awake! What ho, Brabantio! Thieves, thieves!
Look to your house, your daughter, and your bags!
Thieves, thieves!

Enter Brabantio above (at a window).

BRABANTIO   What is the reason of this terrible summons?
What is the matter there?

RODERIGO   Signior, is all your family within?

BRABANTIO   Why, wherefore ask you this?

IAGO   Zounds, sir, you're robbed! For shame, put on your gown!
Your heart is burst. You have lost half your soul.
Even now, now, very now, an old black ram
Is tupping your white ewe. Arise, arise!
Awake the snorting citizens with the bell,
Or else the devil will make a grandsire of you.
Arise, I say!

BRABANTIO   What, have you lost your wits?

RODERIGO   Most reverent signior, do you know my voice?

BRABANTIO   Not I. What are you?

RODERIGO   My name is Roderigo.

BRABANTIO   The worser welcome.
In honest plainness thou hast heard me say
My daughter is not for thee.

RODERIGO   Sir, sir, sir—

BRABANTIO   What tell'st thou me of robbing? This is Venice.
My house is not a grange.

RODERIGO   Most grave Brabantio,
In simple and pure soul I come to you—

IAGO	Zounds, sir, you are one of those that will not serve God if the devil bid you. Because we come to do you service and you think we are ruffians, you'll have your daughter covered with a Barbary horse, you'll have your nephews neigh to you!
BRABANTIO	What profane wretch art thou?
IAGO	I am one, sir, that comes to tell you your daughter and the Moor are making the beast with two backs.
BRABANTIO	Thou art a villain.
IAGO	You are a senator.
BRABANTIO	This thou shalt answer. I know thee, Roderigo.
RODERIGO	Sir, I will answer anything. But I beseech you, If't be your pleasure and most wise consent— As partly I find it is—that your fair daughter, At this odd-even and dull watch o' th' night, Transported with no worse nor better guard But with a knave of common hire, a gondolier, To the gross clasps of the lascivious Moor: If this be known to you, and your allowance, We then have done you bold and saucy wrongs. But if you know not this, my manners tell me We have your wrong rebuke. Straight satisfy yourself. If she be in her chamber or your house, Let loose on me the justice of the state For thus deluding you.
BRABANTIO	Give me a taper. Call up my people. This accident is not unlike my dream. Belief of it oppresses me already. Light, I say, light!

LESSON 3 "I Am Not What I Am"

Dramaturgy and the Hat Trick

❧ _____

PLAY SECTIONS COVERED IN THIS LESSON

1.1.1–73 Iago tells Roderigo he hates the Moor and is angry that a Florentine named Cassio, rather than Iago himself, has been given the post of lieutenant.

LINES: Roderigo, 8; Iago, 64

1.1.161–206 Brabantio is enraged at the news of his daughter's elopement and organizes an armed band to search out Othello.

LINES: Iago, 16, Brabantio, 21; Roderigo, 4

❧ _____

WHAT'S ON FOR TODAY AND WHY

Sharing log entries and choosing hats for each character, students will explore the personalities and relationships in 1.1.

For the hat trick, bring to class a collection of hats, swords, scarves, capes, and props collected from rummage sales, basements, and attics so students can match a hat or prop with each character's personality and use it in acting all subsequent scenes. Any prop that distinguishes one character from another is fine, but there is something about wearing hats that makes students feel less like themselves, and, consequently, less self-conscious about assuming a dramatic role.

Knowing something about the geography and cultures alluded to in the play will help students understand more fully some of the central conflicts in *Othello*. Familiarity with some of the stage history will give them perspective on the way the play is being performed today.

To facilitate research, students will work as teams of dramaturges, specialists who act as consultants to acting companies, especially those doing classical plays, about matters of historical relevance.

WHAT TO DO

1. Log Sharing

Ask for volunteers to read answers to the log questions assigned for homework. Discuss. Clear up any words or passages in the text that proved stumbling blocks.

Ask students to summarize 1.1.1–73 and 1.1.161–206. Discuss what happens in these lines. Have students clarify for each other the fundamentals about who Cassio is, why Iago dislikes him, and how Brabantio's attitude toward Roderigo has changed by the end of the scene—1.1.198, "O, would you had had her!"

Ask students again for opinions about what kind of person they expect to see when Othello appears.

2. Hats

As each character's traits and motivations become clear, choose a hat for him. Discuss the personalities of each character. Don't worry about historical accuracy. Hats are emblematic, not realistic—they are not what someone would really wear, in life or in the play, but indicate something about the personality, occupation, or status of the character. Students can choose which hats go with which character.

Tell the class that as they do the scenes in this unit, actors will wear the hats associated with their character.

3. Dramaturges' Research Topics

Talk about the kind of research actors and directors do to prepare for a production. Give students Handout 4: "Research Topics for Dramaturgy Teams." Assign these topics to individuals or to dramaturgy teams of two to four students, who will prepare five-minute presentations. Stagger the due dates so that the class hears each report when it seems most relevant.

4. Homework

Locate sources for research topics and come to class with any questions or problems.

HOW DID IT GO?

If the hats helped students to focus on character, if students understand the relationship between Iago, Roderigo, and Brabantio, if they have clear expectations and inquisitive attitudes about their *Othello* research, Lesson 3 has gone well.

æ

HANDOUT 4

RESEARCH TOPICS FOR DRAMATURGY TEAMS

Many professional acting companies today have dramaturges, consultants who are responsible for providing directors with all kinds of historical and literary information pertaining to the play.

In *Othello*, there are many issues that would benefit from research. To accomplish this, you will work in dramaturgy teams on the topics below. Note your research topic, the questions it entails, and the due date.

Venice

Where is Venice, and what was it like in the sixteenth century? What was its economic status at that time? If possible, bring pictures of Venice. What was the Venetians' relationship with the Turks? Bring a large map of the Mediterranean and be prepared to show what territory the Venetian Republic and the Ottoman Empire covered.
Possible sources: Any good encyclopedia, and an atlas of European history.
Due date: Lesson 6

Cyprus

Where is it? What was its importance in the sixteenth century? How far is it from Venice? What were the politics of the countries nearest it? Use a map in your presentation.
Possible sources: Encyclopedias.
Due date: Lesson 6

Moors

Who are they? Where did they come from? What were they doing in Europe in the sixteenth century? Are there religious or cultural practices associated with them?
Possible sources: Any good encyclopedia. For more details, try Chapter 6, "The Moors of Venice," in *The Moor in English Renaissance Drama*, by Jack D'Amico (University of Florida Press, 1991), or *Othello's Countrymen*, by Eldred Jones (Oxford University Press, 1985).
Special task: During the weeks to come, when you see references to Othello's Christianity and to the respect in which he is held, note these and bring them to the class's attention.
Due date: Lesson 8

Turks

What was the Elizabethan attitude toward foreigners in general and non-Christians—such as Turks—in particular?

Possible sources: Chapter 4, "Don't Talk to Strangers," in *Shakespeare Alive!* by Joseph Papp and Elizabeth Kirkland (Bantam, 1988) and other works mentioned in *Shakespeare Alive!*'s bibliography.

Due date: Lesson 8

Ira Aldridge

What can you discover about the career of the nineteenth-century American-born black actor Ira Aldridge and his playing of Othello?

Possible sources: Shakespeare in Sable: A History of Black Shakespearean Actors, by Errol Hill (University of Massachusetts Press, 1984) or *Ira Aldridge: The Negro Tragedian,* by Herbert Marshall and Mildred Stock (Arcturus Books, 1968).

Due date: Lesson 18

Paul Robeson

What can you find out about the actor Paul Robeson and how he played Othello in London (1930) and New York (1943)?

Possible sources: Shakespeare in Sable.

Due date: Lesson 18

Recent *Othello* Productions

What can you find about *Othello* productions in recent years? For example, Raul Julia played Othello in Joseph Papp's production in Central Park in 1991; James Earl Jones (with Christopher Plummer as Iago) in New York and other U.S. cities in 1982; Ben Kingsley (with David Suchet as Iago) for the Royal Shakespeare Company in 1985. And there have been many more.

Possible sources: Readers' Guide to Periodical Literature; "Othello on Stage and Screen," by Sylvan Barnett in the 1987 Signet edition of the play; *Othello; Text and Performance,* by Marvin Wine (Macmillan, 1984) for information on British productions.

Due date: Lesson 18

Epilepsy

What are the symptoms of epilepsy? How was it regarded and treated in the Renaissance? Now? Are there conditions that render an epileptic particularly vulnerable to a seizure? Othello has a seizure in 4.1. Is it epilepsy?

Possible sources: A medical encyclopedia, a science teacher, a doctor, or a science journal.

Due date: Lesson 20

LESSON 4

"I Fetch My Life and Being from Men of Royal Siege"

Rehearsing 1.2

PLAY SECTION COVERED IN THIS LESSON

1.2 Brabantio comes with henchmen to arrest Othello, who persuades him to accompany him to the duke, who has summoned Othello to deal with a military crisis.

LINES: Iago, 29; Othello, 40; Brabantio, 34; Officer, 3; Cassio, 17

WHAT'S ON FOR TODAY AND WHY

By preparing short scenes, students will become more secure in the acting process that will carry them through this unit.

WHAT TO DO

1. Research: Progress Report

Spend a few minutes giving support to the research teams and answering questions they may have.

2. Setting Standards for Performance

Remind students that they will approach *Othello* as an acting script, that each of them will be up at intervals to perform a role in a scene, and that for purposes of this unit, performing means reading in parts while on their feet. Students become actors who try to clarify the meaning of the words by moving around a cleared area designated the "stage." Some performances will be spontaneous, some prepared as homework.

Explain that for part of their final grade, each company will present for the class a scene from Act 4 or 5 of the play during the last week of the unit.

3. Acting Companies: Rehearsal

Organize the class into four acting companies. Give each a short scene to perform:

- 1.2.1–32 ("Though in the trade of war" to "what lights come yond")
- 1.2.33–64 ("Those are the raisèd father" to "To who?")

- 1.2.65–100 ("Marry, to—" to "Subdue him at his peril")
- 1.2.101–23 ("Hold your hands" to "shall our statesmen be")

Review orally or write on the board the acting company process:

1. Read round-robin to hear the words, stopping at periods, question marks, semicolons, colons, or exclamation marks.
2. Paraphrase and answer questions about the language. Figure out what's happening.
3. Cast and read again, this time in parts.
4. If needed, cut some of the lines, but only to make the scene clearer. Double up parts or split them in two if you'd like.
5. Get on your feet and add movement. Let the words on the page be your guide.
6. Rehearse until you can communicate the scene to an audience.

As students rehearse, visit each group to field questions and encourage participation. If your costume box has capes, swords, or the like, let students use them. (For swords, use dowel rods, or ask your woodshop teacher or drama coach to show students how to make them. Giving safe, wooden swords to the actors playing Iago, Roderigo, Brabantio, Cassio, and Othello will energize the scene, make it more interesting to watch and easier to perform.)

4. Homework

In addition to their ongoing log assignments, ask students to do this free-writing exercise: Write about a time when you resented someone who received an honor you were hoping to get. How did you feel about the person who received it, and how did you feel about the one who chose the other person instead of you?

HOW DID IT GO?

If students are moving through the steps in their acting companies, they're learning the process. If they recognize the main ideas and conflicts of 1.2 and they are developing a sense of the personalities of Othello, Iago, Roderigo, Brabantio, they are learning the play. Are they beginning to realize that performance is interpretation?

LESSON 5 "Keep Up Your Bright Swords"

Performing 1.2

PLAY SECTION COVERED IN THIS LESSON

1.2 Brabantio comes with henchmen to arrest Othello, who persuades him to accompany him to the duke, who has summoned Othello to deal with a military crisis.

LINES: Iago, 29; Othello, 40; Brabantio, 34; Officer, 3; Cassio, 17

WHAT'S ON FOR TODAY AND WHY

Students will perform the scenes they prepared in Lesson 4. Since they will be seeing several Othellos, Iagos, Brabantios, Officers, and Cassios, for continuity actors may want to wear the designated hats.

WHAT TO DO

1. Acting Companies: Performance

Call the groups together for a performance.

2. First Impressions

After all the performances, students will discuss what they heard and saw.

Possible further questions: We saw Othello for the first time in this scene—is he what you thought he would be? Is he respected by his associates? How do you know?

What contrasts are there between the way Iago, Roderigo, and Brabantio have described Othello and the way he looks and behaves when he actually appears?

3. Interpretation

Informed by knowledge gained in performance, students can answer questions about language and line interpretation. Examples:

- Do you notice basic differences in attitude between Cassio and Iago in their short conversation (1.2.60–65) following Othello's exit?
- Why is Brabantio convinced that Othello must have used witchcraft on his daughter? Why does he have difficulty believing his daughter could run to Othello's "sooty bosom"?

4. Homework

Remind dramaturgy groups doing Venice and Cyprus that they will report in the next lesson. In addition to ongoing log assignments, ask students to:

1. Describe Othello as you see him in your imagination. Say which actor, or type of actor, you would choose to play the role. Find a picture in a magazine that resembles your idea of Othello, or draw your own.
2. Iago swears in line 38 "By Janus." Janus is a Roman two-faced god. Give examples of Iago's two-faced behavior. How might an actor convey this?

HOW DID IT GO?

Did the acting companies perform with improved confidence? Did they show skills at interpreting Shakespeare's language? *Brilliant performance is not the objective.* If both actors and audience were actively involved in the scene, the lesson was successful.

LESSON **6** "She Loved Me for the Dangers I Had Passed"

The Senate Scene on Video

🐦 _____

PLAY SECTION COVERED IN THIS LESSON

1.3.1–342 Before the Senate, Othello defends himself against Brabantio's charge of witchcraft. The duke orders Othello to Cyprus to battle the invading Turks, and allows Desdemona to accompany him.

LINES: Duke, 73; First Senator, 28; Second Senator, 5; Sailor, 4; Officer, 2; Messenger, 10; Brabantio, 65; Othello, 126; Desdemona, 29

🐦 _____

WHAT'S ON FOR TODAY AND WHY

The dramaturges' reports will provide the historical and geographical background useful for understanding the action of 1.3.

Watching the Senate scene on video will propel the class into the unfolding plot and will prepare them both to read it on their own for homework and to see it more clearly so they will be able to discuss it well the next day. Video-watching does not need to be passive, and seeing the scene on film helps develop increased sensitivity to the way a filmed performance, unlike a live one, focuses an audience's attention to one spot. They will realize that the camera actually interprets by what it emphasizes.

If at all possible, use the South African production in this lesson, for this scene is full of lush fabrics, beautiful voices, and wonderful acting.

At the time of this writing, the *Othello*-on-video situation looks like this:

· The 1992 South African production, directed by Janet Suzman and starring John Kani in the title role, is available from Films for the Humanities (1-800-257-5126). Because it is a film of a stage production, the camera doesn't get around much, but otherwise the film is excellent. (Kani's native language is not English; Suzman explains in an interesting introduction that you might want to show later that she wanted an actor who was clearly a "foreigner" to the world he inhabited.)

- The 1981 BBC: The Shakespeare Plays production is directed by Jonathan Miller, stars Anthony Hopkins as Othello, and is available from The Writing Company (1-800-421-4246). The film is useful, as it follows the text closely, but not great in itself. The choice of a white actor in itself raises questions worth discussing. (The British actors' union barred James Earl Jones from playing Othello, but Miller didn't want a black actor anyway.)
- The print of the 1952 Mogador Films/Mercury Productions of Orson Welles's black-and-white film has recently been restored and is now available on videotape from The Writing Company (1-800-421-4246). Welles directed, played the lead, and had a tendency to rearrange the order of the scenes. It was filmed in Venice and Morocco and is worth watching.
- The 1985 Bard Productions version stars an African-American actor, William Marshall, and can be ordered from The Writing Company (1-800-421-4246).
- A videotaped version of the superb 1989 Royal Shakespeare Company production starring Willard White as Othello and Ian McKellen as Iago is at this writing available only in the United Kingdom and in a video format incompatible with American VCRs. When it *does* become available, get it. It's terrific. The setting is a World War I army camp.
- There is no video version of BHE Productions' 1965 film of *Othello* starring Laurence Olivier in black makeup and the young Maggie Smith as Desdemona. There is a filmstrip available from The Writing Company (1-800-421-4246), and the film itself is occasionally shown on cable television.

WHAT TO DO

1. Dramaturges' Reports

Have student dramaturges report on Venice and Cyprus. Adhere to the five-minute time limit.

2. 1.3.1–55

You can save time by summarizing this section for the students. The characters are now headed for Cyprus, a Venetian stronghold, and Othello has been sent for in order to lead the Venetian navy against the invading Turks.

3. Video

Show the video version of 1.3.1–342, through the exit of all but Iago and Roderigo. This takes about fifteen minutes.

Ask students to take a few notes as they watch, to jot down any questions they have about what's going on or observations about differences between what they expected the characters to look like and the actors they see playing the roles. If there is time, you can start the discussion scheduled for Lesson 7 at this point.

4. Homework

Remind students to make their log entries and to read 1.3.55–342.

HOW DID IT GO?   If the students asked engaging questions after the dramaturges' reports and if their comments and questions indicated that they paid active, critical attention to the video, you're on your way.

LESSON 7 **"And I Loved Her That She Did Pity Them"**

Discussing the Senate Scene

ॐ _____

PLAY SECTION COVERED IN THIS LESSON

1.3.1–342 Before the Senate, Othello defends himself against Brabantio's charge of witchcraft. The duke orders Othello to Cyprus to battle the invading Turks, and allows Desdemona to accompany him.

LINES: Duke, 73; First Senator, 28; Second Senator, 5; Sailor, 4; Officer, 2; Messenger, 10; Brabantio, 65; Othello, 126; Desdemona, 29

ॐ _____

WHAT'S ON FOR TODAY AND WHY

The discussion of the Senate scene as seen on yesterday's video will give students a chance to clear up any questions they may have and to explore the ways in which text is translated into performance on film.

A choral reading of Othello's great speech describing his courtship of Desdemona will give everyone a chance to taste these marvelous and justly famous lines. Reading chorally is an excellent way for students to feel, collectively, the power and music of this passage—or of any other great poetry. For those timid about acting, it's a great way for them to immerse themselves, risk-free, in Shakespeare's language.

The brief exercise on "ringing the changes"—asking several different people, in succession, to say the same line, such as Othello's "That I have ta'en away this old man's daughter / It is most true," and making an effort to give it different intonations—will show students how different intonation and delivery of the same line can change its meaning.

WHAT TO DO

1. Discussing the Senate Scene

Ask students to recall the video clip, consult the notes they took about it, then ask questions and suggest answers. Here are some questions to throw in with the students' own:

• To what extent did the actors look like, or sound like, the characters you had imagined? Who would you have cast differently?

• What impression have you of Desdemona? Why?

- Judging only from what you saw and heard in this scene, how do Desdemona and Othello feel about each other? How do you know?
- If you were a director, where would you place Iago in the section of the scene that follows his reentrance with Desdemona? Why?
- If you were the director, is there anything you would ask the actors to do differently?

2. Choral Reading

Othello's great speech beginning "Her father loved me, oft invited me" (1.3.149–96) tells the story of Othello and Desdemona's initial attraction and the dawn of their love. (If students can hold these words in the backs of their minds, they may be able to measure the distance the "noble Moor" falls in the last two acts of the play, a fall reflected in his language as well as his actions.)

Divide the class into two groups, standing and facing each other. Ask the groups to read antiphonally, each group reading to a period, colon, or semicolon, as in the acting circle, only in chorus. This will make clear the rhythm and the variation of the number of lines between stops; both Othello's fourteen-line sentence describing his travels and his half-line "Upon this hint I spoke" benefit from the contrast in length.

Read again. Ask a "silent movie" acting company of three people to mime, during the choral reading, the courtship of Othello and Desdemona in Brabantio's house.

3. Parting Shot

Ask someone to put into his own words Brabantio's parting shot, "Look to her, Moor, if thou hast eyes to see. She has deceived her father, and may thee" (1.3.333–34).

4. Ring the Changes

Have several students say the above lines in turn, each trying for a different intonation. (The repetition may enable them to hear the echo of Brabantio's exit line later in the play, when the words may be having a delayed reaction on Othello himself.) Ask students to be on the lookout for words and images to do with eyes and sight—both literal sight and sight as a metaphor for understanding.

5. Homework

Remind the dramaturgy teams researching Moors and Turks that they will report tomorrow. In addition to their regular log entry, ask students to reread 1.3.55–342 and to answer this additional question in their logs:

- Desdemona makes her first appearance in this scene. What is your impression of her personality? Quote a couple of lines to support your opinion. If you were a director, what actor, or what sort of actor, would you cast in the part? Find a magazine picture corresponding to your idea of Desdemona, or draw your own.

HOW DID IT GO?   Students' questions and comments about the video scene will indicate their involvement, their deepening awareness of the importance of staging in interpreting Shakespeare, and their appreciation of the freedom directors have. If everyone participated in the choral reading and they were able to read together with a sense of the passage's rhythm, they are developing a fluency in reading Shakespeare's language.

LESSON 8 "But Words Are Words"

Searching the Text for Words and Images

The oral presentations on Moors and Turks will give students a background for the geographical, cultural, and historical allusions of *Othello* and help the students understand both Othello's importance as a military leader against an enemy of Venice *and* his status as outsider to Venetian society, despite his Christianity.

To appreciate the richness and complexity of *Othello*'s verbal structure, students will start to track recurrences of particular words and images of thematic significance.

WHAT TO DO

1. Log Sharing

Discuss differences in opinion about Desdemona. Ask students to specify on what lines they base their opinions.

2. Dramaturges' Reports

Student dramaturges report on Moors and Turks. Look at a map of the Mediterranean circa 1600. Have students point out Venice, Cyprus, Rhodes, the Ottoman Empire, and the coast of North Africa, and link them to the situation described in 1.3.1–55.

Discuss what may have accounted for Elizabethan dislike of foreigners, and, possibly, what causes natives of a country to regard foreigners as a threat.

Students should feel free to ask questions following the presentations.

3. Word Search

Write on the board a list of words that appear frequently in *Othello*. Add to or subtract from the list below as you see fit.

soul	honest, honesty
heaven, heavenly	whore, strumpet
hell	love
damn(ed), damnation	monster
faith	hate
Moor	devil
handkerchief	jealous, jealousy

Assign two or three students to each word, asking them to note in their logs the line in which the word appears, line number, and who says it. Ask them to notice who uses the word—or group of words—most and to pay attention to *how* various characters use it. Ask them to record *anything* they notice.

Let students have some class time today to begin their word searches. Have them review the play through 1.3.342 to look for their words, and guide them to careful citation and thorough notes. Explain that at the end of their search they will be asked to come to some conclusions about the cumulative effect of their word and what theme its repetition develops.

For an excellent model of this kind of scholarship, read the discussion of "black" and "white" in Doris Adler's essay "No Cloven Hooves" on page 33.

4. Tools of the Trade

This could be a good time to introduce students to Shakespeare concordances. The best is the *Harvard Concordance to Shakespeare* by Martin Spivak. Concordances provide, for each word, sublists of the plays in which it appears, giving act, scene, and line.

The *Oxford English Dictionary*—often called the OED—is important in gaining an understanding of a word's denotations and connotations. It supplies a history of every word in the English language and supplies examples of different uses of it through time, starting from the year the word first appeared in print. Your students can use as complete an edition as your school can afford.

You may also want to direct them to the *Shakespeare Lexicon and Quotation Dictionary* by Alexander Schmitt, a two-volume set recommended by Stephen Booth as the best "Shakespeare dictionary."

If you or your school is lucky enough to have a software program to turn to for help in searching words and phrases, use it. Whichever tools you choose, give students a few minutes to become familiar with them. Then let students know when and where these tools will be available throughout the remainder of this unit.

5. Homework

Ask students to bring their word searches up to date through 1.3.342.

HOW DID IT GO? Were the dramaturges well prepared? Did members of the class respond to the presentations with questions and comments? Were students intrigued by the prospect of the word search, and did they enjoy the class time spent on it? If so, look forward to the dramatic, culminating activity in Lesson 24.

LESSON 9 "Put Money in Thy Purse"

Introduction to Close Reading, and Iago's Bestiary

ฆ _____

PLAY SECTION COVERED IN THIS LESSON

1.3.343–447 Iago persuades Roderigo to sell his lands and come to Cyprus to pursue Desdemona. In soliloquy, Iago starts to plot against Othello and Cassio.

LINES: Roderigo, 16; Iago, 89

ฆ _____

WHAT'S ON FOR TODAY AND WHY

Now that students are more experienced with the language of *Othello*, they will read in small groups and discuss in great detail a limited portion of text, deliberately trying to wring as much meaning out of it as possible. The point is to look carefully at the language for answers, not to indulge in wild flights of fancy.

For the homework assignment, students will paraphrase a speech of Iago's into their own everyday language. Mary Poole calls this exercise the "Bawdy Method" because she likes to give students license to be exhilaratingly wicked with the language, which Iago is, of course. Do this, if you can. If you cannot, ask them to avoid obscenity but to come up with pungent, contemporary expressions that are modern equivalents of Iago's.

WHAT TO DO

1. Close Reading in Groups

Organize the class into small groups and ask students to read together 1.3.343–447, discussing and answering the questions in Handout 5: "Questions for Close Reading 1.3.343–447."

Circulate and act as a consultant when needed, but for the most part let students come to their own conclusions.

2. Iago's Bestiary

Distribute Handout 6: "Iago's Bestiary." During close-reading time, have students write down the animals/birds/insects Iago names, and, beside them, what they are referred to as *doing*. Students will come up pretty quickly with references to unpleasant, painful actions, and to allusions to trapping and hunting.

Students will keep this handout and continue to make entries as they notice more of Iago's beasts later in the play. When they finish, they are to paste it into their logs. They will want to refer to it in Lesson 20 when they are asked to compare Othello's once-noble language to Iago's bestial speech.

3. Homework

Ask students to reread the final section of 1.3 (343–447), concentrating on Iago's soliloquy, starting at line 426, "Thus do I ever make my fool my purse."

Ask them to write a loose paraphrase of this speech in their logs. Tell them to *be* Iago, to use first person, as in the play, but this time put Iago's words into natural, colloquial, modern speech as if they were saying them themselves. Ask them to avoid limp, wimpy phrases and hackneyed four-letter words. You are the best judge of which words are allowed in your classroom. In any case, encourage *imaginative* language.

HOW DID IT GO? Were the small groups able to handle the close-reading exercise, or did they get bogged down? Did it help them see how much you can find in even a small passage from Shakespeare?

∂

HANDOUT 5

QUESTIONS FOR CLOSE READING OF 1.3.343–447

Answer these questions about *Othello* 1.3.343–447. Use the notes to help you.

347–52   What is Roderigo threatening to do, and why?

351–52   What unusual metaphor does Roderigo use here?

353–54   How old is Iago?

357   Start listing on Handout 6: "Iago's Bestiary" the animals and birds Iago mentions in this scene, and watch for other animals he mentions throughout.

361–75   Try to paraphrase the essence of this long, difficult passage. What evidence is there that Iago sees himself as in control of his life? How does he regard love?

379–80   Comment on Iago's "I have professed me thy friend . . ."

382   "Put money in thy purse" is a figurative expression meaning "You can count on it." What literal meaning has it in this context?

377–400   List the reasons Iago gives Roderigo for believing that the love of Othello and Desdemona cannot last.

411   Iago uses the word "cuckold" for the first time. If you're not familiar with this word, look it up. It's crucial. Watch for it, and for references to cuckolds like "a horned man." Traditionally, the cuckold is represented as having horns. In Italian, the word *cornuto* (horned one) means cuckold, and the term is still one of contempt.

411–12   Paraphrase "If thou canst cuckold him, thou dost thyself a pleasure, me a sport." What are the connotations of the word "sport"—what does his use of it here reveal about Iago's personality?

426   Paraphrase "Thus do I ever make my fool my purse."

427–29   What are the two motives Iago gives here for hanging out with Roderigo?

429–31   Iago gives a new reason here for hating Othello. What is it? Do you remember what the first reason was and when Iago stated it?

431–33   How does he qualify this new reason in these lines?

435   How long would you pause, as an actor, before and after saying "Cassio's a proper man." Be sure to look at the textual note explaining this use of the word "proper."

436–37   What are Iago's stated objectives?

438–39   What plan does Iago arrive at here?

440–41   Why will Othello believe that his wife is betraying him with Cassio?

442–45   Why will Othello believe what Iago tells him? See also lines 433–34.

446   Iago uses the words "hell," "night," and "light" here. Watch for the repetition of these words and words associated with them throughout the play.

❧

HANDOUT 6

IAGO'S BESTIARY

Review 1.3.343–447. Look for animals, birds, insects, and creatures that Iago mentions. List them in the chart below and note what they are doing.

ACT, SCENE, LINE	ANIMALS, BIRDS, INSECTS, OTHER CREATURES MENTIONED BY IAGO	WHAT ARE THEY DOING?
1.1.78	flies	plaguing people—like Brabantio

❧

LESSON 10 "With Foul and Violent Tempest"

Play vs. Opera

ટ**ે**

PLAY SECTION COVERED IN THIS LESSON

2.1 The Turkish fleet is destroyed in a storm. The three Venetian ships arrive safely: first Cassio's, then Iago's (with Desdemona and Emilia), then Othello's. Iago enlists Roderigo's aid in his plot against Cassio.

LINES: Montano, 21; First Gentleman, 3; Second Gentleman, 15; Third Gentleman, 17; Cassio, 54; Messenger, 2; Desdemona, 31; Iago, 150; Emilia, 3; Othello, 30; Roderigo, 8

ટ**ે**

WHAT'S ON FOR TODAY AND WHY

Students will see a clip from Zeffirelli's film of Verdi's opera *Otello*, starring Placido Domingo. The images are more lushly visual than any of the available videos of Shakespeare's play. Furthermore, seeing a piece of the story in a different medium is stimulating and thought-provoking.

Many video stores have *Otello* in stock. It is also available for rent or purchase from Facets Video (1-800-331-6197).

To prepare for tomorrow's discussion, you might want to read Allan Kernan's introduction to the Signet edition of *Othello*, which contains an excellent analysis of the contrast between the civilized city and the outpost in enemy territory.

WHAT TO DO

1. Log Sharing

Ask volunteers to read the free paraphrases of Iago's soliloquy from their logs. Discuss Iago's stated reasons for wishing to destroy Othello and Cassio. How does each of these reasons affect the way he behaves? Would you call these reasons adequate "motives"?

Have students review their log entries for Act 1 and voice what they think are the most important issues. Agree on two or three and write them on the board. Then ask students to state the opinions each of these characters has about each issue: Desdemona, Brabantio, Othello, Iago, the Duke, Cassio.

2. Iago's Bestiary

Ask for volunteers to describe the animals they found and how these animals were behaving.

3. Verdi's Version

Show the opening scene of Verdi's *Otello*. The opera includes none of the events of Act 1 and starts with the point in Act 2 when the storm has scattered the Turkish fleet and Othello's ship is sighted. (From the opening bars to the meeting of Desdemona and Othello is only five or six minutes.)

Discuss how eliminating the action of Act 1 might affect audience reactions to the story. What dimensions did the glimpses of the world of Venice in the play provide that the opera doesn't? Talk about the differences between Venice and Cyprus. Clarify. Who traveled with whom?

4. Homework

Ask students to read 2.1.182–233.

HOW DID IT GO?

If students produced paraphrases of Iago's soliloquy that derived pretty well from the original, and if the opera clip provoked pointed discussion, the class went well.

LESSON 11 "The Riches of the Ship Is Come on Shore"

Actors' Objectives

PLAY SECTIONS COVERED IN THIS LESSON

2.1.1–181 The Turkish fleet is destroyed in a storm. Cassio, Desdemona, Emilia, and Iago arrive on Cyprus. Desdemona, waiting anxiously for Othello, "beguiles the time" by exchanging banter with Iago.

LINES: Cassio, 52; Desdemona, 26; Iago, 42; Emilia, 3; Montano, 21; First Gentleman, 3; Second Gentleman, 15; Third Gentleman, 17; Messenger, 2

2.1.182–233 Iago reacts in an aside to the conversation between Desdemona and Cassio. Othello arrives triumphantly in Cyprus. He and Desdemona greet each other with joy and relief while Iago looks on cynically.

LINES: Iago, 15; Cassio, 2; Desdemona, 5; Othello, 30

WHAT'S ON FOR TODAY AND WHY

Role-playing a scene in contemporary terms will open up some of the hidden dynamics between Desdemona's arrival and Othello's, and introduce students to the concept of subtext before they meet it by name.

WHAT TO DO

1. Acting 2.1.1–181

Michael Tolaydo gives you a sure-fire way to get this scene on its feet. (See "Up on Your Feet with Shakespeare," page 41.)

2. Defining Actors' Objectives

Explain the meaning given to the term "objective" by actors and directors. A character's objective is what he or she is after in that scene—the goal. If he doesn't reach it one way, he will try another. After each attempt, there is a "beat change," a shifting of gears. When the character achieves his objective, there is a beat change, after which he has a new objective. A character's "superobjective" is what he means to have by the end of the play.

In bold and simple terms, have students state Iago's superobjective. Do the same for Othello, Desdemona, and Cassio. Then let students determine each of these character's objectives for 2.1.182–233, the scene they read for homework.

3. Read-Through and Role-Play

Beginning with the stage directions after 2.1.181 ("Cassio takes Desdemona's hand"), ask four students to remain in their seats and read Iago, Cassio, Desdemona, and Othello through 2.1.233 ("Once more, well met at Cyprus"). Then ask four other students to role-play the situation on their feet, using contemporary language. Each actor should have in mind an objective. (Cassio and Desdemona engage in innocent flirtatious conversation, Iago comments on its implications, Othello arrives, Desdemona greets him, and they express their love.) Ask the actors to figure out their own objectives and to explain them to the class.

4. Instant Performance

Ask four different students to get up and read 2.1.182–233 on their feet. Ask a fifth student to be Emilia, who has no lines but is a presence in this scene.

The entire class will be paying close attention to the text so they can advise the actors about objectives and movement.

5. Spotlighting Lines

Ask several people to paraphrase Iago's aside beginning "He takes her by the palm," 2.1.182.

Ask several others to read Iago's lines 2.1.218–20 ("O, you are well tuned now, / But I'll set down the pegs that make this music, / As honest as I am"), ringing the changes as they did in Lesson 7 with Brabantio's curse.

6. Homework

In addition to their ongoing log entries, ask students to

· Pick any short scene in the play so far and imagine you are playing one of the roles. Figure out your character's objective for that scene, and for the play as a whole. Note the scene, write down the objective(s), and tell what the character says that tips off the objective.

HOW DID IT GO?

If those who role-played cooperated to invent contemporary situations that enhanced everyone's understanding of the motivations of Iago, Cassio, Desdemona, and Othello, the understanding of the play continues to grow. If through in-class performance students seemed to grasp the concept of determining objectives, then they are furthering their knowledge about how an actor communicates a character's motives.

18TH-CENTURY ENGRAVING FROM THE FOLGER SHAKESPEARE LIBRARY COLLECTION

LESSON 12   "Knavery's Plain Face"

Iago's Many Voices

⁚

PLAY SECTIONS COVERED IN THIS LESSON

2.1.234–307 Iago convinces Roderigo that Desdemona is in love with Cassio and enlists his aid in causing Cassio's dismissal from his post as Othello's lieutenant.

LINES: Iago, 66; Roderigo, 8

2.1.308–34 Iago fine-tunes his plot against Othello.

LINES: Iago, 27

⁚

WHAT'S ON FOR TODAY AND WHY

To make the speeches easier to manage, and to dramatize the extent to which Roderigo is no match for Iago, students will break down the speeches of 2.1.234–307 in a round-robin reading. By this method they will see that Iago's mind moves at least three times the speed of Roderigo's.

To hear the process by which Iago reasons, students will read Iago's soliloquy in two voices, alternating sentences.

WHAT TO DO

1. Round-Robin Reading

Ask four people to do a reading of 2.1.234–307, the conversation between Iago and Roderigo. One person should be Roderigo and *three* should take turns reading Iago "round-robin," each person reading a sentence.

2. Discussion

Ask: Roderigo is at first astonished when Iago tells him that Desdemona is in love with Cassio. How does Iago convince him?

3. Split the Soliloquy

Ask two people to read aloud Iago's soliloquy, 2.1.308–34 to the end of the scene, alternating sentences.

4. Discussion

Ask: What does Iago mean when he says of Desdemona "Now, I do love her too"? Do you believe Iago when he says, "I fear Cassio with my nightcap too"? Has anyone noticed particular lines in 2.1 that add to, or change, the impression given so far of any character's personality?

Ask students to compare Iago's soliloquy here with his soliloquy at the end of 1.3. Ask if they think Iago's motive has changed in any way from the first to the second soliloquy. (In the first soliloquy, Iago gives sexual jealousy as a motive—"'twixt my sheets / 'Has done my office"— but his main motive is "to get his [Cassio's] place." In the second soliloquy, the motive is plain sexual jealousy, and Iago is plotting "to diet my revenge.")

Coleridge referred to Iago's "motiveless malignity." Do you agree that Iago's "malignity" is fundamentally without motive?

5. Homework—"Catch Iago in a Lie"

Ask students to look over Act 1 and 2.1 and find lines where they think Iago is telling a lie. Have them write these lines in their logs.

Remind students to continue their regular log assignment. Then for extra credit, students can paraphrase Iago's speech starting at 2.1.242 using the method described in Lesson 9.

HOW DID IT GO?   Did the round-robin and two-voice readings help students to understand Iago's speeches? Were students lively in discussion? Engaged—and unfazed—by the questions?

LESSON 13 "With as Little a Web as This . . ."

Introduction to Blocking

PLAY SECTIONS COVERED IN THIS LESSON

2.2 A herald announces that tonight is to be the celebration of both the Venetian victory and of Othello and Desdemona's wedding.

LINES: Herald, 12

2.3.1–39 Othello puts Cassio in charge of the watch and retires for the night with Desdemona. Iago tells Cassio they must first party and tries to persuade him to start drinking.

LINES: Othello, 10; Cassio, 14; Iago, 15

WHAT'S ON FOR TODAY AND WHY

Movement alone can be a powerful interpretive element. "Blocking" is what a director does when he or she decides on each character's physical movement during a scene. The way a director decides to block a scene conveys meaning that can either reinforce or contradict the spoken word. This lesson and demonstration will prepare the class to act the Drinking Scene with increased understanding.

Performing 2.3.1–284 should strengthen the students' interpretive skills and deepen their understanding of Iago's diabolical cleverness, his motives, and his ability to manipulate others.

WHAT TO DO

1. Log Sharing

Call for volunteers to contribute examples of Iago's lies or half-truths.

Ask a student to list Iago's lies on the board as they are mentioned. (The class will probably note that Iago rarely tells outright lies about facts in which he might be caught. He says some things that may or may not be true, about which we have neither contradiction nor verification in what others say or do.)

2. *Othello*'s Shortest Scene

Ask someone to read 2.2, the Herald's speech.

3. Blocking: Introduction

Draw on the board a simple stage diagram like this:

audience

Or, to get the idea across in three dimensions, use a shoebox on its side to represent a stage and different colored buttons for characters moving stage right and stage left.

4. Blocking 2.3.1–39

Ask four to ten volunteers (Cassio, Othello, Desdemona, Iago, and a reasonable number of attendants) to come forward to the acting space in your classroom and prepare to move as silent actors. Ask four more students to read the lines aloud, staying seated. Ask the rest of the class to direct the movements of the silent actors. The stage directions indicate when Othello and Desdemona enter and exit, and when Iago enters, but the class must decide *how* they enter, how many attendants enter, where they stand, whether all or only some exit with Othello, where they stand in relation to each other, and so on.

Your students will have plenty of ideas. If they need encouragement, however, you might want to ask questions such as:

- Does Cassio bow to Othello, or salute, after he is told to look to the watch?
- How do Othello and Desdemona indicate their feelings about each other as they enter and as they exit? Do they stand next to each other as Othello gives Cassio his orders?
- Does Iago bow or salute as he enters?
- How does Iago physicalize the lewd hints he makes about Desdemona?
- How do Cassio's body language and facial expression reinforce his spoken reaction to these hints? If some attendants are still onstage, do they react facially?
- Where is the wine? How does Iago get his cup of wine? Does he pour one for Cassio?

5. Performing 2.3.40–284

Break the class into three acting companies and ask each to prepare to perform 2.3.40–284 (through Cassio's "My reputation, Iago, my reputation").

Have each company appoint a director and decide on who plays what. Ask them to *cut* enough lines to allow the scene to be performed in ten minutes. Let them at it. If they need assistance or encouragement, make a transparency of 2.3.1–48, put it on the overhead projector, and cut it together. Be aggressive. Make plenty of cuts, but keep the essential purpose of the text intact.

Once the scene is cut and groups begin working together, encourage them to use the costume and prop box. The director for each group should be prepared to explain the blocking plan.

Students will probably have fun setting Shakespeare's words to familiar music *or* inventing a song.

Give the companies the rest of the period to prepare.

6. Homework

In addition to their regular log assignment, ask students to answer this question: Can you recall a time when you felt unreasonable hatred for someone? How did you handle these feelings? What reasons did you give yourself for this hatred?

HOW DID IT GO?

If students are *interested* in Iago, if they are able to produce evidence from the text to support their opinions about him, and if they have worked enthusiastically in their companies, the lesson has gone well.

LESSON 14 "Unhappy Brains for Drinking"

The Drinking Scene

❧

PLAY SECTION COVERED IN THIS LESSON

2.3.40–284 Iago gets Cassio drunk, then uses Roderigo to begin a brawl, in which Cassio wounds Montano.

LINES: Othello, 49; Cassio, 43; Iago, 115; Montano, 35; Desdemona, 1; Roderigo, 1; Gentlemen, 1

❧

WHAT'S ON FOR TODAY AND WHY

Comparing the three acting companies' versions of 2.3 will enlarge students' awareness of the different ways this scene might be done.

If possible, arrange to hold today's class in some *large space* like the cafeteria or gym, or outside, in order to have plenty of room.

WHAT TO DO

1. Triple-Threat Performance

Enjoy each of the three acting performances.

2. Discussion

After the performances, let students point out to each other differences in cuts, characterization, pace, and emphasis. Highlight these lines for student response:

- 2.3.34–35 and 2.3.40–43. Cassio knows that he has "very poor and unhappy brains for drinking." What methods does Iago use to tempt Cassio into drinking more than Cassio himself knows he can handle? How does Cassio behave when drunk?
- 2.3.172 and following. What sides of Othello's personality do we see when he comes in to stop the brawl? How did you communicate these?

3. Homework

Ask students to make a log entry.

HOW DID IT GO?

Did each of the three groups prepare the scene thoughtfully? Were they an attentive and involved audience for the other groups' scenes? Did they participate in the discussion following the presentations? Did they have fun carousing and singing a drinking song? If all of these things are happening, learning is too.

LESSON **15** "So Will I Turn Her Virtue into Pitch"

2.3 on Video
The Paraphrase Game

PLAY SECTIONS COVERED IN THIS LESSON

2.3.278–355 Iago advises Cassio to ask Desdemona to plead his case with Othello.

LINES: Iago, 43; Cassio, 35

2.3.356–410 Iago tells of his plan to bring down Cassio by suggesting to Othello that Desdemona is pleading for Cassio because he is her lover. He persuades Roderigo to remain in Cyprus and encourages him to be patient.

LINES: Iago, 48; Roderigo, 7

WHAT'S ON FOR TODAY AND WHY

Watching different video versions of the Cassio–Iago conversation in lines 2.3.278–355 allows students to compare approaches on film and helps them to develop a facility in critical viewing. The South African version, the Bard Productions, the BBC, and the Orson Welles videotapes are all quite different and provide interesting comparisons.

Paraphrasing one or both of Iago's soliloquies in a game format demonstrates that it's possible to have a good time untangling a tough passage.

WHAT TO DO

1. Comparative Video

Select two or more video productions and, before class, cue them up to the Cassio–Iago conversation, from Iago's "What, are you hurt, Lieutenant?" through Cassio's "Good night, honest Iago." The scene lasts only about five or six minutes.

Show the different versions of the scene. Ask the class to make brief notes on the differences they see. Ask one or two people to follow along in the text to see what lines have been cut.

2. Responses

Let the students tell you and each other the significant differences between the versions. If they need prompting, try these: How did the different Cassios act drunk? Act repentant? Which Iago seemed more diabolical? Why? What choices of blocking and gesture contributed to the interpretation? How did the choice of setting affect the performances?

3. Comparative Reading

Ask for two volunteers to read aloud Iago's two speeches: the first soliloquy (2.3.356–83), then his speech to Roderigo followed by another, shorter soliloquy (2.3.391–410).

4. The Paraphrase Game

With a lively, upbeat attitude, play the paraphrase game with one or both of Iago's soliloquies. You're the game-show host. Working through the speech in order and stopping at semicolon or period, question mark or exclamation point, call out a full thought line to each student in turn. Ask them to express their thoughts quickly in contemporary English. If one student hesitates or stumbles or blows the line, pass on to the next. This isn't really one-upmanship; it just keeps them on their toes.

Keep up the pace. Long pauses are out. Give laggards the *Jeopardy* countdown music or the "tick-tick-tick" signal. If a number of students can't paraphrase a line and one finally succeeds, use a corny quiz-show line like "Give this lady the refrigerator!"

5. Homework

Ask students to read 3.1. and 3.2, and 3.3.1–201.

Give them Handout 7: "In Other Words." Ask them to complete it and staple it into their logs.

HOW DID IT GO? Did the responses to watching different videos indicate that students had watched them critically? Have students moved beyond the basic what-happened-here stage to discussions of ideas and images and the connections between them? If the quiz-show paraphrases were fast-paced and lively, chances are that students have a good appreciation of Iago's deviltry and the language he uses to express it.

ॐ

HANDOUT 7

IN OTHER WORDS

Paraphrase the following passages from 2.3 and comment on them.

QUOTATION	WHAT IT SAYS IN YOUR OWN WORDS	COMMENTS
CASSIO: I have lost the immortal part of myself, and what remains is bestial. 2.3.282–83		
CASSIO: O God, that men should put an enemy in their mouths to steal away their brains! 2.3.308–10		
IAGO: She holds it a vice in her goodness not to do more than she is requested. 2.3.340–41		
IAGO: When devils will the blackest sins put on, / They do suggest at first with heavenly shows. 2.3.371–72		
IAGO: Thou know'st we work by wit and not by witchcraft. 2.3.393		
Line of your choice		

ॐ

LESSON **16** "The Green-eyed Monster"

Text and Subtext

PLAY SECTIONS COVERED IN THIS LESSON

3.1 and 3.2 Cassio follows Iago's advice and asks Emilia to arrange a meeting with Desdemona.

LINES: Cassio, 24; Clown, 16; Musician, 5; Iago, 6; Emilia, 14; Othello, 5; Gentlemen, 1

3.3.1–99 Desdemona's interview with Cassio is cut short by Othello's arrival. Desdemona pleads with Othello on Cassio's behalf.

LINES: Desdemona, 63; Emilia, 3; Cassio, 12; Othello, 16; Iago, 5

WHAT'S ON FOR TODAY AND WHY

In their performances so far, students have learned to untangle Shakespeare's language by paraphrasing, asking questions, and determining characters' objectives. They have learned to cut scenes and to add movement. Now they will add voice inflection and subtext, the unspoken meaning under words said aloud.

This is not the first time you have asked students to look for meaning beneath the surface of what is said, but today you will give them the tools of a more formal vocabulary. To prepare for the subtext exchange, write *The "Fred" Scene* on the board, or photocopy it.

WHAT TO DO

1. Reviewing 3.1 and 3.2

Elicit from students comments about their reading assignment and ask them to collaborate on a brief summary of 3.1 and 3.2.

2. Text and Subtext

Ask about the *real* meaning of a speech. What do we mean by the statement "It's not what you say; it's how you say it"? To illustrate, do this exercise, which derives from one developed by Paul Cartier, a member of the Teaching Shakespeare Institute who teaches in Providence, R.I.

Organize three or four pairs of students to do this simple conversational exchange. Ask them to decide on a subtext or "real meaning" for *The "Fred" Scene* and to convey that subtext by means of intonation, stress, pauses and body language like stance, gesture, and eye contact or eye avoidance.

The "Fred" Scene

A. I understand we have Fred to thank for this.
B. Yes, he did it all by himself.
A. It's really just like him.
B. I understand he's a friend of yours.
A. Oh, I wouldn't say that.

A few go-arounds will make clear that, depending on how the lines are said, the speakers might be, among other possibilities, grateful to Fred for giving a surprise party or furious at him for wrecking a car. Depending on the tone of voice used, listeners could assume Fred to be two years old, or twenty, or eighty. The speakers can be wryly anti-Fred or Fred fans, or affectionately amused by Fred's foibles.

3. Subtext in Action

Ask three or four more pairs to say the following lines from 3.3. Have two of these pairs say Iago's lines as though they were unfamiliar with the play and did not know he was a villain:

> IAGO
> Ha, I like not that.
> OTHELLO   What dost thou say?
> IAGO
> Nothing, my lord; or if—I know not what.
> OTHELLO
> Was not that Cassio parted from my wife?
> IAGO
> Cassio, my lord? No, sure, I cannot think it
> That he would steal away so guiltylike,
> Seeing your coming.
> OTHELLO   I do believe 'twas he.

4. Putting Subtext to Work in a Scene

Call for five volunteers to act 3.3.1–99. Give the rest of the class the role of director. Turn the process over to the students, who by now are familiar with the steps:

- Do a round-robin read-through.
- Use questions, discussion, and paraphrase to untangle problem lines.
- Cut lines.
- Add movement.
- Determine the objectives for Cassio, Desdemona, Emilia, Iago, and Othello.

· Isolate several lines (maybe "You do love my lord" or "Well, do your discretion") and practice inflections to match several subtexts.
· Run the scene.

5. The Handkerchief

In the scenes to come it is important to have a *real* handkerchief or scarf as a prop. Ask students to bring several handkerchiefs to class.

6. Objectives and Subtext for the Rest of 3.3

Explain to the class that they will do the rest of 3.3 in relay performances. Organize them into teams and explain that they will go through the steps demonstrated in 3.3.1–99. They will perform only one section of the scene then watch and listen to the rest; therefore, it is important that students convey the scene to the audience in a clear and powerful manner.

As they work out the subtext for the lines in their scenes, ask students to be aware of the techniques Iago uses to undermine Othello's trust in his wife, and to think about why many people call 3.3 "The Temptation Scene."

7. 3.3 Acting Assignments

Give students Handout 8: "The Temptation Scene in Relay." Make assignments. These are ten very short scenes; all except scene 6 are two-character scenes. This array of scenes gives twenty-one people speaking parts. If the class is larger than twenty-one, give some teams directors. Encourage students to cut enough lines so the pace of their scene is rapid.

Students will have the rest of this class day for rehearsal and the next day for performance.

8. Homework

Tell students to study their lines and deliver them out loud to a mirror. Teams of two could rehearse on the telephone.

HOW DID IT GO? Did everyone seem to grasp the point of the text/subtext exercise? Did they apply the concept to the demonstration scene? Was their presentation effective? Did the acting teams for 3.3 get down to work? Did they make progress?

è

HANDOUT 8

3.3—THE TEMPTATION SCENE IN RELAY

Here are 10 short scenes from Act 3. Your groups will prepare one scene and present it to the class. Go through the steps we reviewed in acting 3.1.1–99, with emphasis on voice inflection and subtext. To help you, note the summaries and directions that accompany each scene.

SCENE 1   **3.3.100–146** ("Excellent wretch!" through "I think so too"). Iago starts to poison Othello's mind.

LINES: Othello, 33; Iago, 14

SCENE 2   **3.3.147–200** ("Men should be what they seem" through "who dotes, yet doubts suspects, yet strongly loves!"). Iago goes further in his campaign to make Othello doubt Desdemona's fidelity.

LINES   Iago, 43; Othello, 11

DIRECTIONS: Cut some of Iago's and Othello's longer speeches.

SCENE 3   **3.3.201–49** ("O misery!" through "I am bound to thee forever"). Othello begins to believe Iago's hints.

LINES: Iago, 25; Othello, 24

DIRECTIONS: Aggressively cut Iago's long speeches.

SCENE 4   **3.3.250–82** ("I see this hath a little dashed your spirits" through "My lord, I take my leave"). Othello expresses belief in his wife's honesty, and Iago goes still further with his hints, subtly attacking Othello's sense of self-worth.

LINES: Iago, 25; Othello, 8

DIRECTIONS: In the speech beginning at line 268 (from "Ay, there's the point!") Iago suggests that Desdemona's choice of Othello is unnatural. What are the implications of this? How will the person playing Othello react nonverbally to Iago's lines?

SCENE 5   **3.3.283–320** ("Why did I marry?" through "I'll not believe it"). Othello expresses his doubts. Iago reenters and deepens them, exits again. Emilia and Desdemona enter as Othello is speaking.

LINES: Iago, 13; Othello, 25; Desdemona, 0; Emilia, 0

DIRECTIONS: Decide what fears Othello is expressing when he says "Haply, for I am black / And have not those soft parts of conversation / That chamberers have, or for I am declined / Into the vale of years—yet that's not much— / She's gone." How does Othello react to Desdemona's entrance?

SCENE 6 3.3.321–43 ("How now, my dear" through "I nothing but to please his fantasy"). Othello has begun to doubt Desdemona, and his behavior toward her has changed. Desdemona drops her handkerchief without realizing it, and Emilia picks it up, saying she will have the "work [of the handkerchief] ta'en out" and give it to Iago.

LINES: Desdemona, 10; Othello, 4; Emilia, 10

DIRECTIONS: Use one of the class handkerchiefs. Since what happens in this short scene sets in motion a series of events that results in catastrophe, this acting team should figure out carefully exactly how Othello rejects the handkerchief, how and why Desdemona lets it fall, and how Emilia reacts when she picks it up. Where does Emilia hold the handkerchief when she sees Iago coming?

SCENE 7 3.3.344–82 ("How now? What do you here alone?" through "which thou owedst yesterday"). Iago gets the handkerchief from Emilia and, after she exits, says he will plant it in Cassio's lodging.

LINES: Iago, 24; Emilia, 15

DIRECTIONS: Decide what motivates Emilia to offer Iago the handkerchief after all. (The decision belongs to the actor. Emilia's lines do not explain this.) What is her objective, and how will the actor playing Emilia make it clear? How will the actor playing Iago take the handkerchief from her? Or will Emilia hand it over? The stage directions are not Shakespeare's. You can invent your own.

SCENE 8 3.3.383–434 ("Ha, ha, false to me?" through "I'll love no friend, sith love breeds such offense"). Othello reenters and expresses increasing conviction that Desdemona is betraying him with Cassio.

LINES: Othello, 37; Iago, 15

DIRECTIONS: Speculate about why Othello insists to Iago, "Villain, be sure thou prove my love a whore! / Be sure of it. Give me the ocular proof." Consider the irony of his demand.

SCENE 9 3.3.435–90 ("Nay, stay. Thou shouldst be honest" through "I'll tear her all to pieces"). Becoming even bolder, Iago fabricates a story about how Cassio in his sleep revealed his affair with Desdemona.

LINES: Othello, 15; Iago, 41

DIRECTIONS: Think about the play on the word "honest," meaning both truthful and sexually faithful or chaste. Decide how to say that word.

SCENE 10   **3.3.491–546**   ("Nay, but be wise" through "I am your own forever"). Iago says he has seen the handkerchief in Cassio's hand. Othello's conviction that Desdemona has been unfaithful becomes firm. He and Iago pledge their fidelity to each other.

LINES: Iago, 23; Othello, 32

DIRECTIONS: Work out how to kneel and rise. What props will you use?

LESSON 17 "Ocular Proof"

The Temptation Scene in Relay

❧ _____

PLAY SECTION COVERED IN THIS LESSON

3.3.37–546 Iago, by degrees, gets Othello to believe Desdemona is unfaithful to him with Cassio.

LINES: Iago, 225; Othello, 209; Desdemona, 50; Emilia, 26

❧ _____

WHAT'S ON FOR TODAY AND WHY

Breaking the Temptation Scene into segments and discussing each before going on to the next enables the class to see more clearly the steps by which Iago leads Othello into doubt and frenzied jealousy.

WHAT TO DO

1. Hats and Handkerchief

For continuity, bring out the hats for the various characters to wear then pass off to the next. Use a class handkerchief so that we all follow the "ocular proof."

2. Relay Performances

Call for the performance of the ten short scenes. After each, let students hold a brief recap of what happened. Ask them to say what they think is the most important step taken in each section toward Othello's fall.

3. Discussion

Double time: From the landing in Cyprus, the whole story unfolds in one day and a half. The action is over by the end of the second night in Cyprus. How could Desdemona have "stolen hours of lust" with Cassio? They weren't even on the same ship! Do we, the audience, accept it as possible for her to have been unfaithful?

Ask: Has the use of this double time bothered you at any point? Or did you even notice it?

4. Homework

Remind dramaturges researching Ira Aldridge, Paul Robeson, and *Othello* stage history that they should be ready to give oral presentations during Lesson 18.

Ask students to get their bestiaries up to date.

HOW DID IT GO?

Whether they acted well or not, if the acting teams prepared their sections of the Temptation Scene intelligently and seemed to understand most of what they were saying, if the discussion suggested that students are excited by the play and looking forward to the next step, if nobody stole a glance at a clock or asked what time the period ended—the lesson went well.

LESSON 18 "The Moor Is Far More Fair Than Black"

The Politics of Casting

WHAT'S ON FOR
TODAY AND WHY

Presentations by the dramaturges on Ira Aldridge, Paul Robeson, and the stage history of *Othello* followed by discussion will raise issues that are very much alive today, in both the world of the theater and the "real" world.

WHAT TO DO

1. Listen

Hear the dramaturges' reports on these subjects.

2. Discuss

These reports will probably include the facts that productions of *Othello* have, historically, presented the Moor

- as a "tawny Moor," someone of Middle Eastern descent, wearing white robes; or
- as a "blackamoor," or Ethiopian, a person of African descent.

Ask: What differences in the effect of the play might result from each choice?

Who would be your choice for the role of Othello among the professional actors you know? How important is the actor's skin color? Ethnic origin?

Who would you choose for Iago? What about his skin color and ethnic origin?

3. Homework

Have all students read 3.4, skipping lines 1–22. Issue a casting call for nine volunteers to prepare to read lines, on their feet, the next day. Organize them, or let them organize themselves, into three acting companies for the following scenes. They can practice reading the lines aloud or just get up and do it the next day.

Company 1:3.4.23–115 ("Where should I lose that handkerchief" through Othello's exit). Othello asks Desdemona for the handkerchief and rebukes her when she cannot produce it.

LINES: Desdemona, 36; Emilia, 3; Othello, 54

Company 2:3.4.116–89 ("Is not this man jealous?" through the exit of Desdemona and Emilia). Cassio again asks Desdemona for help, and she explains that Othello does not seem himself. (Encourage them to cut the longer speeches of Cassio and Desdemona and to be able to provide reasons for the cuts.)

LINES: Emilia, 19; Desdemona, 38; Iago, 13; Cassio, 18

Company 3:3.4.190–231 ("Save you, friend Cassio!" to the end of the scene). After Desdemona's exit, Cassio says he has found a strange handkerchief in his lodging. When his lover, Bianca, appears, he asks her to copy the embroidery.

LINES: Bianca, 17; Cassio, 25

HOW DID IT GO?

Were the dramaturge presentations clear and thought-provoking? Was there a good discussion afterward? If so, then students' ideas of interpretation are expanding.

LESSON 19 "There's Magic in the Web"

Passing the Handkerchief

ಜ

PLAY SECTION COVERED IN THIS LESSON

3.4 Desdemona frets about her lost handkerchief. Cassio again asks her to plead his case to Othello, but she puts him off. Cassio, who has innocently found the handkerchief in his room, asks his lover, Bianca, to copy the embroidery work for him.

LINES: Desdemona, 81; Clown, 12; Emilia, 20; Othello, 53; Iago, 9; Cassio, 39; Bianca, 17

ಜ

WHAT'S ON FOR TODAY AND WHY

The emphasis today is on the handkerchief as a supposed "ocular proof" of Desdemona's infidelity, and on its larger symbolic value. To clarify the chain of possession, students will play "Pass the Handkerchief," a mime exercise.

The discussion of gender issues that follows is connected to this: strong reactions to certain well-publicized cases of sexual harassment or accusations of rape have demonstrated how difficult it can be for women to convince men (even some in the U. S. Senate) to accept their version of reality as truth when it comes to sexual matters.

WHAT TO DO

1. Lights Up

See the presentations the three acting companies prepared as homework.

2. Pass the Handkerchief

Find the handkerchief you used for the relay performances of 3.3.

Appoint a narrator to read the script below and ask the rest of the class to direct the volunteers in a demonstration of how this "trifle light as air" goes from person to person in *Othello*.

The Script

· **The handkerchief originally comes to Othello before the action of the play begins, from his mother—who had it either as a gift from an**

Egyptian or as a gift from Othello's father, depending on which account of Othello's you believe.

· Othello gives it to Desdemona, his first gift to her.
· Desdemona tries to bind Othello's head with it, and accidentally drops it.
· Emilia picks it up.
· Iago snatches it from Emilia . . .
· . . . then leaves it in the lodging of Cassio.
· Cassio finds it and gives it to Bianca to copy the embroidery on it.
· Bianca, thinking the handkerchief was given to Cassio by another woman, angrily gives it back to Cassio while Iago and Othello look on unseen.

Using the designated hats for Othello, Desdemona, Emilia, Iago, Cassio, and Bianca will make the passage of the handkerchief easier to follow.

If you have students who are talented in creative movement, add music to the mime and do it as a dance. If there are students who like to write poetry, ask them to accompany the mime with a chant or poem using key words repeated in the scene: "handkerchief," "beast," "monster," "devil," "fiend," "virtue."

3. Gender Issues, Round One

Discuss the ironies of Othello's belief that seeing the handkerchief in Cassio's hand is "ocular proof" of his wife's infidelity.

Ask: In what ways does her encounter with Othello in this scene distress Desdemona? What different ways might an actor play that distress? What explanations does she provide to account for his changed behavior? Why does she feel she must make excuses for him?

Ask the women in the class to comment on Emilia's statement about men: "They are all but stomachs, and we all but food; / They eat us hungerly, and when they are full / They belch us." Ask the men to respond to the women's comments.

Simply airing the issues of gender relations can be illuminating and lively for the class. The discussion will probably be passionate and lively. How you guide it depends on the class's response. Do they agree with Emilia? Do they find her too bitter? Do they find Desdemona too ready to make excuses for her husband? Or do they find Othello's anger natural, given that Desdemona keeps mentioning Cassio?

4. Homework

Ask students to read 4.1. Remind the dramaturges who researched epilepsy that the class will hear their report in the next lesson.

HOW DID IT GO?

Did the "Pass the Handkerchief" mime and discussion help students to see where the handkerchief went and how significant it became to Desdemona, Othello, Iago, and Cassio?

Did men as well as women participate in the discussion?

Do you see evidence that students are being drawn deeper into the tragic misunderstanding that is developing?

LESSON 20 "Is This the Noble Moor?"

Othello's Fall, in Body and in Language

PLAY SECTION COVERED IN THIS LESSON

4.1 Iago continues to inflame the jealousy of Othello, who has a seizure and falls unconscious. Iago converses with Cassio about Bianca, arranging for Othello to stand where he can see but not hear them; he assumes the subject of Cassio's ribaldry is Desdemona.

LINES: Othello, 108; Iago, 134; Cassio, 29; Bianca, 11; Lodovico, 25; Desdemona, 14

WHAT'S ON FOR TODAY AND WHY

The report on epilepsy and the discussion of Othello's breakdown will help students see the shape of the play, and help them understand how far Othello has fallen.

WHAT TO DO

1. Dramaturges' Report: Epilepsy

Hear the report on epilepsy—what it is, and what Elizabethans thought it was.

2. Discussion: Othello's Breakdown

Explore the developments in this scene by asking questions such as:

· What effect does Othello's fit have on an audience?
· How is Iago able to make Othello believe that Cassio is speaking of Desdemona in 4.1.126–63 (from Cassio's "Alas, poor Caitiff!" to Iago's "Before me, look where she comes")? What would you emphasize, as a director, when you rehearsed the actors?
· How, in this scene, does Shakespeare remind us how far we are from Venice and how much Othello has changed?
· Can you find examples to show how Othello's once noble and lofty language is sinking to Iago's bestial level? Refer to your handout on Iago's bestiary. Does Othello use the same kind of imagery in this scene? Can you find lines in Act 1 or 2 that show Othello's noble language and analyze the difference?

3. The Slap

In 4.1, an important man whom we have never seen hurt his wife before now strikes her in public. Ask students: Why does he do it? How do other people onstage react? How do you imagine Desdemona responding physically to the blow? Since she is innocent, why doesn't she defend herself? If you were in Desdemona's position, would you? If not, why not?

Locate the scene on a couple of the videos you have come to like the best and show it. Then continue the discussion.

You might remind the class that in recent years domestic violence is not as hushed up as it once was, and people have become more familiar with the battered-wife syndrome. Countless battered wives have reacted just like Desdemona. Is it part of the play's tragedy that she takes the abuse here—physical and verbal—without protesting publicly?

Some students may come from countries or cultures that consider it a man's prerogative to abuse his wife; hopefully their classmates will provide ardent counterpoint.

4. Homework

In addition to their ongoing log assignment, ask students to read 4.2 and 4.3. Ask two women to play the parts of Emilia and Desdemona in the Willow Scene (4.3.11–117) in the next lesson. It helps if the student playing Desdemona can sing, or at least isn't afraid to try. She can use any melody she likes. Ask them to study their lines and practice reading them aloud.

HOW DID IT GO?

To what degree do students care about Othello and Desdemona and the tragedy that is unfolding? To what degree can they use their minds and bodies and voices to express the tragedy?

LESSON 21 "O These Men, These Men!"

The Willow Scene

❧ _____

PLAY SECTIONS COVERED IN THIS SECTION

4.2.1–198 Othello accuses Desdemona of infidelity and calls her a whore. She turns to Iago for comfort.

LINES: Othello, 71; Desdemona, 66; Emilia, 47; Iago, 14

4.3.11–117 The Willow Scene. Emilia prepares Desdemona for bed, and the two exchange very different views on men and marriage.

LINES: Desdemona, 57; Emilia, 50

❧ _____

WHAT'S ON FOR TODAY AND WHY

Reading parts of 4.2 and 4.3 will carry students more vividly into Othello's irrational torment, and help students get to know Emilia, a wonderful, down-to-earth character who will have her shining moment in Act 5. Students can be moved by Desdemona's song of foreboding if the two students perform it seriously.

To continue to keep students attentive to the language of the play and not merely the action, for homework they will write a poem that includes a line of their own choosing from Act 4.

WHAT TO DO

1. Lights Up

Ask four students to read 4.2.1–198 on their feet and invite comments from the class when they finish. Ask one student to count how many times the word "whore" is used and to comment on that. Discuss the dramatic irony in Emilia's speech in 4.2.153–69 ("I will be hanged if some eternal villain" through "Even from the east to th' west").

2. The Willow Scene

Have the two women who prepared the Willow Scene perform it. (If you wish, let students hear the Willow Song from Verdi's opera *Otello*. It is movingly sung by Leontyne Price on CD—"Verdi's Heroines," RCA RCD1–7076.) Zeffirelli did not include this scene in his film.

3. Gender Issues, Round Two

Hold a free and lively discussion of Emilia's opinions of the male sex as expressed in her concluding speech. What are Desdemona's views? Connect this discussion as tightly as seems reasonable to the one in the preceding lesson. Which of Emilia's ideas are most relevant to the issues raised in Round One?

4. Homework

Tell students that using quotations from Shakespeare can be the inspiration for poetry. Ask them to choose any line from 4.2 or 4.3 and include it in a short poem, which they will write in their logs. The quoted line can appear any place in the poem, and the subject of the poem can, but need not, concern *Othello*. Most students will enjoy hunting for their own lines, but if any feel stuck, you can suggest a few good possibilities, like: "I understand a fury in your words," or "Where either I must live or bear no life," or "How foolish are our minds," or "The world's a huge thing."

HOW DID IT GO?

If students put their best effort into the performances, both watching them and acting in them, the lesson was successful. If nobody groaned about the poetry assignment, you got off really well.

LESSON **22** "Murder's Out of Tune"

Final Casting Call and the Director's Promptbook

❧ _____

PLAY SECTIONS COVERED IN THIS LESSON

5.1 Roderigo attacks Cassio, who stabs him. Iago wounds Cassio in the leg and kills Roderigo.

LINES: Iago, 82; Roderigo, 11; Cassio, 17; Othello, 10; Lodovico, 9; Gratiano, 10; Bianca, 7; Emilia, 5

5.2 Othello smothers Desdemona in bed. Emilia's cries bring Iago, Montano, Gratiano, Cassio, and Lodovico. Othello tries to kill Iago, who kills Emilia. Othello stabs himself. Iago is led away to be tortured.

LINES: Othello, 211; Desdemona, 43; Emilia, 88; Montano, 7; Gratiano, 16; Iago, 12; Lodovico, 43; Cassio, 14

❧ _____

WHAT'S ON FOR TODAY AND WHY

Instead of continuing to present and analyze scenes, the class, organized into a number of acting companies, will experience the rest of the play as actors, directors, or audience. This lesson will be devoted to setting up the companies, presenting the menu of scenes, previewing evaluation forms, and explaining the director's promptbook that each company must prepare.

These scenes are longer than those that students have done before. The instructions for performance are the same except that for this assignment students are encouraged to memorize their lines. Memorization is valuable; students who memorize Shakespeare's lines own a piece of text and are glad they do. If you prefer, you can give extra points for memorization, or require everyone to memorize at least ten (or fifteen, or twenty) of their lines. In any case, actors should be familiar enough with their lines to be able to move freely and look up more often than not.

Handout 9 suggests one way to break down Act 5 into three scenes with a total of eighteen to twenty speaking parts. If you need more, further divide the scenes or split parts, or add scenes from 4.2 and 4.3 to the program. You can speed up and simplify the explanation process by making photocopies of each company's scene.

WHAT TO DO

1. Companies and Casts

Explain to students that they will form themselves into acting companies and perform the remaining scenes of *Othello*. Give them Handout 9: "Acting Companies," which includes instructions and lists of the final three scenes. Let students have a few minutes to organize themselves into companies and choose a scene.

Everyone should be involved in the scene preparation in some way, and everyone should speak at least one line in the course of the performance.

If some or all of each scene is to be memorized, then a prompter for each company is vital. Prompting is just as valuable an experience as acting and requires just as much attention to the text.

2. Promptbooks

Go over all of Handout 9, but give special attention to instruction #8, promptbooks. Professional directors rely on promptbooks to organize and record their decisions about the production in process. Distribute Handout 10: "Director's Promptbook" and Handout 11: "Promptbook Page." Handout 11 is a reproduction of a page from the promptbook for the 1943 New York production of *Othello* starring Paul Robeson.

3. Evaluation Preview

Give students Handout 12: "Scene Evaluation." Let them know from the start how you will grade the acting-company presentations. Point out that these criteria *can* be evaluated objectively, and that acting talent is not one of them. Explain that to encourage teamwork, you will give everyone in an acting company the same grade. (You can, of course, decide to evaluate students individually if this seems like a good idea— as it might if some students in a company had exerted themselves while others goofed off. It's best to start out encouraging the group process, however.)

As a supplement to—or substitute for—your own evaluation, you can ask the members of each company to evaluate themselves and each other on such things as attendance at all scheduled rehearsals, memorizing lines by the agreed-upon date, positive attitude, teamwork, and fulfillment of specific responsibilities. (See *Shakespeare Set Free: Teaching Hamlet and* Henry IV, Part 1, p. 210, for a guide to this kind of self- and peer-evaluation.)

Make clear that this kind of performance evaluation is every bit as valid as a grade on a test or an essay, and that it will demonstrate the depth of their understanding of Shakespeare's text as well as something written. Don't let anyone in your school system talk you out of this, either. *The performance can stand alone as the culminating event of this unit.*

4. Getting Started

Let the acting companies have the remainder of the period to get started on their scenes.

5. Word Search

Remind students that their long-term word-search assignment will be due shortly after the performances in Lesson 26.

6. Homework

Tell students that from now until performance day their homework is to memorize lines and work on promptbooks. Encourage them to read through all of Act 5, not just their own scenes, before performance day.

HOW DID IT GO?

If everyone understands the ground rules of both the scene work and the promptbook, if students haven't squabbled over which acting company they want to be in and have organized themselves well enough to cast their scenes, if everybody is restless to keep going, the lesson has gone as well as can be expected.

FROM THE FOLGER SHAKESPEARE LIBRARY COLLECTION

❧

HANDOUT 9

ACTING COMPANIES

Here is a description of the final scenes in *Othello*. Look them over. Take note of the number of actors required. Join with your classmates and organize an acting company to present one of the scenes. Negotiate with me about who gets to do what scene. You can split long parts or combine short ones, but every student in your group should have a speaking part.

Acting Company 1
5.1 Under cover of darkness, Iago kills Roderigo but only wounds Cassio. There are many possibilities for nonspeaking roles, like litter bearers.
LINES: Iago, 82; Roderigo, 11; Cassio, 17; Gratiano, 10; Lodovico, 9; Bianca, 7; Emilia, 5; Othello, 10

Acting Company 2
5.2.1–203 (through Emilia's "Murder, murder!") Othello murders Desdemona; Emilia enters and discovers this.
LINES: Othello, 120; Desdemona, 43; Emilia, 40
Special warning for Acting Company 2: Professional actors are trained in stage-fight techniques so they can make a staged death or fight look dangerous and real when it is in fact a safe and carefully rehearsed exercise. The students playing Othello and Desdemona will have to figure out a very safe way to do the death. Desdemona can turn her face to the wall and Othello can hold a pillow gently against the back of her head. Then if Othello pretends to be pushing the pillow and Desdemona pretends to struggle, the death will seem real and be effective.

Acting Company 3
5.2.204–435 Montano, Gratiano, and Iago arrive. Emilia tells the truth about the handkerchief and Iago kills her. Othello, realizing his terrible error, kills himself.
LINES: Montano, 7; Emilia, 48; Gratiano, 16; Iago, 12; Othello, 91; Lodovico, 43; Cassio, 14

Instructions for Preparing Your Scene

You will be given three class days to complete this work and memorize your lines. Be productive. Be creative. But above all, be communicative. The rest of the class will rely on your production to know what happens in your scene.

1. Appoint a director or two and cast the scene. When you perform, each person in the company should have a chance to be on stage with at least one line.

2. Read through the scene aloud, at least once, preferably twice. Decide collectively on the cuts, and make the cuts right away. Your scene should not take longer than ten minutes to perform. Read the scene aloud after you've decided on the cuts, timing yourselves, and making necessary adjustments. *Allow extra time*—performing a scene takes more time than just reading it.

3. Talk about characters—what they want in this scene, how they talk and move. This is to be a more prepared and polished performance than the ones you have been doing all along. Give special attention to movement, and memorize your lines.

4. Plan costumes and props. These don't have to be fancy, but should show that you took the trouble to think about what would best convey the impression you are after.

5. Appoint a prompter and establish clear signals about how the prompting will be handled. If actors are not memorizing their lines, write the lines and cues on large note cards to glance at during performance.

6. Give your acting company a name.

7. If you like, plan extra touches like music, sets, programs.

8. Throughout this process, record your decisions in a director's promptbook, due the day the scene is presented. See Handout 10: "Director's Promptbook."

❧

HANDOUT 10

DIRECTOR'S PROMPTBOOK

Every member of your acting company should contribute to the promptbook project. Make sure it is clear who is responsible for what.

Directions for construction

1. Write an *introductory page* for the promptbook in which you explain your overall concept of the scene and how you plan to convey that concept or idea to an audience. In other words, as an acting company, what are you trying to show?

2. Photocopy or type out the scene you have been assigned. *Paste* the scene onto plain or loose-leaf paper that will go into a folder or binder. Leave plenty of margin space around the text in order to write in instructions for the actors.

3. You may *make cuts* in your scene by crossing out lines, but Shakespeare's words *must* appear in their original sequence without changes in their wording or sense. In the margin, explain briefly why you cut the scene as you did.

4. In the margin beside the text, make *production notes* about the way you want the scene to be played. Think about the meaning of and behind each character's words. Include information about tone of voice, gestures, facial expression, and where and how each character will move.

5. Decide how you want to stage the scene and then draw a *diagram of the stage set.* Make a *list of stage properties* for your scene.

6. Design *costumes* appropriate for your concept of the scene. Include a drawing or description of the costumes and a justification for selecting them. Whether you do the scene in modern dress or in another time period, explain your reasons.

7. If your scene needs *special lighting or music,* write a description of a plan for these design elements.

8. Make a *cover* and *table of contents* for your promptbook.

9. Each company's book will be given one letter grade, which each member gets. The books will be evaluated on the basis of completeness, effort, imagination, and accuracy.

❧

HANDOUT 11

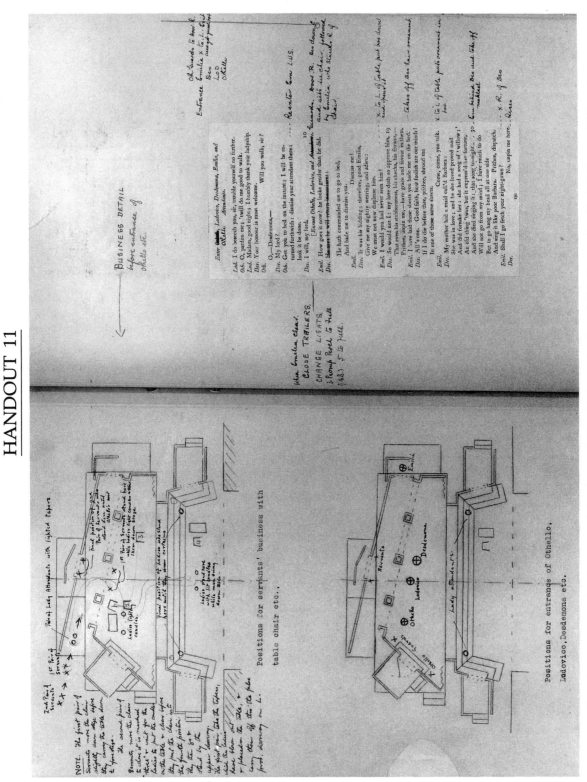

Page from a promptbook prepared for the 1943 New York production of *Othello* starring Paul Robeson. This and many other promptbooks are part of the Folger Shakespeare Library collection.

HANDOUT 12

ACTING COMPANY EVALUATION

ACTING COMPANY: _____

ACTORS: _____

Your performance will be evaluated as a whole, according to the following criteria. To encourage cooperation and collaborative effort, every member of the company will be given the same grade. *Process* is as important as *product*.

	Total Possible	Your Points
1. Memorization and preparation of lines on schedule	20	
2. Concentrated and focused work during rehearsals	10	
3. The imagination and responsibility applied to assembling or constructing your own costume and props	10	
4. Intelligent attention to the text in working out the blocking	10	
5. The clarity, understanding, and expression with which you deliver your lines	10	
6. Cooperation with each other during rehearsals	10	
7. Staying in character during performance	10	
8. Professional demeanor offstage as well as onstage	10	
9. The *energy* with which you perform	10	
10. Extras: bonus points will vary		
	100 TOTAL Possible	Your Points

LESSON 23 "One That Loved Not Wisely, but Too Well"

Acting Company Performances

WHAT'S ON FOR TODAY AND WHY

Students will perform the final scenes in *Othello* today. Encouraging the audience to ask questions of the cast members after each scene will keep everyone involved even when they are not performing.

WHAT TO DO

1. Performances

Be generous in your praise and encourage the audience to do likewise. Call each company in turn. After each scene, let the cast members answer questions from the audience.

2. Promptbooks

Ask all the companies to show their promptbook, and pass them around so each student gets a chance to see what the others have done. Collect them for evaluation.

HOW DID IT GO?

If all the cast members of all the acting companies showed up, if the companies made a sincere effort to produce staged and costumed performances that demonstrated a good understanding of the scenes and of their context in the play, if it was clear that everyone was enjoying Shakespeare—then you can applaud loudly, breathe a sigh of content, and congratulate everyone (yourself included!).

LESSON 24 "Soft You; A Word or Two before You Go"

Shakespeare as Word Opera

As the culminating activity of their word searches (begun in Lesson 8), students will direct performances, ending in tableaux vivants or living pictures that dramatize the words for which they have been responsible. Since they have been keeping a running list of quotations in which the word appears, they will need only ten minutes to prepare. The performances themselves will take two or three minutes apiece. (For a more detailed explanation of the tableau vivant technique, see *Shakespeare Set Free: Teaching* Romeo and Juliet, Macbeth, *and* A Midsummer Night's Dream, p. 163.)

The activity draws attention to the way in which Shakespeare uses words the way an operatic composer uses musical motifs that give an opera aesthetic coherence. Shakespeare used the repetition of a word to create a pattern of sound that has a cumulative effect on ear and mind. Such reiteration gives aural coherence to the play as a whole and suggests the word's thematic importance. It is no accident that words like "love," "Moor," "heaven," "souls," and "devil" are used so often in *Othello.*

The Word Opera, for a class that has studied the play, can serve as a kind of aural review of major motifs and themes. You can remind your students that Elizabethans spoke of going to *hear* a play, not going to see it.

WHAT TO DO

1. Word Opera: Rehearsal

Pass out Handout 13: "Shakespeare as Word Opera," which gives instructions on how to prepare for the word-opera performances. Each team directs a scene around its own word, selecting a line for each actor to say and dramatize. Let them prepare for ten or fifteen minutes.

2. Word Opera: Performance

Groups can decide on the order in which the words should be performed. Then sit back and enjoy the performances.

HOW DID IT GO?   If each student said a line with feeling and followed it up with an appropriate pose, and if the audience let out an "ahhh" of recognition when a tableau vivant was formed, then this has been a worthy follow-up to the performed scenes.

HANDOUT 13

SHAKESPEARE AS WORD OPERA

The point of this activity is to illustrate the way Shakespeare writes for the ear as well as for the mind and the eye. The repetition of a word gradually creates a pattern of sound that has cumulative dramatic effect.

Get together with others who have also been searching "your" word and do this:

1. Pool your lists of lines containing "your" word and choose four to six lines that you all particularly like. Write each of these lines on a separate file card.

2. Recruit enough actors from the class to form a performance company of four to six actors, including yourselves.

3. Give each person in your company one of the cards with a line on it. When it is your company's turn to perform, each actor will say his or her line aloud in succession. You decide the order in which the lines will be said. It is not necessary to preset them in the order in which they appear in the play.

4. When your company performs, each actor will step forward in turn, say his or her line, and then make a gesture or strike a pose that dramatizes in some way the word or the line. Each actor can either stay frozen until all have spoken, or do whatever else the group thinks is most effective.

5. Ideally, when each pose has been struck, the whole company will form a tableau vivant—a living picture—illustrating something about the key word or the effect of its repetition. You can say the word together chorally at the end if you think it makes a good finish.

NOTE: Embellish this performance in any way that seems appropriate. Put your imagination to work. You'll have ten minutes to practice.

LESSON 25   "Here Is My Journey's End"

Drawing Conclusions About the Play

WHAT'S ON FOR TODAY AND WHY

The following exercise, "Seven Statements about *Othello*," challenges students to think about the play as a whole, to consider some debatable opinions about the play, and to take a stand for what they believe to be right—always substantiating their views with close references to the text. It is exciting for students to feel that they know a work well enough to form their own critical opinions. The Seven Statements will lead to some lively classroom debate and, if you wish, form the basis for thoughtful essays.

WHAT TO DO

1. Discussion and Debate

Give students a copy of Handout 14: "Seven Statements about *Othello*," and elicit responses from the students in any way that seems best to you. If your class is small, let students choose whatever statement appeals to them, give them class time to ponder it and prepare a position. Then have each student present a case that will be challenged by the rest of the class. To save time, the handout could be distributed the day before, after the word operas.

Larger classes can be organized into small groups to debate among themselves while you move from group to group enjoying the exchange of views, asking loaded questions, and making sure that all arguments are based on what happens in the play.

(Note: Don't let Statement 1 propel you or your students into that old "tragic flaw" business. See Russ McDonald's "The Flaw in the Flaw" in *Shakespeare Set Free: Teaching* Romeo and Juliet, Macbeth, *and* A Midsummer Night's Dream, p. 8.)

2. Homework

As a final paper on *Othello*, have students either (a) choose one of the statements and write a short essay on it, or (b) write a paragraph each on three or four of the statements, explaining their reasons for agreeing or disagreeing with each and referring to *specific* incidents or scenes in the play to support their conclusions.

HOW DID IT GO?   The noise level in the classroom is a good indicator of the excitement this lesson should generate. Were they touched, excited, and moved by the play? Is the class sorry the Shakespeare unit is over?

HANDOUT 14

SEVEN STATEMENTS ABOUT *OTHELLO*

Below are seven statements about the play—opinions, not facts, that have been voiced by various critics of the play—some of which you will agree with, some not, though some are not as obvious as they may seem at first.

Be prepared to explain your reasons for agreeing or disagreeing with each and refer to *specific* incidents or scenes in the play to support your conclusions.

1. Othello's real problem is his own jealousy.

2. It is very important to the play for Othello to be black.

3. Desdemona is not a wimp. She is a soldier's wife and fit to be so. She has good sense, stubbornness, and courage. She can stand up to Othello for the sake of what she thinks right, even when he is in a dangerous mood and few people would care to face him.

4. Desdemona is not angelically pure. The potential for unrestrained desire must be in her character in order for the drama to work. The more loving she is, the easier it is for Othello to think she has deceived him.

5. Iago is not a "motiveless malignity" as he has been called—a devil who does evil for its own sake. He has a thirst for power and the wit to contrive a way to get it. Desdemona's death is a side effect he did not really intend.

6. Iago's cleverness is not total. He builds into the intricate structure of his plot a piece of terrible stupidity: he fails to understand his wife.

7. The war between Othello and Iago is fundamentally a dispute between the goodness and evil of the world.

Unfinished Business: An African-American Teacher Talks Race and *Othello*

/9j/...(ornament)

DONNA DENIZÉ
ST. ALBANS SCHOOL

I am a woman who has taught for sixteen years in a variety of secondary-school settings—public, private, urban, and rural—and served a three-year term on a state advisory board for all vocational schools in the state of Virginia. I feel it safe to say that I've participated in a representative cross section of our educational institutions; I have witnessed and debated issues of cultural and ethnic diversity as they impact on curriculum choices, teaching methods, and tracking of students. One question investigated in Virginia ten years ago was whether Shakespeare should be taught at all in public and vocational schools since, for many students of immigrant families, English was a second language; at that time, Northern Virginia alone had no fewer than ten different ethnic groups and languages spoken by its student population—Persian, Vietnamese, Spanish, Tagalog, to name only a few. In one public high school I visited, the school's morning announcements were made in six languages.

The common trait shared by all the schools I have worked in or observed is the issue of race or ethnicity—how it is negotiated in all areas of school life, but specifically in social relations, curriculum, and classroom approaches. As an African-American, I have been addressing these same issues in the classroom and out all of my life. I know that such issues require a great deal of skill, patience, understanding, and tactful action. I am cautious about making broad generalizations about matters of race and how they should be treated in America's classrooms. But when Peggy O'Brien asked me to write something about race in the teaching of *Othello,* I put aside my hesitations and decided to write from the personal voice, which is where we all confront this specter in our deepest notions of being.

The Baha'i faith describes racism not only as "the most challenging issue confronting America" but also, as modern science has proven, a "fiction" which devastates society. The term "race," unless it is used in its broadest sense, is a misnomer because we are one human race, not an aggregate of different species.

Racism is the most challenging issue confronting the American community and inevitably American classrooms, where plays like *Othello* provide teachers with a

215

unique opportunity to address constructively what students experience on a daily basis with incidents such as those involving Rodney King and Reginald Denny, and numerous other examples of racial and domestic violence. Our world has only recently seen the end to apartheid, and is still struggling with Haiti, Bosnia, Somalia, Iran, Iraq, and other nationalistic disputes. Race prejudice still bites into the fiber of human relations, wreaking havoc in domestic affairs, as well as in foreign relations. We are still driven by the myth of race. *Othello* provides us all with an occasion to address racism's physical, moral, and spiritual dangers. Whether or not your students are all White or all Black, you know and I know that our society is preoccupied with skin color, appearance, and image. As teachers, we also know the world provides numerous models of disunity, and that it is part of our job to help our students find a unifying vision of the nature of man and society.

Race relations, then, is a topic vitally tied to our identity, not only as individuals but also as society, community, and nation at large. It seems to me that when we approach race, the danger lies in *not talking*—not communicating in such a way that mutual understanding flows among all participants. Too often, in discussions of race, instead of people talking *with* one another, there is a vying for power—individuals struggle to make their points then leave before real thinking happens. So conversations about race often become occasions for talking *to* or *at* others while wearing "ear-muffs"—we can hear others, but we must keep our warmth inside and the outside cold to a minimum. Some incidents in my personal experience might relate better and more clearly how and why I believe that racism is the most challenging issue facing our society at large.

In my life as in many other lives, educational institutions have served to reinforce misconceptions about race and difference. On my first day as a college undergraduate—one of seventy African-Americans—I was asked by other freshmen at dinner, "What are you going to be when you graduate, a jungle bunny?" When I became resident dorm adviser, the jokes in the dorm were ongoing, always said within earshot, but rarely to my face. Finally, when I served on the school's discipline committee, the Dean of Students said to me, in the presence of a number of students and faculty on the school's committee, "You know, normally I hate niggers, but I like you." He then winked to show me that it was just a joke, at my expense. My four years were riddled with incidents of this kind, and since the "offenders" tended to be Irish and Catholic, I grew suspicious of anyone with an Irish name. In addition, the volatile and mutually resentful social relations in the 1970s between Blacks and Irish in Boston had prepared me to be defensive toward White people in general. That led me to select a predominantly Black institution for my graduate study. I was soon to learn, however, that color distinctions—light skin or dark skin—were important there as well.

We all know that education begins in the home before we ever arrive at school. My brother and I were raised on Cape Cod in the 1960s; it was really not cool to have frizzy hair, or to be Black. I remember sitting up nights while my uncle held a hunting rifle, poised and ready to shoot at the first noise from outdoors. We had been summer people but were forced to move to the Cape on a year-round basis since every time we'd return in the summer, we were greeted with doors and windows broken and racial epithets spray-painted on the exterior.

My first encounters in the Cape public schools were strained by racial tensions that neither the White children nor I fully understood. We had absorbed the attitudes of the surrounding home, town, and country, but we didn't have the skills or the intellectual prowess to address our differences of color and behavior with understanding, so some of us settled for imitation. I always seemed to find friends who were White, and, like me, they didn't care as much about color distinctions as they did about our common trials and tribulations of passing the next test and avoiding the Cape's winter boredom. We were as human beings attracted to the differences, though it was another matter to admit such sentiments openly. In conversations among family members, the rituals of "retreat" and "sustain your identity behind a mask" had been long promoted. Blacks did this because it helped us to survive: to ignore the negative, and focus on the positive gifts of one another. This attitude had been a staple in our own family history: cousins were close, and at holiday family gatherings of twenty-five or more stories were told. We'd spend hours talking about recent achievements by family members, or Dr. Martin Luther King, and telling of the one White person or Jewish person—since Jews were considered "other" than White—who had done some outstanding act of common humanity for one of us or for someone we knew. Little time was spent discussing the violence of prejudice, though we all knew those stories too. It was here that I was schooled in the ways of consultation, the talk that revives the human spirit. Talking was a way of making a connection with someone, and after all, we were also doing a lot of laughing, and I perceived that we were uniting the world one heart at a time.

With these familiar family discussions as my model, I was ready to disregard the mask and ask a racial question out loud.

When I was in the fourth grade, I—and every other girl—had a crush on a boy in our class. When no one was around, he'd talk to me in a friendly manner, but in public he would resort to calling me familiar, derogatory, racial epithets. Confused by this behavior and by my own feelings of crush, friendship, and hate, I resolved to confront him. I found him alone on the stairs one day, and I mustered up the courage to ask him point blank "Why do you hate me?" He looked at me and said sincerely and softly, "I don't know." For a moment, we were both lost—our education had not prepared us to deal with something so complex or heartfelt. In acknowledging it, we knew we were doing something forbidden. In that moment of silence, I believe we were both transfixed by the irrational patterns of behaviors between us. We walked away in silence, and never spoke to one another again. He increased his verbal abuse of me in public, and I was ashamed for having tried to talk to him at all. I never told my family because I did not want to hear that I should have kept my mask or should have *known better* than to say anything. But of course, my family also taught me the value of talking as a way of consulting, of bringing understanding to what *seem* like unresolvable issues.

It does seem, however, that some Black people and some White people have been talking *at* and *to* each other for a long time, which indicates that they're both hungry for a kind of true contact beyond the shell of conventionality, but as in my fourth-grade experience, they are still painfully unequipped for handling the difficult moments that inevitably occur in attempts to reach true understanding.

I think the real gaps in discussions of race have been in having methods or skills in navigating the fears or misunderstandings that happen in the difficult moments, moments fraught with a troubled legacy of failure.

Even in the best of circumstances, conversations become a series of elliptical phrases and subordinate clauses: "When insulted, I leave"; "Since you feel that way, I'm through talking"; or "Although you say that, you're wrong." We have had no real models of communication that move us past suspicion into the common ground of justice as a moral principal determining just conduct. Blacks' resentment, though understandable, is *not a solution*, and White indifference, feelings of guilt, or naiveté of the shared past is also *not a solution*. Instead, both attitudes send people into their separatist camps. The rhetoric of race—political correctness, multiculturalism, Black, African-American, or the riches of various ethnic traditions—valuable though it may be in some ways, brings no clearer picture into view, no methods for seeing one another.

Shakespeare's *Othello* demonstrates where we are today in race relations as a society. Perhaps ironically, the depth of my understanding of *Othello* began with the study of *The Merchant of Venice*. A graduate-school professor once said that *The Merchant of Venice* was the scariest of Shakespeare's plays because it so aptly captured the future of human relations; here, the poet was prophet! My question was simple, "Why?" Her answer was not. In a world that comes to confuse the material with the spiritual, every human relationship is tainted. So a father can set his daughter up as a lottery prize; friends base their relations on borrowing and lending money; Christians, engaged in the slave trade, condemn a Jew for desiring a pound of flesh; Portia states her racial bigotry against the Prince of Morocco, and later gives a speech about the quality of mercy, a value that she and the other Christians ultimately fail to enact in their dealings with Shylock. So when all human flesh has a price, a material value, anything is possible.

With this understanding of how human relations and interactions are often driven by vested interests devoid of moral courage, I returned to *Othello* and saw something equally startling that spoke of my own journey for justice and common ground; my American environment had trained me to look for suspicion in "race relations," but not how to strive deliberately, persistently, and with humility for justice among all, justice for both White and Black.

When I stood back from the important but limiting microscope of race relations, I began to see that both Othello and Desdemona were victims of the state, not just victims of Iago. The state, which had to defend at all costs against the common enemy, the Turks, had set the stage for an Iago to work his "medicine." The anxiety of the Duke and the senators about invasion by the Turks—the perennial "other"—reveals the atmosphere of suspicion and fear. I wondered: Why are these guys always running in with reports of a Turkish advance that never happens? What is Shakespeare doing here? Later, I began to think that in such a state of uncertainty, opportunities are rife for an Iago to launch a campaign of misrepresentation against Othello, a campaign full of misconstrued motives and derided aspirations. Iago uses not only racial differences but also regional ones: Cassio is a "Florentine," Desdemona, a "subtle Venetian," all amid the backdrop of the larger fear of the state's weakened, national allegiance against the Turks. In this nationalistic "world" of Venice, Iago could suggest and perpetrate the advantages of being Venetian over Florentine, of being Venetian rather than barbarian Turk, and of being White over Black. Surely, an Iago was bound to occur in such an atmosphere. In the play and in life, an Iago is difficult to recognize because we have abandoned the eyes of justice and view the world from our own vested camps.

The play gave me not only insight but a handbook on how the world has come to view differences in the struggle for economic and political security. I want to lay out in detail some of what I see in *Othello* because I feel that play offers a prime example of how race is used in connection with other prejudices, specifically nationalism. The state to which Othello has done "some service" is itself corrupt in that morality has been subjugated to political gain and national security—vested interests. No understanding of differences, regional, national, or racial, was possible perhaps while the world was consumed by expansionist endeavors. Iago can teach us about the losses, the hindrances to our social progress as a human race. Differences of "race," political affinity, or gender frequently have been tools in the larger pursuit of material gain and economic security. When we are as a society *solely* concerned with what is going on materially outside of ourselves, we ignore that which is spiritually dangerous inside ourselves as individuals.

So what can we learn about the rhetoric of race from Iago's manipulations of differences? Though he uses difference to acquire power, Iago rarely speaks *openly* of others in a derogatory fashion. He works through innuendo, elliptical phrases, and a series of confusing subordinate clauses. Only to Brabantio and Roderigo—those who fail to see with justice, whose motives for action in human affairs are debased already, and who are incapable of appreciating the nature of any ideals—only to them does Iago openly use slander. This was and is the rhetoric of race relations based on bigotry and prejudice. Justified as the fear of invasion might have been, morality took a backseat to material concerns of national sovereignty. Although the state had employed Othello on previous occasions to perform important duties, they knew little of him as a human being.

In terms of nationhood, Othello claims no land as his entire identity, though he is quick to express his pride in African origins. This is not a man who denies his ethnic roots. He is a "wanderer," a soldier, moored to his skill and virtue. Desdemona, who could have had a fair-haired Venetian, chooses to express her allegiance to no land, but to consecrate herself to Othello—his virtue—and she must share the quality in order to recognize it in another. She does, and we are told so by her father, who claims before the Senate that she was ever "a maiden never bold, / Of spirit so still and quiet that her motion / Blushed at herself "; this incredulous father cannot believe that his daughter "in spite of nature, / Of years, of country, credit, everything" could possibly give in to loving "what she feared to look on!" (1.3.112–16) It is clear that racial difference blinded Brabantio to Othello's inner virtues, in the same way that in our world race blinds us to the inner, common realities of spirit. It is also important to acknowledge that his predisposition to view his daughter as a commodity whose virtue would find full realization only in her role as housewife of one of "the wealthy curled darlings of our nation" makes Brabantio incapable of seeing that she would "seriously incline" to hear Othello's life stories.

Despite differences of color, age, and experience, both Othello and Desdemona, devoid of material ownership, choose the island, not of Cyprus, but of dynamic virtues: honesty, trustworthiness, and compassion, on which to build their identities and their union. But they were, as we are, often blind to a larger truth: spiritual values are pitted inevitably against those in society who are withdrawn into the shell of conventionality when dealing with differences, and those whose concerns for political safety and material gain take precedence over humanity's common virtues. Even the *fair-minded* Duke who acknowledges Othello's virtue must turn to pressing affairs of state and leave behind the "mangled matter" that Brabantio wishes to pursue.

In the Duke's action, we see how the taint of foreign affairs manifests itself in domestic relations, and the cost is tragic. A nation declining in moral virtues (Christian Venice) is blind to the ills that a man-made system of nationhood places upon its individual members. In this morally bankrupt climate Othello is encouraged by Iago to suspect first the virtue of Desdemona and finally of himself. Perhaps not surprisingly, Shakespeare does not give us a war, only "the rumors of war," so the issues of race relations are not as easy to dismiss.

Othello's duties were not, in fact, divided between his love for his wife and the political responsibility of protecting the state. As readers, we should examine the peacetime environment and peacetime tensions and then examine a social climate bred for suspicion and anxiety about one another's numerous differences and vested interests. We must scrutinize the individual within our society, which has chronically retreated from moral responsibility in the area of race and gender.

For me, Othello and Desdemona can represent the ongoing conversation between Black and White—an island of peace and unity that many have believed in and seen is possible among all. And do not mistake me here: this unity is not one gained at the cost or loss of anyone's individual identity, ethnic origins, or human dignity. It is not *uniformity*, but the shared human desire for justice, unassaulted by suspicions, traditions, and social training. The impact of social training was brought home to me poignantly by two colleagues who told me of their own classroom dilemmas when teaching *Othello*. One colleague of mine is White and teaches in a midwestern public school. His students are all White. Their response to *Othello* was firm: interracial marriage was immoral; some students refused to read the play, and others even threatened to stop coming to class until they had moved on to new material. Another colleague, an African-American male teaching in a predominantly Black southern public school, said that his students were reluctant to read *Othello* because it was another example of a Black man who desired a White woman.

Clearly, the study of *Othello* provides us with an opportunity to do more than explore a good piece of literature! It's also clear that education must go beyond rote learning and the acquisition of simple skills if we are to fulfill our most noble purpose: to give students the tools to analyze social conditions and their requirements, to engage in community action, and to investigate truth on their own. Education fails if it does not strive to achieve these goals. The true power of education is its ability to transform students into individuals capable of constructively participating in the progress and advancement of the human race. Therefore, it would seem clear that the task facing all teachers today is to free ourselves and our students from prejudices, preconceptions, and reliance on traditional authority. The classroom—and the study of *Othello*—provides us with an opportunity for discovering the truth of our common humanity and oneness by revealing the corrosive, social effects of racism, the spiritual problems and the moral bearings it has upon society.

Perhaps fortunately, there is no prepackaged model for doing this. Teachers must begin by creating an atmosphere where their students can investigate *safely* their own feelings about racial or ethnic difference, and this process begins with ourselves. I've derived creative classroom strategies from my own struggles by asking questions—first of myself, then of my students:

- What have been the barriers to human unity in the past?
- Where and how were these attitudes shaped?
- What are the dangers of treating someone we admire from another ethnic group as an exception to the rule?
- What are the rhetorical patterns between people who have negative attitudes toward racial or ethnic difference?
- In current times, what is social Darwinism and what are the visible effects and the costs of Darwinism on humanity?
- How and where has this philosophy created examples of moral relativism?
- What are our society's attitudes toward racial differences?
- What are our own attitudes toward racial differences?

Finally, I ask students to consider questions posed by yet another colleague:

- Could it be that the things we hate and fear most about ourselves (and about others) are the very things that might save us?
- Could it be that they are keys not only to self-acceptance, but also a source, a measure of our humanity?

In my experience, the best examples of teaching emerge when teachers ask themselves questions. The model for addressing racial matters in a classroom can perhaps be discovered with the creative energy that emerges from questions—our own and our students'. We need to teach our students that there is one race—the human race. The way to achieve this truth remains unimagined. How do we get there? Ask yourself and your students.

Science has long since proven that there is one human race; we are not species different from one another, despite superficial differences in observable physicality, cultural training, language, dress. We must abandon the fictions and false notions of race, Black and White, and see the reality of the oneness of the human race.

As long as students in American classrooms are confronting the problems and the fictions of race relations in American society on a daily basis but with relatively few skills, racism remains the most challenging issue facing us. We must not fail to discuss, consult, and understand. We have something very important to talk about. May we all have something to say.

Whole-Brained Shakespeare

Nancy Goodwin
CLINTON (OK) HIGH SCHOOL

I believe in performance. I have relied on its power to teach Shakespeare for the last ten years. I get warm vibrations when I sit down at my kitchen table with a yellow legal pad and plan the acting activities for an upcoming unit. I crave to see my students caught up in Shakespearean roles. I look forward to the day when a student in my class will say to me as Sarah Johnson did last May, "I've studied Shakespeare every year in high school, but I never understood what I was doing until you got us up acting all those scenes."

If you would have asked me last May, I would have told you in all truth that my commitment to the performance method of teaching was 100 percent. Yet, in the I'll-get-to-it-later part of my brain, I have been aware of reservations. To be sure, the reservations, or so I thought, were in the minds of others—the teacher in Maryland who told me that she would love to "dabble in performance" but she couldn't spare the time from writing, "which students preparing for AP exams have to do every day"; the professor in California who told me that in his college class he let his students prepare the murder scene in *Othello* but he had them present it at night because with all of his lectures and the hourly quizzes there wasn't enough time in class.

The most troubling case of reservations to the performance method involves the man who first taught it to me. Since 1966, Dr. James Yoch, distinguished Shakespeare professor at the University of Oklahoma, has offered students choices in assignments that include writing papers on a play or getting together with classmates to prepare and present a scene from it. At first, students thought of performance as the easy choice. But they soon learned that in envisioning a scene and bringing it to life they were paying much closer attention to Shakespeare than if they had devoted a corresponding thirty or forty hours doing research and writing an essay. The performance component to Dr. Yoch's classes made them respected and popular with adventurous students, so much so that a few of Dr. Yoch's colleagues raised questions about the method. Some insisted that the only valid assignment was a critical paper. Now this story has a happy ending—those who visited Dr. Yoch's classes saw how perfectly the students were engaged with Shakespeare, and saw how performance can take students deeper and more completely into Shakespeare's plays. But in all truth, what troubled Dr. Yoch's colleagues was the suspicion that performance is play whereas real Shakespeare scholarship is done with research, contemplation, and wide reading of criticism. A serious reservation.

I thought I had these reservations pegged. Dr. Yoch's colleagues, the teacher in Maryland, and the professor in California were trapped in what Peggy O'Brien calls the suburbs. They could lecture about semiotic theory as applied to Shakespeare. They could talk about Shakespeare's reliance on Holinshed. They could hint about Shakespeare's love life. They could exclaim with perfect sincerity about Shakespeare's images of blood or water or time. But all this information is *about* Shakespeare. Literally *about*—as in surrounding, as in close but not the same as. People who *do* Shakespeare, who stand before a group of people and say the words and be the characters, know Shakespeare from the inside.

As someone who has sat in lecture halls, taken the notes, done the research, written the papers, and taken pleasure in every step of the process, I am never ready to condemn the suburbs. Rather, I affirm both approaches. Do both. It's wonderful to learn about Shakespeare. It's marvelous to learn by doing Shakespeare. But if I had to choose—well, Shakespeare never wrote plays so people could sit in lecture halls and dissect them. This has been my rock-solid belief for the last ten years.

This summer my rock-solid belief underwent some seismic pressure. Thanks to a National Endowment for the Humanities grant, I had the good fortune to study Shakespeare in Stratford-upon-Avon. It was there, in a Royal Shakespeare Theatre performance of *Twelfth Night*, that I committed the sin for which I had been chastising others. I used scholarship to condemn performance. I had read articles, heard lecturers, and so I knew a thing or two about Orsino. Inert Orsino. He's a god at rest, right? The once-successful duke now discombobulated by love. He spends the first four acts of *Twelfth Night* lounging languidly, listening to slow music, right? Yes. Certainly. These assumptions, learned from books and lectures, were so strong in my head that they were like a checklist, and I sat in the dark theater waiting to see each happen.

I did not see an inert Orsino. From the minute the curtain opened, I saw Orsino's servants dashing this way and that. They ushered in musicians. They looked for something missing. One pulled aside a gigantic antique tapestry, and Orsino strode in, his floor-length velvet robe swirling as he marched about giving orders. His "If music be the food of love, play on" was a command tossed at the musicians on the balcony. At intervals in the speech, he stopped talking and directed the music, his "Enough; no more" was so full of authority, and delivered so abruptly, that it got a laugh.

What? An active Orsino? Doesn't this guy know that Orsino is supposed to portray malaise? I cringe to tell you that after ten years of saying to my students that performance teaches us to find in Shakespeare's text many "right" ways to play a scene, I sat in that theater in Stratford-upon-Avon and thought, "He's got this wrong." Because I had studied *about* Orsino, I thought I knew him better than the actor who took on the responsibility of *being* Orsino. I made just as egregious an error as if I had said to my students, "Believe what you heard in my lecture, and discount what you learned by playing Orsino in classroom scenes."

A day or two later, in an interview session with Clive Wood, the actor who "got it wrong," I ate humble pie. He told us how he developed his take on Orsino. He said he read the script over and over and noticed that in Act 5 Orsino could very well pull a knife on Olivia—"Why should I not, had I the heart to do it, / Like to th' Egyptian thief at point of death, / Kill what I love?" Further, he saw that when Olivia shows preference to Cesario, Orsino might take the "boy" hostage and hold the knife to "his" throat—"I'll sacrifice the lamb that I do love / To spite a raven's heart within a dove."

Mr. Wood said that he asked himself just how Orsino, a noble ruler with an island full of people at his command, could be so off balance. He started thinking of Orsino as possessed by demons, and he got a picture of a man prowling around a big castle with servants scurrying after him; he saw the man as powerful but eccentric, lonely, living in a candlelit world, shouting orders.

So I was wrong. I was wrong to assume that Orsino is absolutely inert, and I was wrong to assume that at the core of my being I really think that performance is closer to Shakespeare than scholarship. In the line of fire, I said, "Down with performance; scholars know best." Once I faced my faulty thinking, I asked myself just how I made the error. Was I mistrusting performers? Was I overvaluing scholars? After much consideration, I discovered that what I was mistrusting was the means whereby I take in information. If I received ideas about Shakespeare from an authority, if I scribbled down notes, if I heard someone string together words that were beyond me, if I smelled the books, if I felt the vellum, if I memorized the seminal points, if I wrote the information in a blue book—this was knowing Shakespeare.

And it is. But it isn't the only way, or even the best way. Actors are smart. Actors learn stuff about Shakespeare that doesn't come from vellum. If I would have given the question half a thought, I would have figured it out. In the course of its two-year run, Clive Wood will play Orsino something like 400 times. That's 400 times to take the stage, say the words, and communicate the thoughts to an audience. Brain hot. Blood pumping. Adrenaline flowing. What is he going to learn about Shakespeare? Which would teach *me* and my students the most—to spend 100 hours in the library and lecture hall or to spend the same amount of time on the stage? Fortunately, I don't have to choose, and neither do actors and scholars, for one does the work of the other. There are plenty of actors who use scholarly research to prepare for roles, and there are plenty of scholars who use performance.

What happened to me when I confronted my prejudice was that I had to examine why I think performance works—for my students and me as well as for a professional actor. Here are my newly examined, stronger-than-ever beliefs:

1. *Holding up the magnet.* I imagine that words are like thousands of magnetized balls bouncing around in some repository of the brain, and, to crudely paraphrase the semiotician Umberto Eco, when we speak, these magnetized words attach themselves to the idea we want to express. Suppose that we reverse the process. Suppose we start with a text, words already attached to a thought by a speaker long ago and far away. We say the words out loud. Maybe they are strange words. We don't understand their meaning. But we say them out loud over and over. Would we not eventually evoke some ideas or feelings that the author originally attached to those words?

Maybe this sounds a little crazy to you. Maybe you think I'm like J. D. Salinger's Franny, who sat in the bathroom in Sickler's and repeated the pilgrim's prayer over and over and over and over in the belief that divine, self-active power would come.

But I believe that saying Shakespeare's words over and over puts me in touch with ideas and feelings I would not have otherwise. I do not presume that these ideas and feelings are exactly the ones Shakespeare had when he put ink and quill to parchment 400 years ago. But they are splendid, and they came from the text, and it is thrilling to see this process happen with Shawn Gilbert, Sylvia Whiteskunk, Jeff King—ordinary teenagers in my classroom in Clinton, Oklahoma.

2. *Reading aloud.* Some people are accomplished readers. They see the words of a play on the page and hear all the voices of all the characters. Others hear nothing. The words go to their brains via a different route. Reading aloud ensures that all of us—from the most skilled readers to the least—hear every word, indeed, every inflection. The ear has ways to the brain the eye does not. Looking at the words on the page and hearing them read aloud doubles the paths to understanding, and it gives all of my students a chance to see the images and think the thoughts that the words suggest.

3. *Repeating.* Shakespeare's language is hard to catch. Often we don't understand it the first time we hear it. That is why every unit in every *Shakespeare Set Free* book is filled with activities that disguise the fact that we are asking students to say the words over and over. We do read-arounds, we rehearse scenes, we memorize lines, we do choral readings—all these are ways to put students in situations where they hear and speak Shakespeare's language often enough to get an idea about what the words are saying.

4. *Moving.* It's hard to learn Shakespeare sitting down. Students will sit in a circle and talk about how they're going to move on performance day, but when I prod them to get on their feet and run the scene there is an amazing difference in how they read, how they engage, how they think.

5. *Reflecting.* Some of Shakespeare's phrases send thoughts crashing into the brain. Other passages take time to piece out. The rhythm of rehearsal, reflection, performance, reflection lets the words work at various speeds.

6. *Reaching an audience.* This is my own theory of how Shakespeare got so good so fast. He was writing for a live audience. He went out onstage, or sent his material out onstage via other actors; he conveyed the words; he got reactions; he revised. Take away the live audience, and this process loses steam. So it is with students. So what if the audience is their classmates? Put them in the position of linking Shakespeare's play to real people, and as they strive to please they breathe life into the words.

One of the best things about performance is also one of the best things about lectures and articles—some of the words and ideas stay with us. This is my hope for you, and for your students as you enjoy the Whole-Brained Shakespeare approach of *Shakespeare Set Free.*